ACCOUNTING
AN INTERNATIONAL PERSPECTIVE

ACCOUNTING

AN INTERNATIONAL PERSPECTIVE

Gerhard G. Mueller
University of Washington

Helen Gernon
University of Oregon

Gary Meek
Oklahoma State University

BUSINESS ONE IRWIN
Burr Ridge, Illinois
New York, New York

Senior developmental editor: Michael E. Desposito
Project editor: Karen M. Smith
Production manager: Diane Palmer
Designer: Mercedes Santos
Art manager: Kim Meriwether
Art studio: Weimer Graphics, Inc.
Compositor: Precision Typographers
Typeface: 10/12 Times Roman
Printer: R.R. Donnelley & Sons Company

Library of Congress Cataloging-in-Publication Data

Mueller, Gerhard G.
    Accounting: an international perspective / Gerhard G. Mueller,
Helen Gernon, Gary Meek.
        p.   cm.
    "Supplement to introductory accounting textbooks"—CIP preface.
    ISBN 0-7863-0007-8
    1. International business enterprises—Accounting. 2. Comparative
accounting. 3. Accounting—Standards. I. Gernon, Helen Moriscato,
date. II. Meek, Gary. III. Title.
HF5686.I56M835   1994b
657'.96—dc20   93-3989

Printed in the United States of America

1 2 3 4 5 6 7 8 9 0 DOC 0 9 8 7 6 5 4 3

To Our Families

We approach the 21st Century knowing that global events will increasingly affect our lives. New nations and new economic powers are emerging. As a result, old alliances are changing, and there are shifts in the well-worn patterns of trade and international commerce. The dismantling of the former Soviet Union, the fast-growing economies of Southeast Asia, the integration of the European Community, and the implementation of the North American Free Trade Agreement all illustrate the dramatic changes that are under way. Advances in computer and communications technology are also having their impact. For example, currency markets are open continuously, 24 hours a day, as they move around the world from New York to Tokyo to London to New York. Foreign exchange trading now stands at $1 trillion per day. Information can travel long distances quickly, and it is increasingly easier and cheaper to get. Indeed, new technology makes the internationalization of product and finance markets possible. Corporations, too, are making themselves over to adapt to the global economy. Flexibility is the key as more and more of them reorganize as networks and stress interdependent alliances and strategic partnerships with other companies, rather than self-sufficiency in all areas. Information, including accounting information, is a critical resource in these makeovers, supporting the linkages both internally and with the outside world.

This book is dedicated to the proposition that the international dimension of accounting is an integral part of the discipline. Accountants who do not understand this dimension are not ready to practice in the world of today and tomorrow. Thus, the authors believe that no accountant is fully prepared without understanding the international aspects of accounting.

This book is also a testament to the positive influence of research. At the time of writing, "research bashing" has become popular. According to this line of thinking, academic research has little or nothing to do with what goes on in the real world. However, this book is largely a synthesis of international accounting research and practice. Nearly everything we say in this book is based on research findings over the past 30 years or so. Thus, research findings are directly applicable to practicing accountants.

Accounting: An International Perspective is designed to be a quick resource for the busy accountant. The book provides a general, nontechnical overview of the subject matter of international accounting, and it is the only book available that serves this purpose. Sophisticated knowledge of accounting is not necessary to understand the contents of this book, so it can also serve as an executive guide for those individuals working in law, finance, or other business-related fields who want to learn more about the main issues in international accounting.

CONTENTS

The book contains 12 chapters, modularized so the reader can pick and choose among them and read them in a different order than they are presented here. Key points, or highlights, are included at the end of each chapter for those who only have time to skim. In addition, each chapter contains several short cases that integrate, and sometimes extend, the material, and a list of additional readings for those who wish to delve further into the subjects. Each list has two or three readings that are fairly easy, while the rest are more difficult.

The first six chapters deal with financial accounting issues. Chapter 1 discusses the factors that influence the development of financial accounting practices and which, therefore, explain the similarities and differences in financial accounting around the world. For example, the legal system and the principal sources of business finance affect how accounting is used in a nation. When factors such as these are similar across nations, accounting also tends to be similar; and when they differ, accounting tends to differ. Chapter 2 describes some of the important areas of difference in worldwide financial accounting practices. Even something as ostensibly simple as cash is a source of difference. Other topics discussed in Chapter 2 are accounting for goodwill, pensions, and inflation. The diversity in accounting that exists among nations has given rise to several institutional efforts to harmonize, or narrow, the range of difference. These efforts are the subject of Chapter 3. For example, the International Accounting Standards Committee, with the support of national and international securities market regulators, is developing worldwide accounting standards. The European Community is also developing accounting and auditing standards. Chapter 4 discusses the various ways multinational corporations report to financial statement users in other countries. These ways range from doing nothing to completely restating financial statements to another set of generally accepted accounting principles. Chapter 5 focuses on disclosure trends, notably some innovative disclosures coming from Europe, several of which are provided on a voluntary basis. Chapter 6 deals with consolidations and foreign currency translation. These related topics are among the most conceptually difficult ones facing accountants today.

International financial statement analysis is the subject of Chapter 7. The diversity in measurement and disclosure practices makes this difficult indeed. This chapter bridges into the next four chapters—Chapters 8 through 11—which deal with managerial accounting issues. Chapter 8 discusses accounting information systems in multinational corporations. The task is to design a system that supports the decision needs in a complex and constantly changing multinational organizational structure. Chapter 9 looks at strategic planning and control, while Chapter 10 is about performance evaluation in multinationals. A major difficulty faced by multinationals is insuring that foreign managers participate in the planning and control process and that they be given the requisite authority to carry out the responsibilities delegated to them. Accountability is another difficult issue—often foreign managers are held accountable for things beyond their control; their operations are treated as profit centers when they are not. The interrelated topics of multinational transfer pricing and international taxation are covered in Chapter 11. Transfer pricing is an important tool in minimizing a multinational's income taxes worldwide, yet its use for this purpose interferes with its role in providing information for decision making and performance evaluation. The book ends with Chapter 12, in which we identify and discuss what we believe to be the most important emerging issues in international accounting.

CONCLUSION

As noted in Chapter 12, the forces of internationalization are irreversible. The key drivers that will keep it going are the increasingly multinational structure of business organizations, the globalization of markets, and the political and regulatory development of regionalism. These forces were alluded to in the first paragraph of this Preface. Related accounting issues include information systems design; performance evaluation in complex, multinational organizational structures; optimal forms of reporting to various user groups around the world; and the development of an accounting esperanto. These are but a sampling of the issues discussed in this book. We hope you find the book both interesting and useful.

Gerhard G. Mueller
Helen Gernon
Gary Meek

CONTENTS

ACCOUNTING
AN INTERNATIONAL PERSPECTIVE

1

AN INTERNATIONAL PERSPECTIVE ON FINANCIAL ACCOUNTING

From a business perspective, accounting is typically defined as a process providing information about various types of enterprises that is useful for making decisions about resource allocations. *Financial* accounting information is oriented primarily toward those parties external to the business enterprise who provide capital to it. Those who have funds to invest or lend may decide where to place their resources based on the *financial reports* (i.e., financial accounting information) that business enterprises prepare. Exhibit 1–1 illustrates this relationship between business enterprises and capital providers. Accounting exists because it satisfies a need—in particular, a need for information. And in order to be relevant to the resource providers, accounting information must be responsive to their needs.

ACCOUNTING AND THE ENVIRONMENT

Accounting is shaped by the environment in which it operates. Just as nations have different histories, values, and political systems, they also have different patterns of financial accounting development. Accounting as we know it in the United States is not like accounting in other countries. Indeed, diversity is what we see. This diversity is an outgrowth of the variety of business environments around the world and the fact that accounting is environmentally sensitive. It is interesting to note, too, that when countries' business environments are similar, their financial accounting systems also tend to be similar.

In a number of countries (such as the United States), financial accounting information is directed primarily toward the needs of investors and creditors, and

1

EXHIBIT 1-1   Financial Accounting Information and Capital Resource Flows

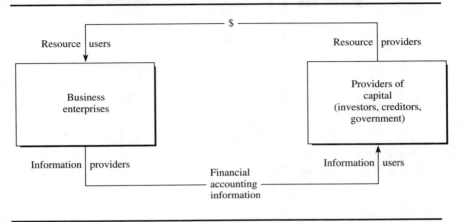

"decision usefulness" is the overriding criterion for judging its quality. However, in other countries, financial accounting has a different focus and performs other roles. For example, in some countries, financial accounting is designed primarily to ensure that the proper amount of income tax is collected by the national government. This is the case in most South American countries. In other countries, financial accounting is designed to help accomplish macroeconomic policies, such as achieving a predetermined rate of growth in the nation's economy. Whether income tax and economic policy information is also useful to individual investors and creditors is somewhat beside the point. For the moment, we are concerned only with the *primary* orientation of a national financial accounting system.

The consequences of national financial accounting differences are all around us. They are reflected in the relative popularity of accounting as a major for university studies, and in the numbers of people with accounting backgrounds becoming senior government officials or top corporate executives. There is a different national emphasis on the use of accounting information in assessing environmental damage liabilities and especially in regulating public securities markets.

A specific illustration of national differences relates total fees (i.e., money charged for services rendered) of a country's largest 10 accounting firms to that same country's gross domestic product (GDP). Exhibit 1-2 shows this relationship for 20 different countries. The ratio for Ireland is more than 60 times greater than the ratio for Japan. Does this mean that financial accounting is considered 60 times more valuable in Ireland than it is in Japan? Another possibility is that Ireland spends too much of its GDP on accounting services, whereas Japan does not spend enough (note that the United States falls near the middle of the range). Whatever the explanation in this specific case, the underlying impact of different national environments is undeniable.

EXHIBIT 1–2   Total Fees of Large Accounting Firms in Different Countries as Percentages of Corresponding Gross Domestic Product

---

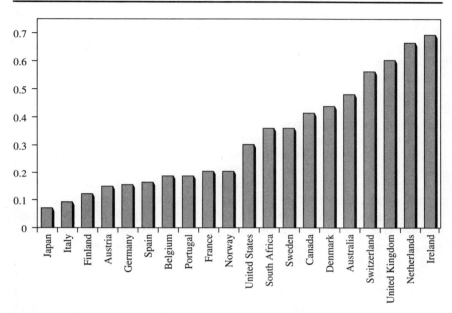

Based on top 10 firms, or all available data where 10 firms were not available.
Based on 1990 data and 1990 GDP. Germany based on West German GDP only.

SOURCE: *1992 International Accounting Databook*. Reprinted from "Special Supplement," *International Accounting Bulletin, September 19, 1992.*

The principal environmental variables that shape the development of national financial accounting systems are examined next.

VARIABLES SHAPING ACCOUNTING DEVELOPMENT

Relationship between Business and the Provider(s) of Capital

The Industrial Revolution in the United States and Britain created a tremendous amount of new wealth in these countries—wealth that spread widely among the general populace. As companies grew, their needs for capital also grew, and the rising middle class became a source of much of this needed capital. What emerged from this phenomenon had an important impact on financial accounting in these two countries. First, the investor/creditor group became large and diverse, and companies acquired a widespread ownership (i.e., many shareholders). Second, the owners became divorced from the management of their companies, and the professional, nonowner manager developed. Investors became essentially uninvolved in the day-to-day running of the companies they owned.

In such an environment, financial accounting information becomes an important source of data about how well a company is doing. Since it is impractical for the shareholders to contact the company president or personally inspect the accounting records, the professional managers provide financial reports to investors and creditors in order to communicate their stewardship over the resources entrusted to them. With such a relationship, it is hardly surprising that financial accounting is oriented toward the information needs of investors and creditors. Financial accounting in Britain and the United States has had such an orientation for many years. Moreover, these countries have large and developed stock exchanges and bond markets. As a result, a great deal of information is disclosed in companies' financial reports; and determining profitability (i.e., management performance) is an objective of financial accounting.

In other countries (such as Switzerland, Germany, and Japan), the environment is characterized by a few, very large banks that satisfy most of the capital needs of business. Ownership also tends to be concentrated. The information needs of the resource providers are satisfied in a relatively straightforward way—through personal contacts and direct visits. Since the business enterprises have to deal with only a few creditors—and maybe even just one—direct access is an efficient and practical way to have the company's financial health monitored. The national governments require some public disclosure, and so companies still prepare financial reports. Not surprisingly, though, they tend not to contain as much information as U.S. companies' reports. And since banks are the primary source of capital, financial accounting is oriented toward creditor protection. One sees, for example, such practices as conservatively valuing assets and overvaluing liabilities in order to provide a "cushion" for the bank in the event of default. These practices also reduce the dividend demands of shareholders.

France and Sweden offer still another orientation of financial accounting. National government plays a strong role in managing the country's resources, and business enterprises are expected to accomplish the government's policies and macroeconomic plans. Governments also actively ensure that businesses have adequate capital and will lend or even invest in companies if necessary. Financial accounting is oriented toward decision making by government planners. Firms follow uniform accounting procedures and reporting practices, which facilitate better government decisions.

Of course, the relationship between a business enterprise and providers of business capital changes quite drastically when new capital is secured in international financial markets. Then the information demands of both domestic and international funds sources have to be satisfied, which typically means going beyond national expectations and customs in providing financial reports. This topic is explored in Chapter 4.

In summary, the following have an impact on a country's financial accounting orientation:

1. Who the investors and creditors—the information users—are (individuals, banks, the government).

2. How many investors and creditors there are.

3. How close the relationship is between businesses and the investor/creditor group.

4. How developed the stock exchanges and bond markets are.

5. The extent of use of international financial markets.

Political and Economic Ties with Other Countries

Accounting technology is imported and exported just as political systems and ideologies are, and countries have similar accounting for this reason. The United States has influenced accounting in Canada due to geographic proximity and close economic ties and because a number of Canadian companies routinely sell shares of common stock or borrow money in the United States. The United States is Mexico's principal trading partner; and, also because of proximity, accounting in Mexico is very much like that in the United States. As a former protectorate of the United States, the Philippines has similar accounting requirements. Finally, accounting in Israel is heavily influenced by U.S. accounting practices as a result of the historical and sociological ties between the two nations. It is interesting to see that Japanese accounting is increasingly feeling the influence of U.S. standards. More and more Japanese firms are raising capital and establishing manufacturing facilities in the United States.

Another significant force in worldwide accounting has been the United Kingdom, principally England and Scotland. Almost every former British colony has an accounting profession and financial accounting practices patterned after the U.K. model. These countries include Australia, New Zealand, Malaysia, Pakistan, India, and South Africa. The British not only exported their brand of accounting but also "exported" many accountants. (In fact, Britain is the only major former colonial power to transfer both its accounting ideas and its accountants.) Former colonies of France and Germany have been similarly influenced by their respective "mother countries," though not quite so profoundly as those of the United Kingdom.

Since the early 1970s, the European Community (EC) has been attempting to harmonize the accounting practices of its 12 member states. Recall from our earlier discussion that Britain, Germany, and France have fundamentally different orientations about the role and purpose of financial accounting. However, as European allies and members of the EC, they have a number of similar economic interests, and they are seriously attempting to bring their accounting practices closer together.

Political and economic ties among nations shape their accounting development; thus, one cannot help but wonder whether the world's growing interdependence will force accounting practices to become more similar.

Indeed, this type of thinking has given rise to the international accounting standards movement. As explored more fully in Chapter 3, the International Accounting Standards Committee (IASC) has become the signal force worldwide to develop international financial accounting standards and seek their widest possible acceptance and use. The International Federation of Accountants (IFAC), among many other activities, develops and issues international auditing standards (also see Chapter 3), which were accepted in 1992 for financial reporting in international financial markets. In Europe, accounting *Directives* are issued by the EC and are incorporated into the national corporate legislation of all EC member countries in due course. Many world agencies like the United Nations (UN), the Organization for Economic Cooperation and Development (OECD), the Association of South East Asian Nations (ASEAN), and the International Monetary Fund (IMF) have operating units specifically concerned with international financial standard setting and reporting. The internationalization of our political and economic environments is directly driving the internationalization of accounting.

Legal System

Many dichotomize the accounting world into those countries with a "legalistic" orientation toward accounting and those with a "nonlegalistic" orientation. The legalistic approach to accounting is predominantly represented by so-called code law countries, and the preponderance of countries with a nonlegalistic approach are the so-called common law countries. Laws in code law countries are a series of "thou shalts" that stipulate the minimum standard of behavior expected. Citizens are obligated to comply with the letter of the law. In most code law countries, accounting principles are national laws; that is, accounting practices are codified much as the tax code is in the United States. These accounting practices and rules tend to be highly prescriptive, detailed, and procedural. Also, the primary role of financial accounting in these countries is to determine how much income tax a company owes the government. Argentina, France, and Germany have legalistic approaches to accounting.

The nonlegalistic approach is usually found in common law countries. Laws are a series of "thou shalt nots" that establish the limits beyond which it is illegal to venture. Within these limits, however, latitude and judgment are permitted and encouraged. Accounting practices in common law countries are largely determined by accountants themselves (rather than by national legislators) and thus tend to be more adaptive and innovative. The United Kingdom and the United States are common law countries.

Levels of Inflation

Accounting in many countries (including the United States) is based in part on the *historical cost principle*. This principle is itself based on an assumption that the currency unit used to report financial results is reasonably stable. In other words, the historical cost principle assumes that the dollar (for U.S. companies) does not change in value—that there is little or no inflation. As one might expect, the less realistic this assumption becomes, the greater the strain on the historical cost principle.

Briefly, the historical cost principle means that companies originally record sales, purchases, and other business transactions at transaction prices and make no adjustments to these prices later. Generally speaking, the historical cost principle affects accounting most significantly in the area of asset values, mainly those assets (such as land and buildings) that the company keeps for a long time. Obviously, the reasonableness of the historical cost principle varies inversely with the level of inflation. Germany and Japan, two of the staunchest adherents to the historical cost principle, have experienced very little inflation in recent years. South American countries, ravaged by inflation problems for years, long ago abandoned any attachment to strict historical cost. Companies in many of these countries routinely write up the values of their assets based on changes in general price levels.

The United States experienced very little inflation in the post-World War II era until the 1970s. Most U.S. accountants were happy with historical cost accounting, and interest in adjusting for changes in price levels was mainly confined to a few academicians. However, once inflation became persistent and high (at least by U.S. standards), interest in measuring the effects of price-level changes on business enterprises began to grow. In 1979 the Financial Accounting Standards Board (FASB), the organization that determines acceptable accounting practices for U.S. companies, required the largest U.S. firms to experiment with ways to account for changes in prices. Eventually, these firms had to report the effects of changing prices in their published annual reports and in filings with the Securities and Exchange Commission (SEC). However, this requirement was rescinded in 1984 as inflation levels in the United States returned to more modest levels.

Interest in incorporating the effects of changing prices into a company's accounting records waxes and wanes with the degree that a country is affected by inflation. Countries with a long history of inflation have already done something about it, while those with low inflation do not even consider abandoning historical cost. Some of the most novel ideas dealing with inflation accounting were proposed in Europe during the 1920s and 1930s, when that continent experienced hyperinflation. More recently, accountants in the United Kingdom and the United States have written some provocative essays about how to account for price-level changes.

Size and Complexity of Business Enterprises, Sophistication of Management and the Financial Community, and General Levels of Education

These factors define the limits of a country's accounting sophistication. Larger, more complex business enterprises have more difficult accounting problems. Highly trained accountants are needed to handle these more difficult problems; accounting cannot be highly developed in a country where general education levels are low, unless that country imports accounting talent or sends bright citizens elsewhere for the necessary training. At the same time, the users of a company's financial reports must themselves be sophisticated—or else there will be no demand for sophisticated accounting reports.

Most multinational corporations are headquartered in the wealthy, industrialized nations (e.g., Japan, Germany, Great Britain, and the United States). These countries have sophisticated accounting systems and highly qualified professional accountants. In contrast, education levels in most developing countries are low and businesses are small; as a result, accounting is primitive. From earlier discussions, however, it may occur to you that if accounting responds to information needs, then accounting in developing countries may very well be at an appropriate level of sophistication under the circumstances. While many accountants hold this view, some feel that the lack of sophisticated accounting ability in less developed countries actually impedes their potential for economic progress. It does appear, though, that newly developed countries (such as Taiwan, South Korea, and Brazil) have been able to overcome their rudimentary accounting expertise. Accounting development and economic development clearly go hand in hand. Just as most of the world can be divided between the "haves" and "have nots," there are accounting "have" and "have not" nations.

ACCOUNTING CLUSTERS

The variables shaping the development of financial accounting overlap to some degree. For example, most code law countries have historically relied on either banks or the government to supply capital to businesses, whereas common law countries have historically relied on their more developed stock and bond markets to satisfy businesses' capital needs. If we accept the idea that accounting is influenced by its environment, then it is logical to expect accounting similarities among countries with similar business environments.

Indeed, nations can be grouped or clustered according to accounting similarities. Before discussing such clusters, however, it is important to emphasize the word *similarities*. No two countries have *identical* financial accounting practices. Each country is a unique mixture of environmental variables that together have influenced the pattern of accounting development in that country. Therefore, in order to cluster countries, one must blur some dissimilarities. However, at a broad level of generalization, four major accounting models can be identified. Countries represented by each model are listed in Exhibit 1–3 and depicted in Exhibit 1–4.

British-American Model

In international accounting circles, one often hears the term *British-American* (or sometimes *Anglo-Saxon*) to describe the accounting approach found in the United Kingdom and the United States. The Dutch approach is quite similar; and, to be more precise, one should really call this model *British-North American-*

EXHIBIT 1–3 List of Selected Countries Comprised by the Four Major Accounting Models

British-American Model

Australia	India	Panama
Bahamas	Indonesia	Papua New Guinea
Barbados	Ireland	Philippines
Benin	Israel	Puerto Rico
Bermuda	Jamaica	Singapore
Botswana	Kenya	South Africa
Canada	Liberia	Tanzania
Cayman Islands	Malawi	Trinidad & Tobago
Central America	Malaysia	Uganda
Colombia	Mexico	United Kingdom
Cyprus	Netherlands	United States
Dominican Republic	New Zealand	Venezuela
Fiji	Nigeria	Zambia
Ghana	Pakistan	Zimbabwe
Hong Kong		

Continental Model

Algeria	Germany	Norway
Angola	Greece	Portugal
Austria	Guinea	Senegal
Belgium	Italy	Sierra Leone
Burkina	Ivory Coast	Spain
Cameroon	Japan	Sweden
Denmark	Luxembourg	Switzerland
Egypt	Mali	Togo
Finland	Morocco	Zaire
France		

South American Model

Argentina	Chile	Paraguay
Bolivia	Ecuador	Peru
Brazil	Guyana	Uruguay

Mixed Economy Model

Armenia	Hungary	Russia
Azerbaidzhan	Kazakhstan	Serbia
Belorussia	Kirgizia	Slovak Republic
Bosnia-Herzegovina	Latvia	Slovenia
Bulgaria	Lithuania	Tadzhikstan
Croatia	Moldavia	Turkmenistan
Czech Republic	Poland	Ukraine
Estonia	Romania	Uzbekistan
Georgia		

EXHIBIT 1-4 Map of Countries Comprised by the Four Major Accounting Models

British-American model

Continental model

South American model

Mixed economy model

Dutch. The United Kingdom, the United States, and the Netherlands are the trend-setting countries for this cluster. Their accounting is oriented toward the decision needs of investors and creditors, and they have large, developed common stock and bond markets, where companies raise large amounts of capital. Education levels are very high, and users of financial accounting information tend to be quite sophisticated. These countries also possess many large, multinational corporations. (Philips, a Dutch multinational, manufactures Norelco brand products. Unilever is a British/Dutch company whose U.S. subsidiary, Lever Brothers, manufactures and sells such products as *All* detergent.) As can be seen from Exhibit 1–3, these three countries represent a sphere of influence over accounting in many other countries as well.

Continental Model

Countries in this cluster include most of continental Europe and Japan. Businesses here have very close ties to their banks, which supply most capital needs. Financial accounting is legalistic in its orientation, and practices tend to be highly conservative. Accounting is not primarily oriented toward the decision-making needs of the capital providers. Instead, it is usually designed to satisfy such government-imposed requirements as computing income taxes or demonstrating compliance with the national government's macroeconomic plan. French-speaking African countries, by-and-large, follow the Continental financial accounting model.

South American Model

The third model includes most countries in South America. With the exception of Brazil, which speaks Portuguese, these nations share a common language—Spanish. They also share a common heritage. What distinguishes the South American model from the British-American and Continental models is the persistent use of accounting adjustments for inflation. These countries have a great deal of experience coping with inflation, and their accounting reflects this. Generally speaking, accounting is oriented toward the needs of government planners, and uniform practices are imposed on business entities. Tax-basis accounting is often used as well for financial reporting purposes.

Mixed Economy Model

The 1989–1990 political upheavals in Eastern Europe and the former USSR have spawned a very environment-specific accounting model seeking to be responsive to both remnants of tight central economic planning and control as well as market-oriented enterprise activities. Where this model applies, enterprises typically operate dual accounting systems. One track produces information for managers used to the former system oriented toward a command economy and relying heavily on uniform charts of accounts and budgeted rather than actual financial information. (Refer to the discussion at the end of this chapter on accounting in Communist countries.) The other track has a capitalist markets orientation, tries to emulate the British-American accounting model, and seeks to provide information primarily for investors, bankers, and corporate financial analysts from capitalist countries. Reconciling these two very different conceptual approaches to financial accounting is difficult if not impossible. Among the big challenges for the mixed economy model are joint venture accounting, establishing values for productive assets for the privatization of economic units, education and organization of effective local and national accounting professions, and regulatory control over needed accounting development. The UN Centre for Transnational Corporations is particularly active in supporting the mixed economy model.

Emerging Models

Aside from the four major accounting models just described, two others are in early developmental stages. One is the Islamic model. It has a theological base in that it prohibits, for example, any recognition of interest on money. Current market values are favored as measures of business assets and liabilities. This model has not yet evolved to the point where it represents a comprehensive pattern (or framework) of financial accounting.

Another emerging model might be called the International Standards model. Its roots lie in the international harmonization of financial accounting—especially for multinational corporations and international financial markets participants. Quite a few large corporations already note that their annual financial reports are in conformity with international financial accounting standards. The international standards movement was briefly mentioned earlier in this chapter and is discussed more fully in Chapter 3.

Accounting in Communist Countries

This chapter focused on the non-Communist world. We end it with a brief description of accounting in Communist countries, such as Cuba. Communist governments own all productive resources (no private ownership) and supply all capital needs; therefore, it stands to reason that high uniformity is required and that the primary users are government planners. Uniform accounting is necessary for tight central economic control. Financial statements are not prepared for outsiders but for various agency administrators and government planners. Financial reports normally include budgetary information.

In contrast to capitalist economies, the basic inputs to production in command (i.e., Communist) economies are not purchased (nor are outputs sold) on open markets. The states allocate firms a specified quantity of resources, and firms are expected to produce a predetermined level of output. Success is not measured by the amount of income earned; rather, the emphasis is on achieving production quotas and on determining production costs. Since private ownership of productive resources is absent, valuing fixed assets is not emphasized as much as it is in capitalist economies. Indeed, financial accounting per se does not exist; what we refer to as *managerial accounting* comes closer to illustrating the overall accounting scene in Communist regimes. China, of course, is the present bulwark of the Communist world. Her basic accounting systems are fully consistent with Marxist principles. If market economy concepts and practices ever gain the upper hand, the command economy accounting model will begin to wither away.

CONCLUSION

One should not say that the accounting in one country is of better quality than the accounting in another country. Accounting exists because it fulfills a need, and as long as accounting satisfies the needs of its user groups, it is doing what it is supposed to do. Accounting develops in and is nurtured by its environment. That the world is a potpourri of accounting practices reflects the diversity of uses to which it is put.

KEY POINTS

1. Accounting is shaped by the environment in which it operates.
2. Among the key environmental variables affecting accounting development are (*a*) the relationship between business and the providers of capital, (*b*) political and economic ties, and (*c*) the legal system.
3. Most nations can be grouped into one of four accounting "models" or types: (*a*) British-American, (*b*) Continental, (*c*) South American, or (*d*) Mixed Economy.
4. Accounting differs around the world because it serves different primary information needs: (*a*) decision making by capital market investors, (*b*) collecting taxes, or (*c*) compiling government statistics.

CASES

By Guess and by Gosh

Terri Parker is a financial analyst for foreign financial statements at a large U.S. pension fund. As a matter of policy and investment diversification, the pension fund invests between 15 and 20 percent of its assets in offshore corporate financial securities.

Terri is frustrated. "We're doing well with these foreign securities, but more often than not we select them and monitor them mostly by guess and by gosh," she fumes. "Often, I don't fully understand their financial statements; our executive director doesn't understand them, nor does our board of directors. Why can't big corporations around the world use the same financial accounting and reporting standards? Somebody ought to do something!"

Questions

1. Why do financial accounting standards used by large corporations differ from country to country?
2. What is Terri likely to do about a foreign financial report (written in English) that she cannot understand?
3. Whose responsibility is it "to do something" about this situation?

The Swiss Solution

The financial vice president of a U.S. multinational corporation recently returned from a business trip to Switzerland. While there, she had occasion to learn about Swiss accounting practices, and she came home with some ideas for changing her own company's financial reports.

"I like what I saw over there," she said. "The annual report that we send to our shareholders is getting fatter and fatter each year, and the costs are getting out of hand. The Swiss don't see the need to disclose nearly as much information as we do, and they seem to be no worse off for it.

"For example, rather than a complete balance sheet and income statement, only selected items are revealed. One company just showed its gross profit and net income. The people at that company felt that if they revealed total sales and the details of their operating expenses, they would be giving competitors a lot of information about how they run their company. I think they have a point.

"Swiss companies also use balance sheet 'reserves' to cushion their bad years. They set up reserves in good years by making deductions from income. Then, in 'off' years, income is increased by reducing these reserves. It's just a way to smooth out the good and bad years as far as reporting to stockholders is concerned.

"They're also a lot more conservative than we are. They tend to undervalue assets and overvalue liabilities. I'm not so sure *that's* such a good idea, but I think our company might do well to adopt the accounting practices I mentioned earlier."

Questions

1. What specific differences between Swiss and U.S. accounting did the financial vice president observe?

2. What environmental differences help explain the differences she found?

3. Do you agree with her that the company ought to adopt lower levels of disclosure and the use of reserves? Why or why not?

4. Illustrate with journal entries how using reserves can "smooth out" the good and bad years.

Law and Order Accounting

"I'll tell you, Günter. Here's what's wrong with German accounting."

Tim O'Reilly has been on assignment at his accounting firm's office in Cologne, Germany, for two weeks. During this time, he has reviewed the financial statements of a number of German companies in order to learn something about German accounting practices. He's learned enough so far to know that German accounting is a lot different than accounting back home in the United States.

"For one thing, too many German companies prepare their statements in German. Hey, Günter, the language of international business is English. How do these companies expect people who don't understand German to read their financial statements?

"For another, you guys give incredible amounts of detail about a lot of things that most people don't care about and not enough information about stuff that's really important. I saw one statement that listed every blasted subsidiary owned by the company—it was a six-page list. But that same company reported nothing at all about how much profit it earned in various parts of the world or how much was made by product line. And German balance sheets and income statements are so detailed, it's really hard to get the 'big picture.'

"Why companies seem to undervalue assets and overvalue liabilities is beyond me—all that does is understate net income. Why, it's almost as if you're being overly conservative on purpose. The companies always say that their financial statements 'comply with the law,' but what the heck does that mean, Günter?"

Questions

1. What specific differences between German and U.S. accounting practices has Tim observed?

2. What environmental variables help explain the German accounting practices that Tim noted?

3. Do you agree with Tim that there is something "wrong" with German accounting?

ADDITIONAL READINGS

Barrett, G.R. "Is Accounting Becoming the First Truly International Profession?" *Journal of Accountancy* (October 1992), pp. 110–13.

Gray, S.J. "Towards a Theory of Cultural Influence on the Development of Accounting Systems Internationally." *Abacus* (March 1988), pp. 1–15.

Hudack, L.R. and L.L. Orsini. "A Note of Caution to Users of Japanese Financial Reports: A Demonstration of an Enlarged Exogenist Approach." *International Journal of Accounting* 27 (1992), pp. 15–26.

O'Malley, S.F. "Accounting across Borders." *Financial Executive* (March/April 1992), pp. 28–31.

Pratt, J. and G. Behr. "Environmental Factors, Transaction Costs, and External Reporting: A Cross-National Comparison." *International Journal of Accounting* (Spring 1987), pp. 1–24.

Smith, L.M. and D.R. Lassila. "Ranking of International Accounting Topics by Multinational Business Firm Practitioners." *Issues in International Business*, Montclair State College (Spring 1989), pp. 24–32.

United Nations Centre on Transnational Corporations. *Accounting Development in Africa: Challenge of the 1990s.* New York: UNCTC, 1991, 200 pp.

2

DIVERSITY IN FINANCIAL ACCOUNTING PRACTICES

In Chapter 1, we discussed the principal environmental variables that shape the development of national financial accounting systems. We identified:

1. Relationship between business and the provider(s) of capital.
2. Political and economic ties with other countries.
3. Legal system.
4. Levels of inflation.
5. Size and complexity of business enterprises, sophistication of management and the financial community, and general levels of education.

Chapter 3 is devoted to the idea of worldwide harmonization of the existing country-by-country financial accounting diversity. What is this diversity, and is it really problematic? Why is the enforcement of accounting rules and regulations a national activity? Who wins and who loses from national diversity in financial accounting practices? Questions such as these are explored in this chapter.

REDUCING DIVERSITY WITHIN COUNTRIES

Until the Great Depression of 1929 through 1930, companies everywhere could freely choose the accounting methods and rules they thought appropriate for their individual situations. In a 1927 book entitled *Main Street and Wall Street*, William Z. Ripley, then Harvard professor of political economy, described his review of U.S. corporate annual reports in these terms:

Confronted with a great pile of recent corporate pamphlets on my table, the first impression is of their extraordinary diversity, in appearance, size, content, and intent. One premier concern, the Royal Baking Powder Company, fails to register any fiscal information at all, in as much as it has never issued a balance sheet or financial statement of any kind whatsoever for more than a quarter of a century. . . . Akin to it is the Singer Manufacturing Company, which handles 80 percent of the world's output of sewing machines. Neither hide nor hair of financial data for this firm is discoverable in the usual sources of information. The dance-card, bald balance-sheet, or picture-book variety of corporation report follows hard upon these examples of complete reticence. . . . Yet colored pictures of factories, brightly lighted at night,—as some of these must well have been in view of their extraordinary success,—tell no tales.[1]

Companies in the United States were incorporated under state law statutes, which generally contained only superficial accounting and financial reporting requirements. Code law countries had more elaborate corporate law provisions, but also literally nothing on accounting and financial reporting. This was a world of terrible misinformation and noncomparable financial statements. Essentially, corporate managements picked accounting and reporting rules that often pictured their companies financially better than they were in fact (this is called *window dressing* in accounting).

Remedies began to surface soon after the Great Depression. Countries subscribing to the British-American model of financial accounting created committees or boards of professional practicing accountants (certified public accountants [CPAs] in the United States; chartered accountants [CAs] in Canada and the United Kingdom) to recommend *generally accepted accounting principles* (GAAP) to be used within each country. In the United States, enforcement was assigned to the Securities and Exchange Commission (SEC), which is a federal government agency created to regulate all domestic markets for financial securities. Enforcement in the United Kingdom is more indirect in that it occurs mainly through litigation and other court processes.

Countries subject to code laws (i.e., those following the Continental and South American models) revised their respective companies' laws to require compliance with various accounting provisions and the orderly publication of financial statements.

Developing accounting and financial reporting methods and rules is called financial accounting *standard setting* (see Chapter 3). As mentioned in Chapter 3, the Financial Accounting Standards Board (FASB) sets financial accounting standards in the United States. There were 112 FASB standards at the end of 1992. Together with standards set before the FASB was established in 1973, these pronouncements constitute GAAP in the United States.

Other countries have different approaches to producing accounting standards. Exhibit 2–1 provides a comparative summary for five countries.

Most industrialized countries and a few developing countries have their own

---

[1]William Z. Ripley, *Main Street and Wall Street* (Houston, Tex.: Scholars Book Co., reprinted 1972), pp. 162–64.

EXHIBIT 2–1   Financial Accounting Standard Setting in Five Countries

---

Germany relies very heavily on legislation, particularly company law, and on taxation; accounting standards tend to be especially conservative and have very detailed provisions with respect to presentation and valuation.

France also depends on legal and tax decrees, although to a lesser degree than Germany; the concept of ''substance over form'' has little impact since it is assumed that following the rules will produce a ''true and fair view.''

Japan is a third country that draws heavily on legal and tax directives, so much so that the private sector has little direct involvement in setting accounting standards; in many ways, Japan's legal and tax systems follow those in Continental Europe.

In the **United Kingdom**, private-sector influence is very strong; standards tend to set out broad principles, with some latitude as to the details.

In the **United States,** the private sector is also the primary source for accounting standards, but with input and influence from the SEC; standard setting is a particularly lengthy process and, in addition to basic pronouncements, there is much detailed guidance.

SOURCE: International Capital Markets Group, *Harmonization of International Accounting Standards.* A paper prepared by the International Federation of Accountants with the assistance of Federation Internationale des Bourses de Valeurs and the International Bar Association Section on Business Law, 1992, p. vii.

accounting standard setting boards or committees. By and large, these organizations have been successful. They have greatly reduced accounting and financial reporting diversity within countries and have forged clearly recognizable and nationally acknowledged country-by-country GAAP. The big concern now is that the GAAP of no two countries are the same. This means that financial information does not travel well internationally.

WHY FINANCIAL ACCOUNTING PRACTICES DIFFER BETWEEN COUNTRIES

Accounting and financial reporting are not the same everywhere. The three trigger factors described and explained so far in this book are:

1. Major environmental variables that impact accounting development in any one national setting.
2. Adherence to a particular financial accounting model (by choice, affinity, or historical accident).
3. Approach to and process of national financial accounting standard setting.

There is a fourth critical factor that has to do with the very nature of accounting. This factor relates to all the uncertainties modern business must cope with. Here is how a group of experts describes what is going on:

Financial statements, which are designed to portray the financial position and results of operations, are prepared at least annually. Businesses nowadays are involved in transactions which extend over significant time periods, and which have inherent uncertainties associated with them. As a result, at any accounting date there are often significant transactions which have not been completed, and where the final outcome is uncertain. This means that preparers of financial statements must make estimates about future events in order to apportion costs and revenues to the appropriate financial periods. Thus estimates have to be made about future costs and revenues on long term contracts, on future pension costs, asset lives, and on many other matters. These are inherently difficult problems. There are not necessarily 'right' answers, and it is therefore not surprising that countries deal with them in different ways.[2]

Conservatism, one of the cornerstones of financial accounting around the world, is one way to cope with these uncertainties. However, the extent to which conservatism affects accounting practices varies. As noted in Exhibit 2–1, for example, German accounting is especially conservative. U.K. accounting, on the other hand, is much less conservative.

Thus, we have diversity from one set of GAAP to another among different countries. This diversity may well be justified in terms of one or a combination of the four trigger factors mentioned, but the same diversity creates barriers for international financial information flows. It is one of the primary issues in international accounting.

SOME EXISTING PRACTICE DIFFERENCES

When dealing with international accounting at a basic level, it is inappropriate to illustrate existing practice differences with elaborate examples. Therefore, *general* discussions of three technical topics follow the overview, which is presented first.

The subject matter of financial accounting divides itself into two dimensions— *measurement* and *disclosure.* Measurement concerns economic events and transactions whose effects are reflected directly on the three basic financial statements (i.e., the balance sheet, income statement, and cash flow statement). If an accounting entity borrows money from a bank, the amount of the debt is measured, and both the cash received and the debt payable are reflected on the next balance sheet and cash flow statement. Similarly, when a payroll comes due, all employee pay obligations are measured and social security/unemployment insurance/private pension contributions and other indirect employment costs are added to arrive at an appropriate amount for employment expenses on the next income statement. Measurement activities like these drive all formal accounting systems.

Aside from measurements themselves, readers of financial statements want to

---

[2]International Capital Markets Group, *Harmonization of International Accounting Standards.* A paper prepared by the International Federation of Accountants with the assistance of Federation Internationale des Bourses de Valeurs and the International Bar Association Section on Business Law, 1992, p. 3.

EXHIBIT 2-2   Selected Definitions of Cash and Cash Equivalents

Definitions Used in Pronouncements Guiding Preparation of Cash Flow Statements	Area of Application
Cash and demand deposits and highly liquid investments (monetary assets)	South Africa United States of America
Cash and demand deposits and highly liquid investments less bank overdraft	United Kingdom and the Republic of Ireland
Cash and demand deposits and highly liquid investments less short-term borrowings (net monetary assets)	New Zealand Canada IASC

SOURCE: R. S. Olusegun Wallace and P. A. Collier, "The 'Cash' in Cash Flow Statements: A Multi-Country Comparison," *Accounting Horizons*, December 1991, p.49.

know which measurement methods were used and if there are items of interest that somehow could not be measured directly. Difficult-to-measure things include future effects of strikes, mergers, and product development. Also included are environmental protection effects, charitable commitments, or comparisons with another country's GAAP. These are often reported in supplemental disclosures, apart from the basic financial statements. Chapter 5 discusses disclosure issues. Accounting measurements are addressed in the rest of this chapter.

Assets and liabilities are subject to often significant measurement differences around the world. Take something as simple as cash. Most corporate balance sheets have a caption like "cash and cash equivalents." What does this cover? In the United States, demand deposits and highly liquid investments are included. In other countries, bank overdrafts are subtracted instead of being reported separately as short-term borrowings. Exhibit 2-2 reveals some of the existing differences.

Of course, there is the additional problem of translating national currencies (see Chapter 6). Multinational corporations (MNCs) do business in many different countries and therefore have various bank accounts in as many countries. Companies like Kodak, Nestlé, or Procter and Gamble sell their products in more than 100 different countries and therefore have bank accounts in as many national currencies. To bring them all together into a single balance sheet requires *measuring* them in terms of a single currency. In other words, for Kodak, all forms of cash equivalents must somehow be translated (i.e., remeasured) to U.S. dollars. What foreign exchange rate is appropriate for this purpose? Should one represent the resulting total as a U.S. dollar amount when, in fact, the majority of the funds involved is denominated in other national currencies?

If we have so much difficulty with a straightforward item like cash and cash equivalents, it is little wonder that even more substantive issues are encountered in relation to inventories, depreciable assets, intellectual properties, software, research and development, capitalized borrowing costs, leased properties, intercorporate investments, and other assets.

The liabilities side of the accounting equation is equally complex. For decades, accountants have debated how to measure income tax accounting effects when financial accounting differs from tax accounting (i.e., within the British-American model only, since financial and tax accounting are highly similar in all of the other models). If a company takes relatively larger expense deductions for income tax purposes in connection with depreciation or some long-term contracts (and therefore postpones taxable income), should a *deferred income tax* effect be measured and put on the balance sheet? If the answer is yes, is this item a liability like accounts or notes payable?

International liabilities measurement differences exist with respect to leasing contracts and contingencies like the eventual outcome of pending lawsuits. Recognition of employee pension liabilities is covered later in this chapter. The U.S. introduction of measuring employers' obligations for postretirement benefits other than pensions (SFAS No. 106) is likely to add yet another dimension to international financial accounting practices diversity, since such benefits are not universally available and covered by government programs in most code law countries. There is little international agreement on how to account for future contracts in the commodities markets, interest rate swaps and similar arrangements in the financial markets, and hedging operations in the foreign exchange markets. Joint venture obligations are also a real measurement problem.

When it comes to measuring business net income or loss, things are still more complicated. The main sources of diversity in this area are:

1. Avoidance of the income statement altogether: for example, taking unusual gains and losses, merger premium payouts, or certain financing transactions directly to owners' equity on the balance sheet.
2. Creation of secret reserves (off-balance sheet assets and overstated liabilities) in the name of prudence and conservatism in order to ''manage'' periodic business income reported to outsiders.
3. Impact of legal requirements that may necessitate setting up legal reserves to protect some tax advantages, treating executive bonuses and stock options on or off income statements, or dictating accruals by legal formula rather than economic effect.

In the preceding paragraphs, we have identified about two dozen accounting topics for which country-by-country measurement differences exist. International accounting textbooks treat these differences in some detail. Many articles and monographs present overviews of selected items in tabular arrangements. Exhibit 2–3 is an example.

We now turn to three specific cases.

Goodwill

When a company buys another company, a business division, or some other business enterprise, it typically anticipates greater benefits than the fair market values of the net assets acquired. Maybe an added team of executives will bring about

EXHIBIT 2-3   Selected Accounting Treatments in EC Countries

Country	Funds Flow Statement	Equity Method	Revaluation Reserves	Reserve Account		
				Statutory	General	Hidden
Belgium	No	Rare	Yes	Yes	Yes	Some
Denmark	Yes	Yes	Yes	Yes	Yes	Some
France	Yes	Yes	Yes, countrywide	Yes	Yes	Prohibited
Germany	Rare	Prohibited	No	No	No	No
Greece	No	Rare	Yes, countrywide	Yes	Yes	Some
Ireland	Yes	Rare	Yes	No	No	Prohibited
Italy	Yes	Rare	Yes	Yes	Yes	Some
Luxembourg	Rare	Rare	No	Yes	Yes	Rare
Netherlands	Yes	Yes	Yes	Yes	Yes	Prohibited
Portugal	Rare	Rare	Yes, countrywide	Yes	Yes	Some
Spain	Rare	Rare	Yes, countrywide	Yes	Yes	Some
United Kingdom	Yes	Yes	Yes	No	No	Prohibited

SOURCE: L. Sundby and B. Schwieger, "EC, EZ?" *Journal of Accountancy*, March 1992, p. 71.

major synergy, maybe certain patents or processes lend themselves to higher profit potential, or maybe market access is at stake. Whatever the anticipated benefit, to the extent that purchase price exceeds total fair market value, something called *goodwill* is created (*negative goodwill* may occur in bargain purchases).

Considerable diversity exists among countries on whether purchased goodwill should be carried on balance sheets, and if so, whether it should be amortized and how it should be amortized.

Probably the most authoritative recent comparative GAAP study was initiated by the Office of the Chief Accountant of the SEC when it asked the Big Six accounting firms to survey and compare certain key accounting standards and practices in the United States to those of certain other major countries. The accounting for goodwill, among other items, was surveyed by Arthur Andersen & Co. Exhibit 2-4 presents its findings.

The goodwill accounting diversity is aggravated by a taxation effect. For instance, goodwill amortization is not tax deductible in the United States, United Kingdom, or the Netherlands, but it is deductible in Canada, Japan, and Germany (post-1986). Obviously, the diversity involved affects business practices and therefore global competitiveness. If a company can permanently shield its income statements from goodwill amortization, it will report comparatively higher net earnings and thereby gain a competitive advantage.

Pensions

Individual and employer-provided private pension plans are common in the United States but not elsewhere, since government sponsored pension schemes

EXHIBIT 2–4   Accounting for Goodwill in Selected Countries

	Option to Expense Immediately	Option to Charge to Equity	Amortization Period	Straight-Line or Accelerated
Australia	No	No	20 years*	S/L
Canada	No	No	40 years*	S/L
France	No	Rare	20 years	S/L
Germany	No	Yes	5 years	S/L
Italy	Yes	Yes	10 years*	S/L
Japan				
Legal merger	Yes	No	5 years*	S/L
Consolidation	No	No	5 years	S/L
The Netherlands	Yes	Yes	5 years	Accelerated
United Kingdom	No	Yes	Rare	Rare
United States	No	No	40 years*	S/L
International Standards				
Existing standards	No	Yes	Not specified	Not specified
Proposed standards	No	No	20 years*	S/L

*Maximum amortization period.

SOURCE: Arthur Andersen & Co., Coopers & Lybrand, Deloitte & Touche, Ernst & Young, KPMG Peat Marwick, and Price Waterhouse, *Survey of International Accounting Practices*, 1991, p. 3.

predominate in most countries. This fact alone triggers accounting practice differences. In addition, some pension plans are based on defined contributions, where defined amounts are paid in periodically and the employee receives whatever has accumulated at the time of retirement. Alternatively, there are defined benefit plans. Here, the contractor (employer or government) agrees to make specified payments to retired employees in the future and then must contribute enough assets to cover the required future payouts. This is a major source of GAAP differences between countries. Along procedural lines, the United States is the only country that requires annual revaluation of all pension plan obligations. Revaluations every three years are the international norm. Also, U.S. pension accruals are high by international comparisons. This means that comparative net earnings reported by U.S. companies are relatively lower.

To provide some insight into country-to-country pension accounting differences, Exhibit 2–5 contains excerpts from comparisons reported in the 1991 *Survey of International Accounting Practices*. The three issues selected are necessarily technical, but they also illustrate well the point of existing international diversity.

Recognition of Inflation and Other Price Changes

Financial accounting in most countries is based in part on the *historical cost principle*. This principle is based on the assumption that the currency unit used to report financial results is reasonably stable—that is, there is little or no inflation.

As a result, strict historical cost accounting does not recognize the effects of inflation or other price changes. Keeping assets valued at their original transaction prices avoids having to make subjective determinations about how much more or less they are worth now compared to some earlier time. Accountants have traditionally believed that objective accounting information is more reliable than subjective information and, therefore, more useful.

However, as discussed in Chapter 1, severe inflation is a potent force that can strain the historical cost principle. Dramatic price changes make historical cost accounting information less believable and, therefore, less useful. The reasonableness of the historical cost principle varies inversely with the severity of price changes.

There are two basic approaches to accounting for changing prices. *General price level (GPL) accounting* (also known as constant dollar accounting) uniformly changes the values of assets and liabilities to reflect the general change in the currency unit's purchasing power. While transactions are initially recorded at their historical costs, they are later notched up or down by changes in the currency's general purchasing power. As a result, the items on the balance sheet and income statement are reported in units of the same purchasing power. *Current value accounting,* on the other hand, changes the historical costs of assets to their current values and recognizes corresponding expenses at the current cost of obtaining the services represented by those expenses. Current value accounting has several variations, of which *current cost accounting (CCA)* is the most widely accepted. (For our purposes we consider current cost accounting to be synonymous with current value accounting.)

Only a very few countries *require* that the effects of changing prices be incorporated directly into the accounting records and financial statements. This points out that while inflation can put a severe strain on the historical cost model of accounting, historical cost nevertheless has a strong hold on accounting practices. Historical cost is still the predominant basis for preparing financial statements. The GAAP of some countries, though, allow companies to reflect the effects of changing prices if they choose to do so. And the GAAP of still other countries suggest that the impacts of fluctuating prices be disclosed supplementally—apart from the main financial statements.

The International Accounting Standards Committee (IASC) recommends in *Standard 29,* "Financial Reporting in Hyperinflationary Economies," that when a company is reporting in the currency of a country experiencing very high levels of inflation, the financial statements should be restated to reflect the purchasing power of that currency unit at year-end. In other words, *Standard 29* requires comprehensive GPL accounting for a company reporting in the currency of a "hyperinflationary" economy.

South America.   South American countries base their approach on general price level accounting. They have contended with high inflation rates for a long time and, as a result, accounting for changing prices is an issue too serious for their accountants to ignore.

EXHIBIT 2–5 Pension Accounting Aspects in Selected Countries

United States	International†	Australia	Canada	France
Assumptions				
Each represents management's best estimate.	Should be appropriate and compatible; modified from time to time.	Determined in the aggregate, on a long-term basis; infrequently adjusted.	Each and in the aggregate represent management's best estimate, reassessed annually.	Each represents management's best estimate modified only to reflect lasting, significant deviations from actual experience.
Future compensation levels				
Required assumption based on management's best estimate.	Incorporate an assumption about projected salary levels to date of retirement.	Ranges within 6% to 10% and promotional adjustments.	Required assumption based on management's best estimate.	Estimate future benefits as accurately as possible; broken into cost of living adjustment and merit seniority increases.
Prior service cost				
Amortized (straight line) over the average employees' remaining service lives.*	Recognized systematically over a period approximating the average of the expected remaining working lives of participating employees.	Amortized over employees' remaining service lives.	Amortized in a rational and systematic manner over an appropriate period, usually the expected average remaining service life of employees.	Annual service cost is adjusted to reflect the effects of the amendments; amounts amortized over remaining active life of plan participants, but method of amortization is not specified.

*U.S. GAAP does not allow immediate recognition of prior service costs from plan amendments unless the employer does not expect to realize any future economic benefits from that retroactive plan amendment. Since this situation is very uncommon, this summary reflects the predominant practice of amortizing such amounts.

†IAS requirements are based on the existing standard, IAS 19, Accounting for Retirement Benefits in the Financial Statements of Employers, and the proposed amendments, as set forth in the Statement of Intent, Comparability of Financial Statements.

‡Italian accounting standards do not specifically address defined benefit plans. Therefore, Italian companies look to IAS 19 for guidance, the requirements of which are listed herein without consideration of any proposed amendments thereto.

SOURCE: Arthur Andersen & Co., Coopers & Lybrand, Deloitte & Touche, Ernst & Young, KPMG Peat Marwick, and Price Waterhouse, *Survey of International Accounting Practices,* 1991, p. 49.

Germany	Italy‡	Japan	The Netherlands	United Kingdom
Long term, often set or influenced by law; infrequently adjusted.	Should be appropriate and compatible; no specific guidance on individual assumptions; modified from time to time.	Most are regulated by law and are infrequently adjusted.	Established on an item-by-item basis; infrequently adjusted.	Actuary's best long-term estimate; reevaluated at each valuation date.
Not included in plan assumptions.	No specific guidance.	Within a specified range, set by law.	Not included in plan assumptions.	Required assumption based on actuary's best estimate.
Immediately recognized.	Either immediately recognized or allocated systematically over expected remaining working lives of participating employees.	Either amortized over a reasonable period of time (and amortization method is not specified) or immediately recognized.	Immediately recognized; may be recorded as a direct charge to shareholders' equity.	Normally amortized over remaining working life or average working life of plan participants, but method of amortization is not specified.

Argentina, Bolivia, Brazil, and Chile require companies to comprehensively restate their financial statements on the basis of changes in general price levels. Several others require that fixed assets be revalued at certain intervals for changes in the price level. (Since fixed assets are not replaced as often as current assets, their historical costs are more likely to be out of date with persistently high price changes.) Depreciation expense is calculated on the restated values of fixed assets. A few other South American countries also accept such restatements. Interestingly, in Bolivia and Brazil, a company's *taxable* income is also computed after making inflation adjustments—something most tax authorities would never allow.

The Netherlands.   Accounting in the Netherlands is heavily influenced by business economics (or *microeconomics*, the study of the behavior of individual economic agents, such as business firms, and the markets in which they operate). A fundamental notion in business economics is that the input values of a company's goods and services must be less than their selling prices in order to maintain long-run profitability and, hence, ensure survival. The Dutch professor Theodore Limperg (1879–1961) is often called the father of replacement value theory, from which current cost accounting is derived.

CCA is not required in the Netherlands but is strongly encouraged by the Netherlands Institute of Registeraccountants either as supplemental information or by incorporation into the primary financial statements. While most Dutch companies continue to use historical cost accounting, many of the large ones prepare comprehensive current cost financial statements. Those that use historical cost often disclose current cost information supplementally.

United States and the United Kingdom.   The recent history of accounting for price changes is similar for the United States and the United Kingdom. Both countries experienced what were for them unusually high levels of inflation during the 1970s. By 1980, both had standards in effect to provide information in financial statements about the effects of changing prices. In the United States, the FASB published *Statement 33*, "Financial Reporting and Changing Prices." It required large publicly held companies (approximately 1,300 in all) to supplementally disclose selected financial statement items on both current cost and general price level bases.

This requirement proved to be highly controversial. Many companies preparing the information protested that it was too costly to produce and that it was unreliable. There were also a number of studies that assessed the usefulness of the required disclosures. Most of these studies concluded that the disclosures provided little if any benefit to users beyond the primary historical cost financial statements. The FASB finally decided that the costs of preparing and reporting the information were not worth the benefits, and in 1986, *Statement 89* was issued making the disclosures voluntary rather than mandatory.

Statement of Standard Accounting Practice (SSAP) 16, "Current Cost Accounting," was issued in the United Kingdom in 1980. It was a comprehensive current cost approach and applied to all public and nationalized companies, plus private companies above a certain size—altogether, 5,000 to 6,000 companies. Companies could either prepare (1) primary financial statements based on historical cost, with current cost financial statements as a supplement, (2) primary financial statements based on current cost, with historical cost financial statements as a supplement, or (3) current cost financial statements only, with selected historical cost items disclosed.

SSAP 16 was as unpopular in the United Kingdom as *Statement 33* was in the United States, and for this reason, a new standard was proposed in 1984. Unlike *SSAP 16*, it did not call for dual financial statements. Instead, it suggested limited current cost disclosures of such amounts as depreciation, cost of goods sold, and fixed assets. The proposal represented a more flexible, simplified, and less comprehensive approach to accounting for changing prices than *SSAP 16.* Moreover, it called for these disclosures only from large corporations. As a result, it would have been less universally applicable. However, the 1984 proposal proved to be just as controversial as *SSAP 16,* and all the while compliance with *SSAP 16* by U.K. companies was deteriorating. As a result, it was made nonmandatory in 1986.

CONSEQUENCES OF WORLDWIDE ACCOUNTING DIVERSITY

Enough evidence is available to conclude resolutely that GAAP differ (at times substantially) from country to country. Whether this is good or bad depends on the points of view of a variety of interest groups.

Corporate Management

Managers of companies with strictly domestic operations care little. As long as national GAAP are relatively clear, useful, and broadly applied, most medium-sized and small companies feel well served by the accounting rules they have to contend with. In this regard, there are no problems.

MNCs see it differently. They face global competition every day and find that working with many different national GAAP requirements is a costly proposition. They also sense that accounting diversity affects competitiveness. If a European corporation can bid for a U.S. acquisition target company and immediately write off all premium payouts to owners' equity, it might outbid an equally interested U.S. corporation that must amortize the same premium payouts as goodwill through subsequent income statements. MNCs like "level playing fields" for their global operations. Distorting factors cause barriers and retaliation.

MNCs also worry about accounting for similar events and transactions in a

mnc = Multi-national Corp.

similar manner. If a given set of business activities allows reporting higher net income under one set of GAAP in comparison with another set of GAAP, management immediately seeks to compensate for such accounting effects so that corporate borrowing costs and prices for the corporation's shares and bonds remain unaffected. Given a choice, some MNC managements will attempt to use another country's GAAP if they think the other GAAP are better known and understood than their own. As discussed in Chapter 4, MNCs want to be understood by their customers, bankers, labor unions, suppliers, government regulators, and other interested parties.

Investors

Portfolio investors and their agents, financial analysts, probably dislike international accounting diversity the most. Instant global communications and overall cheap and quick access to global financial markets have made cross-border investing very attractive. Since national business cycles are not synchronized around the world, advantages are available from judicious diversification of investments involving different national securities markets. Financial misinformation short-circuits this process.

Investors experience frustrations when they do not understand whether financial statements merely look similar or are in fact similarly prepared (see the first case in Chapter 1). Underwriters consistently report that worldwide accounting diversity causes some underwriting (i.e., pricing of new securities issues) difficulties. If investors, analysts, and underwriters indeed experience difficulties with GAAP diversity, financial markets are not as efficient as they could be and therefore returns to investors are less than they ought to be. This is a powerful indictment of GAAP diversity.

Accounting Professionals and Regulators

Some have suggested that accounting professionals, especially those in the Big Six professional firms, like diversity because it generates fees for them all the way from assisting in setting up new business units for their clients in different GAAP territories to restating financial reports from one set of GAAP to another (see Chapter 4). GAAP diversity also makes cross-border auditing more costly and therefore raises auditing fees. Even though not demonstrated by reliable research, it stands to reason that at least some accounting professionals gain from the GAAP diversity factor.

Accounting regulators, as guardians of the public interest, would like to have full authority over all GAAP and financial reporting of companies whose securities are publicly held or whose size is so large that the public interest is affected. But regulations are primarily enforced through national laws and national legal systems. Therefore, a national focus is inevitable for accounting regulation—at least for the time being. Moreover, national regulators want discretion over national GAAP. International or any other GAAP are beyond their reach of influence and hence unacceptable. Nationalism is an issue here. Do you want others (i.e., non-nationals) to have determining influence over the GAAP you are required to use? Many countervailing forces come to bear on this point.

CONCLUSION

Worldwide diversity in financial accounting and reporting exists. Four specific reasons explain this diversity. In some instances, the diversity among national GAAP is significant; in others it is not. There are some winners and some losers as a result of the diversity condition. When diversity reaches the point of misinformation, it becomes dysfunctional. National environmental factors together with national laws and national accounting standard setting systems will make some degree of GAAP diversity inevitable. However, in domestic terms, national GAAP have reduced practice diversity. A similar degree of diversity reduction may be desirable on the international level. Harmonization of accounting practices is aimed at such reduction and is explored in Chapter 3.

KEY POINTS

1. International diversity springs from a number of sources. Four examples are: the environmental variables that impact accounting development; the adherence to a particular financial accounting model; the way accounting standards are set; and how uncertainties are reflected.

2. There is diversity in both measurement and disclosure practices. Three key measurement differences are accounting for goodwill, pensions, and inflation.

3. Many people believe that differences in accounting are not neutral in their effects—that is, they affect business decisions, produce an "unlevel playing field," and impact the global competitiveness of companies.

4. There are winners and losers as a consequence of worldwide accounting diversity. Corporate managements and investors often believe they are hurt, but at least some professional accountants probably gain from the diversity.

CASES

Whose Money?

The world's portfolio investors are heteromonetary when it comes to earning the highest possible returns on their investments.

Sigwan Fund is composed entirely of U.S. investors. It is incorporated in Delaware and pays dividends strictly in U.S. dollars. However, all of its assets are invested in the common stocks of Sigwan companies listed on the SWSE—the Sigwan Stock Exchange. The Sigwan national currency is the Sigi, which is fully convertible and internationally quite stable.

"All of our record-keeping and accounting practices ought to be in U.S. dollars and U.S. GAAP," snorts Clint Hill, the fund's general manager. "After all, the United States is our cradle, and that's where we are ultimately accountable. Forget all this Sigi nonsense."

"Wrong, wrong, and wrong again," retorts Benno Hellborn, the fund's CFO. "Everything we have is fully invested in Sigwan securities denominated in Sigis. This is what determines our future viability! We must report using Sigwan GAAP and Sigi currency units. Economic reality absolutely dictates this."

Questions

1. Do you agree with Mr. Hill or Mr. Hellborn? Defend your response adequately.
2. Why is the choice of national GAAP and/or national currency an issue in these circumstances? Is the issue contrived?
3. From the perspective of the fund, an identity question bears on the GAAP choice. Does this choice push the fund toward a U.S. or a Sigwan identity? As a fund investor, would you have any preferences?
4. Should Sigwan or U.S. regulators be able to determine appropriate GAAP choices for the Sigwan Fund? Please explain your answer adequately.

National Agendas for Accounting

"As a national accounting regulator, I owe allegiance only to my country and its citizens. I will work long hours and expend all the personal energy I have to assure that the best possible accounting information reaches everyone in the economic marketplace in my country. I have some empathy for what other governments and their accounting regulators want to achieve, but this is at best a secondary concern. International efforts always end up watered down and catering to the lowest common denominator. The only way to stay on top is to show the flag and rally around it."

Questions

1. What benefits, if any, have been achieved from following the perspective advocated by the person quoted?

2. Given only the information you presently have, would you support the creation of additional national accounting standard setting authorities in countries that now don't have such agencies?

3. Does cross-country accounting diversity really influence global business competition? Defend your answer in two or three brief paragraphs.

4. If you were master/mistress of the universe, how would you go about reducing the present level of accounting practice diversity around the world?

The Current Cost Conundrum

Antje Larson is a senior accountant for a large U.S. multinational corporation. She has just attended a seminar in Europe, where she learned that the Netherlands allows firms to use current cost accounting as the basis for their primary financial statements. On the flight back to the United States, she thinks about what her boss's reaction would be if she proposed that the corporation they work for adopt this practice.

"Why, that's a bunch of nonsense," her boss would probably say.

"For one thing, prices are rising, and current cost accounting produces lower net income in those circumstances. Lower net income means two things: (1) investors are going to be less willing to provide our company with the capital we need and (2) since my bonus is based on company profits, my bonus will drop. For another thing, our company purchased a lot of property a number of years ago, and its value has gone up substantially since then. With historical cost, I only have to report the prices we paid for the property. With current cost, I have to show what it is worth now. If we tell *that* to our shareholders, they may start clamoring for us to sell it and pay the extra money out as a dividend.

"Besides, current cost data are too subjective. It's a proven fact that investors demand hard, objective numbers from accountants. Current cost information is so unreliable, investors would either not use it at all or they would misinterpret it."

Questions

1. Would Antje's boss be correct in contending that the lower net income accompanying current cost accounting would make it harder for the company to raise investment capital? How about the bonus contention?

2. Would investors misuse current cost information? Would they not use it at all?

3. Should shareholders be kept in the dark about the current value of the company's assets?

4. In what other way(s) might the company reveal current cost information besides incorporating it into the primary financial statements?

ADDITIONAL READINGS

Andersen, Arthur & Co., Coopers & Lybrand, Deloitte & Touche, Ernst & Young, KPMG Peat Marwick, and Price Waterhouse, *Survey of International Accounting Practices.* New York: Authors, 1991, 56 pp.

Brown, P. R. and C. P. Stickney, "Instructional Case: Tanaguchi Corporation," *Issues in Accounting Education* (Spring 1992), pp. 57–79.

Coopers & Lybrand, *International Accounting Summaries: A Guide for Interpretation and Comparison.* New York: John Wiley & Sons, Inc., 1991, paginated by section. Annual update supplements available.

Doost, R. K. and K. M. Ligon. "How U.S. and European Accounting Practices Differ." *Management Accounting* (October 1986), pp. 38–41.

International Capital Markets Group, *Harmonization of International Accounting Standards.* London, England: International Bar Association, 1992, 67 pp.

Stewart, M., "Accounting Down Under." *CPA Journal* (October 1989), pp. 62, 64–65.

Wallace, R. S. O. and P. A. Collier, "The 'Cash' in Cash Flow Statements: A Multi-Country Comparison." *Accounting Horizons* (December 1991), pp. 44–52.

3

HARMONIZATION OF FINANCIAL ACCOUNTING DIVERSITY

Chapter 1 explains how certain environmental variables shape the development of accounting in a particular country. It also provides a rationale for the worldwide diversity of accounting practices—since accounting reflects the environment in which it operates and since environments differ around the world, it follows that accounting will also be different around the world. The worldwide diversity in financial accounting practices is addressed in Chapter 2.

One way to reduce diversity (i.e., bring harmony) is to set and then enforce common standards for all concerned. Standards we all know about include speed limits on streets and highways, appropriate labeling of consumer products, and grades awarded to college and university students. Accounting and auditing standards play key roles in financial reporting (see Chapter 4).

ACCOUNTING AND AUDITING STANDARDS

Accounting standards are the rules for preparing financial statements: that is, the "generally accepted accounting principles" (GAAP) that specify the type of information that financial statements ought to contain and how that information ought to be prepared. Accounting standards define what are acceptable and unacceptable financial accounting practices.

Auditing standards are the rules governing how an *audit* is performed. An audit of financial statements is the technical process by which an independent person (the auditor) gathers evidence to form an opinion about how well a set of financial statements conforms to GAAP. In most countries, a particular group of accountants is legally sanctioned to conduct financial statement audits. In the United States, for example, it is the certified public accountant (CPA). In the United

Kingdom, it is the chartered accountant; in the Netherlands, the register accountant; and in Germany, the Wirtschaftsprüfer. Financial statements conforming to GAAP are said to be "reliable," and reliable information is an important ingredient in good decision making.

Accounting standards and auditing standards are interrelated. Accounting standards presumably define what is *useful* financial information. Auditing standards guide an auditor in determining whether it is also *reliable*. Useful and reliable financial information puts investors, creditors, and others in a position to make better decisions.

Accounting has been called the language of business. That analogy is accurate, since accounting is a form of communication. As with all types of communication, though, misunderstandings can arise unless meanings are reasonably clear.

To counteract the possibility of misunderstood financial communications, approximately 40 countries have created their own national financial accounting standard setting mechanisms. This has harmonized financial accounting diversity *within* countries. Unfortunately, international diversity continues to exist. This diversity results in a general lack of comparability in financial reports from one country to the next. As a result, there is a risk of misunderstanding when financial statements are communicated transnationally. The ensuing problems for users and preparers of financial reports are outlined in Chapter 4.

The problem of different auditing standards is more subtle. Fundamentally, an audit assures users that they can trust the information communicated by the financial statements. However, if auditors around the world are not comparably trained or if they do not observe comparable standards, then their work varies in quality. As a result, the inherent reliability of financial statements also varies.

The existence of different accounting and auditing standards affects the decisions of resource providers to the extent that they fail to either understand or trust the messages communicated by financial statements. A number of international and regional organizations recognize this problem and are endeavoring to harmonize accounting and auditing standards to the extent possible. This chapter discusses the work of these organizations. First, however, we quickly review the three major bodies involved directly in accounting and auditing standard setting in the United States. These organizations indirectly influence accounting in other countries as well, due to the United States' leading position in the accounting world.

U.S. ORGANIZATIONS

The U.S. *Securities and Exchange Commission* (SEC) is a U.S. government agency charged with ensuring adequate accounting and reporting standards for companies whose securities are publicly traded in the United States. The SEC's primary concern is to protect investors from potential losses resulting from insufficient or incorrect financial information. The SEC is empowered to write accounting standards for so-called publicly held companies, although it has typically deferred this task to the Financial Accounting Standards Board. Any corporation whose securities are publicly traded in the United States (even a non-U.S. firm) must abide by the rules of the SEC. The SEC's reporting requirements for non-U.S. firms are similar, though not identical, to the reporting requirements for U.S. companies. In this way, it also exerts influence over the financial reporting of some companies from other countries.

The *Financial Accounting Standards Board* (FASB) is the principal body that writes the generally accepted accounting principles by which the financial statements of U.S. companies must be prepared. The official pronouncements that establish GAAP are known as *Statements of Financial Accounting Standards (SFAS)*, and those issued so far concern such diverse topics as accounting for leases (*Statement 13*), reporting the effects of changing prices (*Statement 33*), foreign currency translation (*Statement 52*), and employers' accounting for postretirement benefits other than pensions (*Statement 106*). The FASB has also produced a conceptual framework that deals with theoretical and conceptual issues and is intended to provide an underlying structure for future accounting standards. The conceptual framework pronouncements are called *Statements of Financial Accounting Concepts*. Moreover, in various policy statements, the FASB has committed itself to full consideration of international perspectives in all of its work.

The FASB is a private-sector body (i.e., not a government agency) supported financially by several professional, business, and accounting groups. The board is composed of seven full-time members, who are aided by a staff of some 50 technical specialists plus administrative and other support personnel.

The *American Institute of Certified Public Accountants* (AICPA) is an organization of about 300,000 CPAs. CPAs engage in a number of accounting activities including preparing tax returns, giving tax advice, and conducting audits of financial statements. The AICPA publishes standards to aid auditors in their examinations. *Statements on Auditing Standards* cover such issues as how to plan an audit and supervise assistants, how to report audit findings, the use of statistical sampling on an audit, and what to do when the auditor discovers fraud. Like the FASB, it is a private-sector body.

PROS AND CONS OF INTERNATIONAL ACCOUNTING AND AUDITING STANDARDS

Every international accounting textbook and most international accounting research studies contain long lists of benefits and costs arising from international accounting and auditing standard setting. Among the alleged benefits, these sources mention greater international comparability of financial reports most often. Financial executives think that a more level playing field will result if international accounting standards are widely used—with reference to items such as cross-border mergers and acquisitions, and securing financing outside the home country. Some economists believe that such standards would improve global business competition, and some international agencies (e.g., UN) advocate international standards as a form of assistance to developing countries. In a more operational sense, international standards may reduce bookkeeping costs and allow more efficient preparation of financial statements.

Researchers have identified still other benefits: for example, reconciliation of sometimes adversarial interests between preparers and users of financial statements. Standardization is thought to bring more efficiency to analysis and use of financial reports and, pointedly, increase the credibility of the entire financial reporting system.

Of course, there are also those who object to the very idea of international accounting and auditing standards. In the early 1970s, critics condemned international standard setting as a solution too simple for a problem too complex. Other challenges point to inherent differences in national backgrounds and traditions, the potential breach of national sovereignty, politicalization of the entire field of accounting, plus standards overload if both national and international standards have to be applied concurrently.

A senior U.S. corporate officer gives this perspective:

> Harmonization of international accounting principles is unlikely to come about. Too many different national groups have vested interests in maintaining their own standards and practices which have developed from widely different perspectives and histories. There is not a single powerful champion of the proposal for harmonization. There is no authoritative body with the ability to mandate the adoption of Global GAAP. . . . I have argued that Global GAAP is unlikely to be achieved due to the institutional impediments in the standards setting process and because there is no demonstrated need in order to fuel the growth of robust international capital markets.[1]

Nevertheless, the movement toward international standards for accounting and auditing is growing.

INTERNATIONAL ORGANIZATIONS

We now turn to the international and regional organizations involved in harmonizing accounting and auditing standards within their respective spheres of influence. The organizations discussed can be categorized according to several key variables, and you may want to keep them in mind as you read:

1. Is the organization concerned with accounting standards, auditing standards, or both? Some organizations are trying to harmonize the form and content of financial statements, while others are concerned with professional accountants themselves and the way they do their work.

2. Are the organization's members governments of countries or professional accounting groups from different countries? This sometimes affects the

---

[1]R. K. Goeltz, "International Accounting Harmonization: The Impossible (and Unnecessary?) Dream," *Accounting Horizons*, March 1991, pp. 85–88.

political pressures bearing on the organization's deliberations and the types of interests that the organization represents.

3. Is the organization's effort regional or international in scope? Regional efforts may stand a greater chance of success, since the participants are likely to have more in common than those of a broader based, international effort.

International Accounting Standards Committee

The *International Accounting Standards Committee* (IASC) was formed to develop worldwide accounting standards. Many differences in financial reporting practices among the world's corporations do arise legitimately from differences in business environments. However, not all differences can be thus explained.

Accounting evolves rather slowly, and larger multinationals have literally transcended the environments of their native countries to reflect a global business environment. (Toyota, for example, probably has more in common with General Motors than it does with small Japanese companies.) Yet most multinational corporations still retain the accounting practices of their native countries.

In essence, the IASC is trying to harmonize the world's accounting standards and eliminate those differences that cannot be explained by environmental variables. Even though international standards are meant for all companies, they are especially relevant for multinational corporations.

To date, the IASC has issued 31 *International Accounting Standards* (IASs). Those mentioned elsewhere in this text are:

Standard 14, "Reflecting Financial Information by Segments."

Standard 15, "Information for Reflecting the Effects of Changing Prices."

Standard 21, "Accounting for the Effects of Changes in Foreign Exchange Rates."

Standard 27, "Consolidated Financial Statements and Accounting for Investments in Subsidiaries."

Standard 29, "Financial Reporting in Hyperinflationary Economies."

The IASC was formed in 1973 by an agreement of the leading professional bodies in Australia, Canada, France, Germany, Japan, Mexico, the Netherlands, the United Kingdom and Ireland, and the United States. It now represents more than 100 accountancy bodies from 78 countries, which are listed in Exhibit 3–1.

Unlike some of the organizations discussed later, governments do not belong to the IASC—it is a private-sector body with representatives from professional accounting organizations. In one sense the IASC is an international counterpart to the U.S.'s FASB.

The International Accounting Standards Committee is governed by a board consisting of representatives from 13 countries, including the founding member

---

EXHIBIT 3-1 Countries Represented by the IASC

Australia	India	Panama
Austria	Indonesia	Paraguay
Bahamas	Iraq	Philippines
Bahrain	Ireland	Poland
Bangladesh	Israel	Portugal
Barbados	Italy	Singapore
Belgium	Jamaica	South Africa
Bolivia	Japan	Spain
Botswana	Jordan	Sri Lanka
Brazil	Kenya	Swaziland
Canada	Korea	Sweden
Chile	Kuwait	Switzerland
Colombia	Lebanon	Syria
Cyprus	Lesotho	Taiwan
Denmark	Liberia	Tanzania
Dominican Republic	Libya	Thailand
Ecuador	Luxembourg	Trinidad and Tobago
Egypt	Malawi	Tunisia
Germany	Malaysia	Turkey
Fiji	Malta	United Kingdom
Finland	Mexico	United States of
France	Morocco	America
Ghana	Netherlands	Uruguay
Greece	New Zealand	Yugoslavia
Hong Kong	Nigeria	Zambia
Iceland	Norway	Zimbabwe
	Pakistan	

---

countries listed earlier. Before approving a *Standard*, the board exposes it for public comment for six months and seeks input from all IASC member bodies. The board meets several times a year in a different city in order to secure a variety of viewpoints. For example, recent meetings have been held in Copenhagen, Sydney, Seoul, and Chicago.

Compliance with IASC *Standards* is voluntary, since the IASC has no power to enforce them. Nevertheless, support for the IASC and recognition of its *Standards* are growing around the world. The IASC is increasingly viewed as an effective voice for defining acceptable "world class" accounting principles. For example, Japan began requiring financial statements prepared on a "consolidated" basis after the IASC issued its initial pronouncement on the topic (see Chapter 6 for more details on consolidation of financial statements). If all multinational corporations observed IASC *Standards*, significant harmonization would occur. Striking examples are accounting for the costs of income taxes and employee retirement benefits. Cash basis, rather than accrual basis, accounting for these two kinds of business costs is commonly used in many countries. However, IASC *Standards* require accrual accounting for both of them.

The IASC's most ambitious project to date is its comparability project. Announced in 1989 as *Exposure Draft 32*, this undertaking is aimed at eliminating most of the choices between various alternative accounting methods allowed under existing IASs. Broad support exists for this project. Financial analysts, attorneys, bankers, labor unions, and other business groups have expressed approval of the process involved. IOSCO (defined in the following section), a key international agency, has voted to support IASC and the comparability project. By the end of 1992, the IASC had agreed on the elimination of alternative treatments for 22 difficult accounting issues. Implementation will occur through revisions of existing IASs affected.

Regarding future activities, IASC has committed itself to a number of propositions. These include (excerpts only):

As the need arises, IASC will develop new International Accounting Standards and revise existing International Accounting Standards. IASC has, however, made clear that it will spend less time on new Standards. It is unlikely that there will ever be more than forty current International Accounting Standards (current projects will take the total to about 35).

* * * * *

Multinational companies will make greater use of International Accounting Standards particularly when they wish to raise capital in foreign markets.

* * * * *

There will be more co-operation between the standard setting bodies of different countries which will lead to mutual recognition of the accounting requirements of different countries. This will only be successful if each country's requirements conform with International Accounting Standards so IASC will be a key part of that process. Therefore, IASC and national standard setting bodies will work together to:
• Improve International Accounting Standards.
• Narrow the differences between the existing requirements of different countries.
• Narrow the differences between national requirements and International Accounting Standards.

* * * * *

The world-wide accountancy profession will continue to play a major part in the work of IASC. The business community and the users of financial statements will also play a greater part in the work of IASC.

International Federation of Accountants

The *International Federation of Accountants* (IFAC) was formed in 1977 to develop a worldwide accountancy profession. Its purpose is similar to that of the AICPA except on a global basis; that is, it is mainly concerned with professional

---

EXHIBIT 3–2   IFAC's Mission Statement

The International Federation of Accountants (IFAC) is the worldwide organization for the accountancy profession. The mission of IFAC is the development and enhancement of the profession to enable it to provide the public interest with services of consistently high quality.

To achieve this goal, IFAC will pursue the following objectives:

- Enhance the standards and development of the profession by issuing technical and professional guidance and by promoting the adoption of IFAC and IASC pronouncements.

- Promote the profession's role, responsibilities, and achievements in advancing the interests of member bodies and in serving the public interest.

- Foster a strong and cohesive profession by providing leadership on emerging issues, coordinating with regional organizations and member bodies and assisting them to achieve strategic objectives.

- Assist with the formation and development of national and regional organizations that serve the interests of accountants in public practice, commerce, industry, public sector, and education.

- Liaise with international organizations to influence the development of efficient capital markets and international trade in services.

---

accountants rather than accounting principles. Its members are drawn from professional accounting bodies in over 75 countries. Exhibit 3–2 shows IFAC's mission statement and the related action goals.

IFAC's International Auditing Practices Committee issues *International Standards on Auditing* (ISAs), designed to harmonize the way audits are conducted worldwide. IASs issued to date include *Standard No. 1* on the objective and scope of an audit, *No. 6* on studying and evaluating the accounting system, *No. 8* on audit evidence, *No. 13* on the auditor's report, and *No. 25* on materiality and audit risk. Its Education Committee works toward harmonizing the qualifications for becoming a professional accountant, while its Ethics Committee tries to make the codes of professional ethics in various countries more compatible with each other. For example, the Education Committee has published a comprehensive *Guideline (No. 9)* dealing with the education and training needed to become an accountant. The Ethics Committee has developed the *Code of Ethics for Professional Accountants*, which covers, among other items, accountants' integrity, objectivity, and independence, as well as the confidentiality of information obtained during the course of an audit.

Every five years, IFAC organizes a World Congress of Accountants, the 14th of which was held in 1992 in Washington, D.C. Eighteen countries are represented on IFAC's governing council, and general assemblies of the organization are conducted every two and a half years. Council terms are also two and a half years.

Acceptance of IFAC pronouncements received a major boost when the International Organization of Securities Commissions (IOSCO) voted in 1992 to accept

ISAs for purposes of multinational registrations and filings with securities commissions. The strength and influence of IOSCO derives from the fact that the organization is comprised of senior securities administrators from about 50 countries. The SEC is a member of IOSCO.

Also in 1992, IFAC forged a strong linkage with the International Organization of Supreme Audit Institutes (INTOSAI). This organization brings together top public-sector auditors from most of the world's independent nations. Nearly all UN member countries are also INTOSAI members. The organization has just begun to issue public-sector auditing standards—which is the linkage to IFAC.

United Nations

The interest of the *United Nations* (UN) in accounting and reporting reflects its wider interest in the effects of multinational corporations on the world economy. In 1982, an advisory group reaffirmed a set of *Guidelines* issued in 1977 listing financial and nonfinancial disclosures that multinational corporations ought to provide. Among the suggested financial disclosures are an income statement and balance sheet, expenditures on research and development, and the amounts of new investments in fixed assets. Recommended nonfinancial disclosures include information about employment and transfer pricing policies. While these *Guidelines* have yet to be adopted by the UN itself, they will likely serve as a checklist for countries to use in requiring information of multinationals located within their borders.

One should recognize that the United Nations is a political forum to which nearly every nation belongs. It is heavily represented by Third World countries, which are not very industrialized and are often suspicious of the heavily industrialized countries (such as the United States) and their large, multinational corporations. Third World countries are particularly concerned about being exploited. Thus, an implicit objective of the UN disclosure *Guidelines* is to get multinational corporations to provide sufficient information so governments of developing nations can better judge their social performance.

Current financial accounting and reporting endeavors at the UN are carried out by its Intergovernmental Working Group of Experts on International Standards of Accounting and Reporting. This Working Group holds annual working sessions in March of each year. The proceedings of each such session are published as *International Accounting and Reporting Issues: 19xx Review*. For example, the *1991 Review* numbers 244 pages and contains a wealth of information aside from UN-specific items. It covers such topics as activities of international and regional organizations, current developments in 44 different countries, and various technical topics like accounting for environmental protection measures.

Organization for Economic Cooperation and Development

The *Organization for Economic Cooperation and Development* (OECD) is an organization of 24 governments of nearly all industrialized countries: Australia,

Austria, Belgium, Canada, Denmark, Finland, France, Germany, Greece, Iceland, Ireland, Italy, Japan, Luxembourg, the Netherlands, New Zealand, Norway, Portugal, Spain, Sweden, Switzerland, Turkey, the United Kingdom, and the United States. Its purpose is to foster economic growth and development in member countries, and it principally acts as a vehicle whereby member countries consult with each other about general economic matters that concern them all, such as balance of payments or exchange rate problems.

In 1976, the OECD issued a code of conduct for multinational corporations that includes guidelines for voluntary disclosures of financial information. More recently, the OECD began looking at the accounting principles in member countries with a view toward encouraging greater harmonization and comparability of accounting and financial reporting. The OECD intends to act only as a catalyst, however. It has neither the resources nor the desire to actually write generally accepted accounting principles. OECD conferences and seminars are high quality international accounting events. Among its various publications is the *Accounting Standards Harmonization* series (e.g., *No. 5*, "Consolidated Financial Statements," 1988).

REGIONAL ORGANIZATIONS

European Community

The *European [Economic] Community* (EC), formerly known as the European Common Market, was formed in 1957 by the Treaty of Rome and now has 12 members: Belgium, Denmark, France, Germany, Greece, Ireland, Italy, Luxembourg, the Netherlands, the United Kingdom, Spain, and Portugal. The EC's major aims are the free flow of goods, persons, and capital; a customs union; and harmonization of laws. To encourage capital movement and capital formation, the EC is harmonizing the generally accepted accounting principles of member countries. The accounting harmonization effort is a part of a broader program by the EC to harmonize the many types of policies related to economic activities. In order to achieve its harmonization objectives, the EC has issued various *Directives,* which are EC laws that member states are obligated to incorporate into their own national laws. The EC efforts are unique in history and, as they are accomplished, they will fundamentally alter how individuals and businesses conduct their activities within this region. Since these harmonization efforts have the full weight of law behind them, the provisions are mandatory for any company doing business there. Anyone with business dealings in Europe (accountants included) should monitor EC developments as they unfold.

Recall from Chapter 1 that there are some fundamental dissimilarities among the EC countries. A very important one is the distinction between a legalistic/nonlegalistic accounting orientation. The legalistic orientation produces highly prescriptive, detailed, and procedural accounting, while nonlegalistic accounting is more innovative and adaptive to business situations. Another fundamental dissimilarity is the role accounting plays in society. Accounting in the Netherlands, United Kingdom, and Ireland is oriented toward the decision needs of investors and creditors. Determining profitability in order to judge how well management has run a company is the significant purpose of accounting. Accounting practices in Germany, Luxembourg, and Belgium are overly conservative and designed mainly to protect the interests of banks. France has uniform accounting designed to facilitate the decision making of government planners.

Through 1992, four EC *Directives* have been issued that have major financial reporting consequences. They are:

Fourth Directive, issued July 26, 1978, basically addressing format and content of financial statements (i.e., constituting EC GAAP).

Directive to Publish Interim Financial Statements, issued February 15, 1982, calling for the publication of six months' interim financial reports within four months of the end of an accounting period.

Seventh Directive, issued June 13, 1983, comprehensively addressing the issue of consolidated financial statements (see Chapter 6).

Eighth Directive, issued April 10, 1984, covering various aspects of the qualifications of professionals authorized to carry out legally required (statutory) audits.

Both the *Fourth* and *Seventh Directives* contain provisions at variance with U.S. generally accepted accounting principles. The *Fourth Directive*, for instance, allows capitalization (and maximum five-year amortization periods) of research and development expenditures, and does not require cash flow statements. In the United States, R&D costs are expensed outright, and cash flow statements are mandatory. Thus, for U.S. companies operating in the EC, new and different financial statements may be necessary to comply with these *Directives*. In addition, larger, closely held U.S. companies operating in the EC will be required to make their financial statements public, even though they do not have to do so in the United States.

Given the significantly different business environments and cultures among the EC member countries, it should not be surprising to find that the EC is experiencing some implementation problems with its accounting and financial reporting harmonization efforts. Italy finally adopted the *Fourth Directive* in 1992. This was 14 years after ratification! Also, all EC *Directives* allow various alternative choices to each adopting member country. For example, abridged financial reporting is allowed in some EC jurisdictions but not in others. Segment disclosures (*SFAS No. 14* in the United States) are optional in all member countries. Therefore the implementation status of each *Directive* in each EC country is as important as the *Directive* itself.

Nevertheless, developments in the EC bear watching. They represent the only active accounting harmonization effort in the world with the force of law behind it. If the effort is successful, one may be more optimistic about the chances for international harmonization. If the effort fails, then achieving worldwide harmonization of accounting is doubtful. Even though it is premature to venture a realistic assessment, the greater EC internal markets integration presently underway seems likely to promote European accounting harmonization. Thus, European developments might become increasingly important to world developments in accounting.

Other Regional Organizations

The *African Accounting Council* was formed in 1979 with the aims of harmonizing accounting practices, upgrading accounting education, and exchanging ideas among member nations. Its members are the *governments* of 27 African countries. National *professional* accounting institutes in the Gambia, Ghana, Liberia, Nigeria, Senegal, and Sierra Leone have jointly formed the *Association of Accountancy Bodies of West Africa*. The *Asociación Interamericana de Contabilidad* is comprised of accountancy bodies from 21 nations in North and South America, though it is primarily concerned with South American accounting issues. Technical accounting papers are presented at group conferences every two or three years. The *ASEAN Federation of Accountants* is an accounting organization of the six members of the Association of Southeast Asian Nations (ASEAN)— Brunei, Indonesia, Malaysia, Philippines, Singapore, and Thailand. Its purpose is to advance the status of the accounting profession in these nations, but it eventually expects to reconcile divergent accounting principles among its members.

The *Confederation of Asian and Pacific Accountants* has representatives from the accounting bodies of some 20 Pacific Rim nations. Its purpose is to develop a coordinated regional accounting profession, and one day it expects to tackle harmonizing accounting standards. The major professional accounting association in Europe is now the *Fédération des Experts Comptables Européens* (FEE—Federation of European Accountants). FEE was established in 1986 as the successor organization of two groups, one with EC ties and the other Europewide. There is a tradition of extensive study groups, conferencing, and publishing activities for the European associations. For example, in 1992 FEE published a major survey and analysis of accounting and disclosure practices of over 400 European companies. It is reasonable to expect significant FEE involvement in international accounting matters.

These six organizations are regional in scope and primarily concerned with the accounting profession rather than accounting practices. However, some eventually expect to harmonize accounting practices at a regional level. The activities of the regional accounting organizations have as their main thrust the exchange of information and discussion of common problems at conferences.

HARMONIZATION SCENARIOS[2]

Harmonization of accounting, auditing, and financial reporting has many dimensions—regional versus global, voluntary versus mandated, piecemeal ver-

---

[2]This section is adapted from the newsletter, *IASC Insight*, December 1991, p. 5.

sus comprehensive, political versus professional, and so forth. What will emerge as the most likely development path for the near future? There are three possibilities.

One scenario is the use of *bilateral agreements*. Under this approach, two or more countries agree to recognize each other's national standards on a reciprocal basis. This would have to be done politically and is likely to be difficult to achieve where national standards differ greatly (e.g., between Japan and the United States).

Mutual recognition on a regional level is a second possibility, for instance, between the EC and North America. Here the clout of regional economies would come to bear—again mainly through political channels. This approach also places accounting professionals and their professional organizations in secondary roles.

A third scenario places harmonization at the doorsteps of *private, professional groups* such as IASC and IFAC. They hammer out internal agreements on key issues and then negotiate acceptance with regulators and other political bodies.

The accounting world of the 1990s contains actual examples of each of these three scenarios. At the time of this writing, it appears that the third alternative enjoys a slight edge. But all harmonization efforts require much time and energy, and all are fraught with pitfalls. Moreover, harmonization is a continuous process. Former IASC Chairman Arthur Wyatt observed:

> We all must understand that harmonization is not an effort to remake the accounting and auditing world in the image of any one culture. While it is clear that emerging standards in both accounting and auditing reflect the needs of those economies that rely on a diverse source of capital providers, those standards will hopefully emerge as a blending of the best standards found in practice and a rejection of notions tried and found wanting. The fact that the standards that are emerging will require some adjustments to practices found in all societies should be of some comfort to those who fear the process is dominated by a single culture.[3]

CONCLUSION

The fact that so many groups are involved in accounting harmonization efforts indicates sizable support for the effort. The question of whether harmonization of either accounting principles or auditing practices is necessary may seem silly. The basic rationale for harmonization was expressed earlier. Differences in accounting principles mean that the financial statements of companies from different countries not only look different but impart different information. This basic lack of comparability may cause investors and creditors to make poor decisions. Similarly, if accountants of different nations do not perform audits the same way, then the assurances they give about the reliability of financial information cannot be regarded equally by financial statement users.

---

[3]*Ibid.*

Nevertheless, some accountants question the desirability of an organized accounting harmonization effort. They argue that artificially imposing international harmonization on disparate business environments will strip accounting of its basic utility. Chapter 4 shows how companies pay a penalty when they do not provide investors and creditors with the kind of information desired. Similarly, if the inherent reliability of the accounting information is suspect, investors and creditors impose additional penalties on the companies providing the information. Thus, the argument goes, if investors and creditors really want comparable and reliable accounting information from multinational corporations, these companies are obliged to give it or else face the prospects of higher interest costs or lower common stock prices. So, is the work of the IASC, IFAC, EC, and others useless and wasteful? The answer to that depends on whether one believes that accounting principles and auditing practices can be harmonized on their own by the "invisible hand" of free market forces.

Regional harmonization efforts will be successful to the extent that they reflect environmental similarities among countries. The same is true of international efforts. Harmonization cannot be artificially imposed from above; there must be support from below. The regional and international harmonization efforts will continue. It seems reasonable that the combined wisdom of several nations' accountants can produce better accounting and auditing practices than can a single nation alone.

KEY POINTS

1. Among the alleged benefits of international accounting and auditing standards are improved financial statement analysis brought about by greater comparability and a level playing field for multinational financing and cross-border transactions. However, there are practical and other difficulties in achieving their acceptance.

2. The International Accounting Standards Committee aims to narrow, or harmonize, existing accounting diversity through its financial reporting standards. While compliance with IASC standards is voluntary, support for the IASC is growing, especially since the issuance of *Exposure Draft 32*.

3. The International Federation of Accountants develops auditing, ethical, and educational standards to be observed by the accountancy profession worldwide.

4. The European Community (EC) is the most important regional group involved in setting accounting and auditing standards. EC *Directives* are mandatory for any company doing business there.

CASES

Going International

Mike Reynolds is at a business luncheon with Kate Avila. He is the chief financial officer (CFO) of Bopar, Inc., and she is a Big Six partner in charge of Bopar's independent audit. They are discussing the makeup of this year's Bopar annual report.

"Our company is becoming more and more internationally oriented," observes Mike. "About 40 percent of our sales are outside the country. We have listed our stock on six different foreign stock exchanges, and we borrow a lot of money from international banks. Maybe the time has come to refer to international accounting standards in our annual report."

Kate cautions by urging careful consideration. She explains, "In the United States, we have no control over IASs. What happens if they come up with a standard simply unacceptable to Bopar? Will you then drop the reference to international standards? That would really be a red flag to financial analysts all over."

"We understand that," Mike counters. "But our research indicates that CPC International, Exxon, FMC Corporation, IBM, and General Electric, for example, refer to IASs in their respective annual reports. Here is FMC's 1991 annual report version:

Management Report on Financial Statements

The statements have been prepared in conformity with accounting principles generally accepted in the United States and are consistent with standards issued by the International Accounting Standards Committee.

"I know. I know," says Kate. "It's your annual report for sure. But I don't really see any benefits from referencing IASs—I see mainly risks. Please think carefully before you jump."

Questions

1. Do you support Mike or Kate on this issue? Defend your answer briefly.

2. What are the likely benefits to Bopar from publicly referring to IASC pronouncements?

3. How do two other U.S. companies reference IASs in their annual reports? (Hint: You may wish to use a computerized database in your business administration library to answer this question.)

4. Should the SEC require all publicly traded U.S. companies to refer to IASs in their respective annual reports? Why or why not?

International Harmonization: Pro or Con?

You are provided the following arguments for and against establishing a harmonized set of international accounting standards:

Pro:

Harmonizing accounting standards internationally will improve the comparability of accounting information around the world and thereby eliminate one source of misunderstanding in transnational financial reporting. More comparability will better the analysis of financial statements; this will, in turn, lower interest rates and improve resource allocation. A single set of financial accounting standards will also save corporations time and money, since they will no longer have to prepare multiple sets of financial statements. Finally, establishing international standards will raise the quality of accounting in many countries.

Con:

Harmonized international accounting standards are unnecessary, since the worldwide competition for investment funds is propelling harmonization to the extent that investors desire it. Corporations in need of funds are compelled to provide financial statement users—the resource providers—with what they want or else pay a penalty in the form of higher interest rates or lower common stock prices. If user needs are similar internationally, then harmonization will result as a matter of course, without an organized effort. If they are not, then requiring a single set of accounting practices may actually worsen the situation. Accounting is relevant only when it is responsive to the environment in which it operates. Imposing harmonization could very well strip accounting of its usefulness in many situations.

Question

Write two paragraphs stating your position on the desirability of establishing a harmonized set of international accounting standards.

A Conflict of Standards

"Good grief, you accountants sure know how to make life miserable." These are the words of Heather Maxwell, president of Stillwater Technologies, Inc. (STI), a publicly held U.S.-based multinational corporation. Heather has just learned from STI's corporate controller that STI must prepare a second set of financial statements conforming to the *Fourth* and *Seventh Directives* of the European Community (EC).

"Why can't we just use our U.S. reports?" Heather asks. "If they're good enough for the SEC, they ought to be good enough for the EC, too."

"Well, they're not," replies the controller. "The EC *Directives* require not only a different way of presenting our financial statements but also some extra disclosures that we don't currently put in our reports."

Heather then asks, "What if we follow International Accounting Standards

Committee *Standards?* Will that keep us from having to prepare two sets of financial statements?''

"No," says the controller. "Neither the SEC nor the EC accepts IASC *Standards* in place of its own. The SEC won't accept EC *Standards,* and the EC doesn't accept the SEC's.''

Heather responds, "I just don't see the benefit of preparing EC financial statements. They'll cost us a lot of money and, as far as I'm concerned, we have excellent financial reporting right now.''

Questions

1. Why must STI prepare financial statements that conform to the requirements of the Securities and Exchange Commission (SEC)?

2. Why must STI prepare financial statements that conform to the requirements of the European Community (EC)?

3. Does it make sense for STI to prepare two sets of financial statements? Why or why not?

4. What does the controller mean by the statement, "Neither the SEC nor the EC accepts IASC *Standards* in place of its own. The SEC won't accept EC *Standards*, and the EC doesn't accept the SEC's''?

5. Is there any way that STI can overcome the conflict described above? If so, how? If not, why not?

ADDITIONAL READINGS

Fleming, P. D., "The Growing Importance of International Accounting Standards," *Journal of Accountancy* (September 1991), pp. 100–106.

Gernon, H.; S. E. C. Purvis; and M. A. Diamond, *An Analysis of the Implications of IASC's Comparability Project.* Los Angeles, Cal.: School of Accounting, University of Southern California, 1990, 115 pp.

Sundby, L., and B. Schwieger, "EC, EZ?" *Journal of Accountancy* (March 1992), pp. 71–76.

Tay, J. S. W., and R. H. Parker, "Measuring International Harmonization and Standardization," *Abacus* 26, no. 1 (1990), pp. 71–88.

United Nations Centre on Transnational Corporations, *International Accounting and Reporting Issues: 1991 Review*, New York: UNCTC, 1992, 244 pp.

Van Hulle, K. and K. U. Leuven, "Harmonization of Accounting Standards: A View from the European Community," *European Accounting Review* (May 1992), pp. 161–72.

Wyatt, A. R., "An Era of Harmonization," *Journal of International Financial Management and Accounting* (Spring 1992), pp. 63–68.

4

FINANCIAL REPORTING IN THE INTERNATIONAL ENVIRONMENT

Financial accounting practices in a country are determined by a number of environmental variables that interact in a complex way. As discussed in Chapter 1, these variables include the following:

1. Relationship between business and the provider(s) of capital.
2. Political and economic ties with other countries.
3. Legal system.
4. Level of inflation.
5. Size and complexity of business enterprises, sophistication of management and the financial community, and general levels of education.

Companies prepare the financial statements in their annual reports directed toward the needs of their primary users. Financial statements not only look different but report different information, depending on whether the primary user group is, for example, the investor, the creditor, or the government. Moreover, even if companies in different nations orient their financial statements toward similar user groups, there are still likely to be differences in accounting practices and in the way that the annual reports appear. For example, companies from the United States and Great Britain orient their annual reports to the decision needs of investors, but there are still a number of differences in the two countries' accounting and reporting practices.

Transnational financial reporting refers to reporting across national boundaries or, more specifically, to reporting financial results to user groups located in a country other than the one where the company is headquartered. A U.S. company is engaged in transnational financial reporting whenever it sends an annual report to a citizen of another country. If you write to a German company and receive its annual report, transnational financial reporting has occurred.

Transnational financial reporting has been encouraged by two phenomena. The first may be termed the *global financing strategies* of multinational corporations. Global financing includes (1) listing a company's capital stock on stock exchanges outside the home country, (2) selling bonds in various countries, and (3) arranging for loans with foreign banks. Multinational corporations no longer look exclusively to the stock markets, bond markets, and banks of their respective home countries to raise capital. They go wherever the money is most available and cheapest. The second phenomenon is *transnational investing*; those with funds to invest buy the stocks and bonds of foreign companies in addition to those in their own nation. Thus, the multinational corporation (as the resource user) and the investor/creditor (as the resource provider) are responsible for these twin phenomena.

During the 1980s, a truly global financial market began to emerge. The increase in international financial transactions is rather startling. For example, consider the following: (1) Between 1980 and 1990, cross-border transactions in equity securities increased from $120 billion to $1.4 trillion per year. (2) In 1982, international bonds outstanding amounted to $259 billion; by 1991, the amount was $1.65 trillion. (3) From 1980 to 1991, the balance of international bank loans outstanding increased from $324 billion to $7.5 trillion.[1]

Transnational financial reporting presents a unique problem to both the multinational corporation (as the information provider) and the investor/creditor (as the information user). When a company prepares a financial report for users in its own country, it can reasonably assume that the users understand (1) the general orientation of financial accounting in that country, (2) the particular accounting practices that the company employs, (3) the language in which the annual report is written, and (4) the currency unit used to present the financial statements. However, any or all of these four items may be different when a company sends a financial report to users in another country. More and more corporations and investors are facing transnational financial reporting problems as both financing and investing are increasingly globalized.

RESPONSES BY USERS

Exhibit 4–1 is the 1991 income statement for the German retailer, Douglas Holding. Suppose that a friend of yours suggests that Douglas would be a good company to invest in, and so you write Douglas, ask for, and receive its annual report. What would immediately strike you after opening the annual report is that it is written entirely in German. In looking at the financial statements, you also

---

[1]"Fear of Finance, A Survey of the World Economy," *The Economist*, September 19, 1992, pp. 6, 9.

EXHIBIT 4–1   Douglas Holding Income Statement

Konzern-Gewinn- und Verlustrechnung

	Anhang		1991	Vorjahr
		DM	DM	TDM
1. Umsatzerlöse				
a) Bruttoumsatzerlöse	(18)	3.040.242.587,92		2.594.562
b) in den Umsatzerlösen		− 359.721.860,56		− 304.177
enthaltene Umsatzsteuer				
			2.680.520.727,36	**2.290.385**
2. Sonstige betriebliche Erträge	(19)	150.247.638,47		124.800
3. Aufwendungen für Roh-,	(20)	− 1.517.372.660,37		− 1.298.799
Hilfs- und Betriebsstoffe				
und für bezogene Waren				
4. Personalaufwand	(21)	− 511.074.098,32		− 424.050
5. Abschreibungen auf		− 94.637.536,20		− 85.359
immaterielle Vermögensgegen-				
stände des Anlagevermögens				
und Sachanlagen				
6. Sonstige betriebliche	(22)	− 464.803.603,50		− 387.148
Aufwendungen				
7. Beteiligungsergebnis	(23)	216.368,13		20
8. Abschreibungen auf	(24)	− 5.191.798,28		− 10.377
Finanzanlagen und auf Wert-				
papiere des Umlaufvermögens				
9. Zinsergebnis	(25)	− 12.463.844,62		− 8.845
10. **Ergebnis der gewöhnlichen**			**225.441.192,67**	**200.627**
Geschäftstätigkeit				
11. Steuern vom Einkommen	(26)	− 129.754.154,83		− 116.203
und vom Ertrag				
12. Sonstige Steuern	(27)	− 11.338.922,50		− 10.925
13. **Jahresüberschuß**			**84.348.115,34**	**73.499**
14. Gewinnvortrag aus dem Vorjahr		213.468,00		216
15. Einstellungen in		− 29.951.373,04		− 27.622
Gewinnrücklagen				
16. Gewinnanteile		− 15.980.461,49		− 11.653
anderer Gesellschafter				
17. Verlustanteile		1.870.251,19		1.560
anderer Gesellschafter				
18. **Konzerngewinn**			**40.500.000,00**	**36.000**

---

notice that all of the amounts are expressed in deutsche marks (DM). The report looks different from U.S. companies' reports (compare Exhibit 4–1 to Exhibit 4–2, the 1991 income statement of Coca-Cola Company), so you may also suspect that Douglas uses German accounting practices. Unless you can read German, know German accounting practices, and are familiar with the mark, you will probably have a difficult time understanding Douglas's annual report. As a result, you may decide not to invest in Douglas since it would be ''too much trouble'' to ex-

EXHIBIT 4–2 Coca-Cola Company Income Statement

Consolidated Statements of Income *The Coca-Cola Company and Subsidiaries*

Year Ended December 31, (In thousands except per share data)	1991	1990	1989
Net Operating Revenues	$11,571,614	$10,236,350	$8,622,287
Cost of goods sold	4,648,385	4,208,850	3,548,570
Gross Profit	6,923,229	6,027,500	5,073,717
Selling, administrative and general expenses	4,604,184	4,075,936	3,347,932
Operating Income	2,319,045	1,951,564	1,725,785
Interest income	175,406	169,985	205,035
Interest expense	192,515	230,979	308,034
Equity income (1991 reduced by $44 million related to restructuring charges recorded by CCE)	39,975	110,139	75,490
Other income—net	41,368	13,727	66,034
Income from Continuing Operations before **Income Taxes**	2,383,279	2,014,436	1,764,310
Income taxes	765,277	632,532	571,471
Income from Continuing Operations	1,618,002	1,381,904	1,192,839
Equity income from discontinued operation	—	—	21,537
Gain on sale of discontinued operation (net of income taxes of $421,021)	—	—	509,449
Net Income	1,618,002	1,381,904	1,723,825
Preferred stock dividends	521	18,158	21,392
Net Income Available to Common Share Owners	$ 1,617,481	$ 1,363,746	$1,702,433
Income per Common Share			
Continuing operations	$ 2.43	$ 2.04	$ 1.69
Discontinued operation	—	—	.77
Net Income per Common Share	$ 2.43	$ 2.04	$ 2.46
Average Common Shares Outstanding	666,472	668,570	691,962

See Notes to Consolidated Financial Statements.

tract the information you need from the annual report. You may very well pass up a good investment opportunity, although you will never know it.

Of course, you may also take other courses of action. One would be to get someone to translate the report into English, while you learn all you can about German accounting practices. (Several large CPA firms publish such information, and books are also available on the subject.) At a minimum, this choice would be time-consuming and could even cost you money if, for example, you had to pay someone for the translation. And having done this, the accounting information would still not be directly comparable to that of a U.S. company. In most cases, it is impossible for a *user* to restate financial accounting information so that it conforms to the accounting practices of another country. Another course of action is to forgo trying to understand the Douglas annual report and instead rely on the advice of an expert, such as a stockbroker. In fact, investment firms employ people to analyze foreign companies' annual reports and to make recommendations about which companies seem to be good ones to invest in. Such analysis involves a high level of sophistication.

Many accountants are concerned about the effects that an unfamiliar language, monetary unit, and accounting practices may have on investors and creditors. They fear that resource allocation decisions may be based on misunderstanding and, as a result, that these decisions may not be optimal. This is one reason why accountants are trying to harmonize accounting practices around the world. (This effort is discussed in Chapter 3.)

RESPONSES BY MULTINATIONAL CORPORATIONS

What about multinational corporations? Don't they have a role to play in trying to minimize misunderstandings? Indeed they do. Just as the users of financial reports may take various courses of action to overcome the problems associated with transnational financial reporting, so too do companies approach the problems in various ways. We can classify five approaches that multinational corporations take to accommodate foreign readers of their financial reports:

1. Do nothing.
2. Prepare convenience translations.
3. Prepare convenience statements.
4. Restate on a limited basis.
5. Prepare secondary financial statements.

Do Nothing

A corporation that sends the same financial statements to the foreign user as it does to the domestic user has done nothing to accommodate the foreign user. The financial statements are written in the native language and use the native currency unit and accounting principles. This approach puts the entire burden of understanding the financial report on the user, and it more or less assumes that the report for readers at home is useful to readers in other countries as well. The income statements for both Douglas Holding and Coca-Cola illustrate the do-nothing approach.

This is the most common approach of multinational corporations. Why would a corporation choose to seemingly ignore the information needs of its foreign readers? First of all, if the company raises very little capital outside the borders of its home country, the added expense of taking one of the other four approaches may not be worthwhile. While global financing is becoming more commonplace, many corporations that manufacture and sell products multinationally still raise most of their capital in a single nation—the home country. These companies perceive little benefit in preparing financial statements for readers other than those at home.

Second, some multinationals are able to entice international investment in their securities even though they leave their financial statements in their original form. One way they accomplish this is by selling large blocks of their securities directly to sophisticated overseas investors, such as pension funds. (Such sales are called *private placements*.) Or they may meet directly with investment firms, referred to earlier, to encourage the firms to recommend investments in their securities. Large investment firms, especially, employ analysts who are skilled at interpreting financial statements in their original form. Either way, these multinationals attempt to attract foreign investors without incurring the extra costs associated with the other forms of transnational financial reporting.

A third reason why a multinational corporation may choose to do nothing is that the language, currency unit, and accounting principles of its home country are well known and understood around the world. This is true, for example, of U.S. and U.K. companies, which almost always take this approach. U.S. and U.K. accounting standards are highly regarded and generally understood in other parts of the world. Both the U.S. dollar and the British pound are international currencies, and the English language is referred to as the "language of business." Thus, financial reports useful to native readers may very well be useful to foreign readers.

Prepare Convenience Translations

Convenience translations are financial statements translated into the foreign reader's language. They retain the home country's accounting principles and currency unit, however. Exhibit 4–3 (p. 58) is an example of this approach. It is the income statement of ENTEL-Chile, a Chilean telecommunications firm. Note that while the income statement is in English, it still uses Chilean accounting principles and the Chilean peso.

This approach is a relatively inexpensive accommodation to the foreign readership. Companies taking this approach typically prepare English, French, German, and, perhaps, Spanish language versions (as appropriate) of their annual reports. Presumably, any interested reader will understand one of these languages. The user is saved the bother of dealing with an unfamiliar language but must still understand another country's accounting practices and monetary unit. Companies usually prepare convenience translations in order to enlarge the scope of investor/creditor interest beyond the borders of their home country, and they are a low-cost alternative to the do-nothing approach. For this reason, convenience translations are also commonly used with private placements or to attract the attention of foreign investment firms, as discussed above.

Prepare Convenience Statements

This approach takes convenience translations one step further. Not only are the financial statements translated into the language of the foreign reader, but the monetary amounts are also expressed in the reader's currency. However, the accounting principles of the home country are still used to prepare the financial reports. Exhibit 4–4 (p. 59) is an example of a convenience statement for the Japanese electric wire and cable manufacturer, Sumitomo Electric Industries. (Notice that yen amounts are translated into dollars at the year-end exchange rate. An exchange rate is simply how much of one currency it takes to buy so much of another currency. At Sumitomo's year-end, the exchange rate was Yen 140.95 = U.S.

EXHIBIT 4–3   ENTEL Income Statement

CONSOLIDATED INCOME STATEMENTS
for the years ended December 31, 1990 and 1989
(Expressed in thousands of Chilean pesos)

	1990 Th.$	1989 Th.$
OPERATING INCOME		
Operating revenue	50,710,403	46,786,607
Costs of operation	(20,649,220)	(17,819,847)
Gross profit	30,061,183	28,966,760
Selling and administration expenses	(6,065,016)	(5,977,660)
Operating income	23,996,167	22,989,100
OTHER INCOME (EXPENSE):		
Interest income	526,995	542,147
Other income	1,644,172	2,294,483
Interest expenses	(1,821,427)	(1,833,394)
Related companies losses	(107,043)	(25,804)
Other expenses	(773,514)	(233,261)
Price-level adjustment	(854,586)	518,244
Other income (expense), net	(1,385,403)	1,262,415
Net income before tax	22,610,764	24,251,515
Income tax	(1,962,780)	(1,085,258)
NET INCOME	**20,647,984**	**23,166,257**

$1.00, and so all amounts initially expressed in yen are simply divided by 140.95 to arrive at the dollar figures.)

Convenience statements lose much of their foreign appearance, and unless users realize that another country's accounting principles are used, they will be misled into thinking that the financial statements can be directly compared to those of companies of their home country. Naturally, readers can comprehend their own language and currency better than those of another country, but they must still be able to understand the accounting practices used in the *company's home country* in order to derive actual meaning from the annual report.

Restate on a Limited Basis

Compared to the first three, this approach represents a significant step toward accommodating the information needs of foreign readers. The disclosure is in the footnotes section of the company's financial statements. Normally, a company reconciles the net income amount shown on its income statement (prepared using its home-country accounting principles) to a net income amount based on the accounting principles of the reader's country, and often the company restates the

EXHIBIT 4–4   Sumitomo Electric Industries Income Statement

CONSOLIDATED STATEMENTS OF INCOME
Sumitomo Electric Industries, Ltd.
For the years ended March 31, 1991 and 1990

	Millions of yen		Thousands of U.S. dollars (Note 1)
	1991	1990	1991
Net Sales (Note 7)	¥1,113,720	¥1,001,037	$7,901,525
Cost of Sales (Note 7)	919,077	828,273	6,520,588
Gross profit	194,643	172,764	1,380,937
Selling, General and Administrative Expenses	119,615	108,625	848,635
Operating income	75,028	64,139	532,302
Other Income (Expenses):			
Interest and dividend income:			
Unconsolidated subsidiaries and affiliates	2,438	2,294	17,297
Other	12,873	9,336	91,330
Interest expense	(17,343)	(12,509)	(123,044)
Equity in net income of unconsolidated subsidiaries and affiliates	4,767	4,519	33,821
Gain on sale of securities, net	3,704	4,802	26,279
Other, net (Notes 4 and 11)	(12,866)	(14,887)	(91,281)
	(6,427)	(6,445)	(45,598)
Income before income taxes	68,601	57,694	486,704
Provision for Income Taxes (Note 8)	36,997	31,063	262,483
Net income	¥ 31,604	¥ 26,631	$ 224,221

	Yen		U.S. dollars (Note 1)
Per Share of Common Stock			
Net income—Primary	¥ 44.79	¥ 38.18	$ 0.318
—Fully diluted	41.78	35.25	0.296

See accompanying Notes to Consolidated Financial Statements.

balance sheet figures as well. However, sometimes a company restates only selected financial statement items. The annual report is typically written in the reader's language, but the currency may still be that of the company's country.

Companies adopting this approach feel a clear need to communicate with their
foreign annual report users. If a significant number of investors or creditors are
located in other countries and if the company's accounting practices diverge significantly from those found in the reader's country, then the need is real. Companies following this approach must keep more than one set of accounting records.
Fortunately computerized accounting systems can significantly reduce the cost
and inconvenience of this approach!

A number of companies adopt this approach. The disclosure of the Swedish
company Electrolux in Exhibit 4–5 (p. 61) is illustrative. Notice that Electrolux
reconciles both net income and shareholders' equity from Swedish to U.S. ac-

counting principles. In addition, balance sheet amounts expressed using Swedish and U.S. accounting principles are shown side by side, on a comparative basis.

Prepare Secondary Financial Statements

This represents a further accommodation to the users of a company's financial statements. Companies continue to prepare their primary financial statements for the home user with the home country's language, currency, and accounting principles. For foreign readers, however, the company completely restates its financial report to conform to another set of accounting standards.

In practice, the other set of accounting standards used most often is either the generally accepted accounting principles (GAAP) of the United States or the standards of the International Accounting Standards Committee (IASC). U.S. GAAP are the most detailed and extensive in the world, and they are generally regarded as "world class" in quality. As a result, many multinationals choose U.S. GAAP when they prepare their secondary financial statements. However, as discussed in Chapter 3, the IASC is increasingly accepted as the voice for acceptable worldwide accounting standards. (As a practical matter, there are few instances where U.S. GAAP conflict with IASC Standards.) Japanese multinationals preparing secondary financial statements tend to use U.S. GAAP, whereas European multinationals that prepare secondary financial statements tend to adopt IASC Standards.

Secondary financial statements are meant for sophisticated, worldwide users. What makes a company go to so much trouble to accommodate the foreign reader? As with the previous approaches, it all comes down to whether the perceived benefits exceed the costs. Multinationals preparing secondary financial statements are normally from countries where accounting is legalistic in its orientation. For them, the British-American model of accounting, with its emphasis on presenting useful information to investors and creditors, is more likely to attract widespread international investment than is their home country's legalistic model of accounting. (IASC Standards and, of course, U.S. GAAP reflect the British-American model of accounting discussed in Chapter 1.)

Exhibit 4–6 (p. 62) is the 1991 consolidated income statement of Komatsu Ltd., the Japanese heavy equipment manufacturer. Notice that three years' worth of data are presented in Japanese yen, while the 1991 amounts are translated into U.S. dollars. Exhibit 4–6 also reproduces Komatsu's footnote indicating that U.S. GAAP are used. Exhibit 4–7 (p. 63) is the 1991 consolidated income statement of the Swiss pharmaceutical company Roche. Two years' worth of data are presented in Swiss francs. The footnote describing the use of IASC Standards is also reproduced in Exhibit 4–7.

WHOSE ACCOUNTING PRINCIPLES?

Restating financial statements to another set of accounting standards, as in limited restatements and secondary financial statements, has its critics. Some believe that financial statements are meaningful only if they are consistent with the underly-

EXHIBIT 4–5   Electrolux Limited Restatement (from Swedish to U.S. Accounting Principles; Amounts in Millions of Swedish Krona)

11 American accounting principles (US GAAP)

The consolidated accounts have been prepared in accordance with Swedish accounting practice, which differs in certain significant respects from American accounting principles (US GAAP). The most important differences are described below:

Write-ups on assets

In certain situations, Swedish practice permits write-ups of fixed assets in excess of acquisition cost. This does not normally accord with US GAAP.

Adjustment for acquisitions

In accordance with Swedish practice, the Group reports negative goodwill as a liability which is taken into income in accordance with a schedule based on the acquired company's earnings capacity. According to US GAAP, negative goodwill should be deducted from the value of acquired long-term assets and reported as income over the useful life of these assets.

In accordance with Swedish practice, the tax benefit arising from application of tax-loss carryovers in acquired companies is deducted by the Group from the current year's tax costs. According to US GAAP, this tax benefit should be booked as a retroactive adjustment of the value of acquired assets.

Pensions

As of 1989, the new American recommendations for pensions known as FAS 87 (Employers' Accounting for Pensions) have been applied for pension plans outside the US. In accordance with this recommendation, future salary increases, inflation and other factors must be taken into account for computation of the projected benefit obligation. The computed Swedish provision for PRI pensions is not adjusted for future salary increases, but this is offset by the lower discounting rate applied for computation of the provision for PRI pensions in comparison with FAS 87. The initial difference arising from the first application of FAS 87 (January 1, 1989) is amortized over the future average employment period, so that the effect on net income is insignificant. Other important differences have been adjusted in accordance with US GAAP.

Other benefits

In addition to pensions, some of the Group's subsidiaries, principally in the US, provide employees with benefits in the form of health care and life insurance subsequent to retirement. Recommendation No. 106 of the US Financial Accounting Standards Board (Employers' Accounting for Post-retirement Benefits Other Than Pensions), issued in 1990, requires a provision in the accounts for the estimated future commitment represented by these benefits. This recommendation permits application of various types of transitional methods and will be introduced by 1993 at the latest for the Group's US subsidiaries and by 1995 for the other companies.

It has not yet been decided when and according to which method the Group will adopt this recommendation. The Group is currently studying the transitional effects, which are estimated at USD 200–250m for Group operations in the US. The transitional effects for Group companies outside the US are not expected to be material. This change in accounting principles will have no effect on liquidity.

Deferred taxes

Taxation and financial reporting are affected during different periods by certain items. Swedish accounting principles do not require reporting of deferred taxes on timing differences. Electrolux reports deferred taxes on the most important timing differences, which refer mainly to untaxed reserves. A 30% tax rate is applied. US GAAP requires that such taxes be reported for all significant differences and that deferred taxes be computed at the rates which applied during the period when the timing difference arose.

Application of US GAAP would have the following approximate effects on consolidated net income, shareholders' equity and the balance sheet:

A. Consolidated net income	1991 SEKm	1990 SEKm
Net income as reported in the income statement	377	741
Adjustments:		
Acquisitions	78	−65
Pensions	34	–
Deferred taxes	−77	147
Other	−8	−3
Interest on convertible loan after taxes	–	1
Approximate net income according to US GAAP	404	821
Approximate net earnings per share, according to US GAAP (number of shares in 1991 and 1990: 73,233,916)	5.50	11.20

B. Shareholders' equity	1991 SEKm	1990 SEKm
Shareholders' equity as reported in the balance sheet	15,758	16,565
Adjustments:		
Minority interests	3	−23
Revaluation of fixed assets	−169	−142
Acquisitions	−1,028	−1,109
Pensions	−34	−199
Deferred taxes		
Difference in tax rates	−975	−944
Other items	−159	−67
Total adjustments	−2,362	−2,484
Approximate shareholders' equity according to US GAAP	13,396	14,081

C. Balance sheet

The table below summarizes the consolidated balance sheets prepared in accordance with Swedish accounting principles and US GAAP.

	According to Swedish principles		According to US GAAP	
	1991 SEKm	1990 SEKm	1991 SEKm	1990 SEKm
Current assets	38,394	40,243	41,127	43,731
Real estate, machinery and equipment	18,357	19,247	17,833	18,655
Shares and participations	569	560	569	560
Long-term receivables	400	428	400	428
Goodwill	3,948	4,256	3,250	3,547
Other fixed assets	661	1,059	693	1,130
Total assets	62,329	65,793	63,872	68,051
Current liabilities	25,177	27,412	27,881	30,912
Long-term liabilities	19,834	19,804	19,904	20,012
Deferred taxes	1,309	1,706	2,443	2,717
Minority interests	251	306	248	329
Shareholders' equity	15,758	16,565	13,396	14,081
Total liabilities and shareholders' equity	62,329	65,793	63,872	68,051

EXHIBIT 4–6   Komatsu Income Statement

Statements of Consolidated Income

Komatsu Ltd. and Subsidiaries
For the years ended March 31, 1991, 1990, and 1989

| | Millions of yen | | | Translation into thousands of U.S. dollars (Note 1) |
| | Year ended March 31 | | | Year ended March 31 |
	1991	1990	1989	1991
Revenues				
Net sales	¥ 988,897	¥887,108	¥792,809	$7,013,454
Interest and other income	39,633	31,936	27,129	281,085
Total	1,028,530	919,044	819,938	7,294,539
Costs and expenses				
Cost of sales	718,714	657,554	590,550	5,097,263
Selling, general, and administrative	194,420	167,047	161,403	1,378,865
Interest	26,218	20,744	17,959	185,943
Other	4,163	13,427	6,386	29,525
Total	943,515	858,772	776,298	6,691,596
Income before income taxes, minority interests, and equity in earnings	85,015	60,272	43,640	602,943
Income taxes (Notes 1 and 13)				
Current	40,330	37,026	25,056	286,028
Deferred	7,150	(2,344)	(1,024)	50,709
Total	47,480	34,682	24,032	336,737
Income before minority interests and equity in earnings	37,535	25,590	19,608	266,206
Minority interests in profits or losses of consolidated subsidiaries—net	(610)	(265)	(313)	(4,326)
Equity in earnings of affiliated companies—net	(5,667)	1,957	1,538	(40,192)
Net income	¥ 31,258	¥ 27,282	¥ 20,833	$ 221,688
	Yen			Cents
Earnings per share (Note 1)				
Primary	¥30.5	¥26.6	¥21.3	21.6¢
Fully diluted	30.4	26.6	20.3	21.6

See the accompanying notes to consolidated financial statements.

Note 1: Basis of Financial Statements . . . [T]he accompanying consolidated financial statements have been prepared on the basis of accounting principles generally accepted in the United States of America.

ing environmental variables from which accounting in a company's home country is derived. (The variables affecting accounting development are discussed in Chapter 1.) According to this view, the first three forms of transnational financial reporting make more sense, since they retain the accounting principles of the company's home

---

EXHIBIT 4–7   Roche Income Statement

Consolidated statements of income
in millions of Swiss francs

	1991	1990
Sales	**11,451**	9,670
Cost of goods sold and delivered	**(4,865)**	(4,309)
Gross profit	**6,586**	5,361
Marketing and selling	**(2,504)**	(2,080)
Research and development [15]	**(1,727)**	(1,444)
Administrative	**(747)**	(609)
Other operating income/(expense), net	**(222)**	141
Financial income, net [16]	**651**	83
Income before taxes	**2,037**	1,452
Taxes [17]	**(531)**	(496)
Income before minority interests	**1,506**	956
Income applicable to minority interests [10]	**(24)**	(8)
Net income	**1,482**	948

Note: Basis of preparation of financial statements   The financial statements of the group are based on the separate financial information of the group companies prepared for the year ending 31 December using the accounting policies summarized below which are in accordance with the criteria of recognition and measurement formulated by the *International Accounting Standards Committee.*

---

country. In essence, the argument is that the effects of business decisions, as reflected in financial statements, cannot be separated from the accounting principles used to measure and originally record these decisions. The alternative view is that comparability improves investor decision making, and so one of the last two forms of transnational financial reporting is more appropriate. (International diversity is the subject of Chapter 2, while efforts to enhance comparability are discussed in Chapter 3). This conceptual conflict presents a dilemma for both users and multinational corporations involved in international financial reporting.

BEWARE THE FOREIGN FINANCIAL STATEMENT

So far, we have discussed the problems confronted by financial statement users when they are provided information that is not in their native language, their native currency, or prepared according to accustomed accounting principles. We have also discussed what corporations do to help financial statement users overcome these problems. Even if readers get financial statements in a language, currency unit, and based on accounting principles that they can understand, they must still consider that the inherent reliability of financial statements can vary because of different auditing standards worldwide. (This issue was discussed in Chapter 3.)

Finally, it should be noted that financial practices (as opposed to accounting practices) and business decision making differ around the world, and readers of foreign financial statements must understand how the business environment in a corporation's home country affects the firm's financial reports. This is especially critical if the user is comparing the accounting numbers of companies from different cultures.

One device used to analyze financial reports is *ratio analysis*. Ratios of key items on the financial statements are calculated to determine such things as riskiness, ability to pay off debts, and profitability. For example, a commonly employed ratio is the debt/asset ratio (total liabilities divided by total assets). Since liabilities must be paid off with company assets, the lower this ratio is, the greater is the company's ability to pay off its debts and, therefore, the safer the company is perceived to be. Generally speaking, creditors should be more willing to lend money to, and investors should be more willing to invest money in, companies with lower debt/asset ratios.

However, applying ratio analysis internationally can be deceptive. For example, Japanese companies tend to have significantly higher debt/asset ratios than comparable U.S. companies, even after Japanese financial statements are restated to conform to U.S. accounting principles. In Japan, the debt/asset ratio is an indication of how much confidence the banks have in a company. Companies have low debt/asset ratios because they are unable to get any more credit from the banks. Rather than demonstrating a risky company, in Japan the reverse is true—companies with high debt/asset ratios are generally safer![2]

What this tells us is that comparability still may not exist even if financial statements are prepared on the basis of comparable accounting standards. Because many business practices are culturally based, they are bound to have an impact on companies' financial statements. One must know something about the business environment of a company's home country in order to fully understand the company's financial statements.

International financial statement analysis is explained more fully in Chapter 7.

CONCLUSION

Transnational financial reporting arises when a corporation sends its financial statements to users residing and working in other countries. When this happens,

---

[2]Frederick D. S. Choi et al., "Analyzing Foreign Financial Statements: The Use and Misuse of International Ratio Analysis," *Journal of International Business Studies*, Spring/Summer 1983, pp. 113–31.

one issue that the corporation faces is that the financial statements it prepares for users in its own country may not serve the needs of users in another part of the world. Financial statements are a communications device, and when a company does not communicate effectively with its audience, it pays a penalty. The penalty arises because failure to fully understand a multinational corporation's financial statements (in whole or in part) increases the risk associated with providing capital to that multinational. When the communications breakdown is severe, the resource providers simply refuse to provide funds to the multinational. However, less extreme penalties that the corporation may pay are higher interest costs or lower common stock prices. The multinational will accommodate its foreign audience if it believes that it can reduce the penalties of nonaccommodation. How the company responds to information needs depends on how it views its own cost/benefit equation—the company will try to balance the increased cost of additional accommodation to its financial statement users against the potentially lower penalties that the users may impose.

KEY POINTS

1. Global financing and investing give rise to transnational financial reporting— financial reporting across national boundaries.

2. Multinational corporations bear costs when financial statement users in other countries fail to understand their reporting.

3. The five approaches to transnational financial reporting are (*a*) do nothing, (*b*) prepare convenience translations, (*c*) prepare convenience statements, (*d*) restate on a limited basis, and (*e*) prepare secondary financial statements. The first three approaches retain the home country accounting principles, while the last two restate to another set of principles.

4. Users must also understand how the business environment of a corporation's home country affects the financial statements.

CASES

The Mexican Investment

"Holy cow," thought Travis. "What do I do now?"

For some time Travis Dunn had been considering investing in a few shares of a foreign company. Because he had heard so much about the positive effects of the North American Free Trade Agreement, he thought he would get in on the ground floor by buying some shares of Mexican companies likely to benefit from the agreement.

Travis mailed letters to a number of Mexican firms, asking for a copy of their most recent annual reports. He figured that after analyzing the financial statements he would be able to choose the best one.

He anxiously awaited the responses, but the first one he received was nothing like what he expected. "It's all in Spanish," he thought with dismay. (Travis's knowledge of Spanish ended with ordering beer and locating the public facilities.) "I can't even tell the balance sheet from the income statement. Let's see—pesos . . . Oh yeah, that's the Mexican currency, but I can't remember how many pesos it takes to get a dollar. Analyzing this company is going to be tougher than I realized."

Questions

1. Which example of transnational financial reporting is Travis confronting here? Why might this Mexican company take this approach?
2. What must Travis do to make the financial statements more understandable?
3. Where can he go to learn about Mexican accounting principles?

How Best to Report?

A Swiss multinational corporation has decided to list its common stock shares internationally, for the first time. Sarah Morgan, who works for a large, international accounting firm, has been hired to advise the corporation on how to adapt its annual report so that it effectively serves the information needs of the prospective investors. "I can have a report ready by the end of the week," Sarah confidently exclaimed.

Before developing her report, Sarah prepared the following background information:

> Swiss financial reporting is legalistic in its orientation. It is highly conservative in that the law specifically permits the undervaluation of assets or the creation of secret reserves. Within reason, these practices are generally accepted in tax law. Banks are the primary source of finance and because they are able to obtain information from companies firsthand, disclosure levels are low and Swiss financial statements have a pervasive air of secrecy surrounding them. German is the dominant language spoken in Switzerland and the Swiss franc is the currency unit.

Help Sarah write her report by answering the following questions.

Questions

1. What are the advantages and disadvantages of each of the five approaches to transnational financial reporting?

2. What criteria should a multinational corporation consider in choosing which approach to take in reporting to its foreign readers?

3. As described above, how suitable is Swiss accounting for reporting to investors on a worldwide basis?

4. Which approach to transnational financial reporting should this corporation take? Why?

N.V. Cirts

You receive the following convenience statement from the Dutch firm, N.V. Cirts.

N.V. CIRTS
Balance Sheet
December 31, 1993

Cash	$ 26,000	Payables and reserves	$ 54,000
Inventory	65,000	Common stock	40,000
Fixed assets	142,000	Retained earnings	109,000
		Revaluation surplus	30,000
	$233,000		$233,000

N.V. CIRTS
Income Statement
For the Year Ended December 31, 1993

Sales		$470,000
Cost of goods sold		282,000
Gross profit		188,000
Salaries	$69,000	
Depreciation	18,000	
Tax expense	42,000	
Other expenses	21,000	150,000
Net income		$38,000

By reading the footnotes accompanying the financial statements, you discover two key differences between the accounting principles employed by Cirts and what would be generally accepted in the United States. First, Cirts uses current cost accounting in valuing its inventory and fixed assets and in expensing cost of goods sold and depreciation. Second, included in "other expenses" is a $5,000 charge for "unanticipated losses," which management recorded in case an unforeseen catastrophe arises in the future. In past years a total of $17,000 had been recorded; as a result, there is now a $22,000 "reserve" included in "payables and reserves" on the balance sheet. (Neither the charge for unanticipated losses nor the reserve is allowed by U.S. generally accepted accounting principles.)

N.V. Cirts also discloses in its footnotes that the historical costs of inventory and cost of goods sold are $53,000 and $240,000, respectively. If historical cost were used, the fixed assets would have a net book value of $124,000, and depreciation expense would be $16,000.

Questions

1. Prepare a secondary set of financial statements conforming to U.S. generally accepted accounting principles (GAAP).

2. Compare Cirts's financial statements prepared on the basis of Dutch GAAP with the financial statements conforming to U.S. GAAP (i.e., compare the statements given to you with those you prepared for question 1). Which set makes Cirts appear to be healthier financially? Which set best reflects economic reality? Why?

3. Suppose the information provided was insufficient to make Cirts's financial statements conform to U.S. GAAP. How could you compare Cirts's financial condition to that of a U.S. company in the same industry?

4. If Cirts's financial statements were mailed to you in the United States, would you assume that they conformed to Dutch or U.S. GAAP? Why? What items on the balance sheet and/or income statement provide clues that the statements do not conform to U.S. GAAP?

ADDITIONAL READINGS

Archer, S., and S. McLeay. "Financial Reporting by Interlisted European Companies: Issues in Transnational Disclosure." In *International Pressures for Accounting Change*, ed. A. G. Hopwood. Hertfordshire, England: Prentice Hall International (U.K.), 1989. pp. 73–115.

Berton, L. "No Comparisons." *The Wall Street Journal* (September 1989), p. R30.

Biddle, G. C., and S. M. Saudagaran. "Foreign Stock Listings: Benefits, Costs, and the Accounting Policy Dilemma." *Accounting Horizons* (September 1991), pp. 69–80.

Choi, F. D. S., and R. M. Levich. "Behavioral Effects of International Accounting Diversity." *Accounting Horizons* (June 1991), pp. 1–13.

Slipkowsky, J. N. "The Volvo Way of Financial Reporting." *Management Accounting* (October 1988), pp. 22–26.

Tonkin, D. R., ed. *World Survey of Published Accounts*. London, England: Lafferty Publications, 1989. Chapters 1 and 2.

Wygal, D. E.; D. E. Stout; and J. Volpi. "Reporting Practices in Four Countries." *Management Accounting* (December 1987), pp. 37–42.

5

DISCLOSURE PRACTICES AROUND THE WORLD

The term *disclosure*, in its broadest sense, encompasses the release of any piece of information about a particular company. It includes everything contained in the company's annual report, press releases, newspaper and magazine stories, and so on. However, this chapter is more narrowly focused. It is about disclosures contained in annual reports or, more specifically, annual report information besides that in the main financial statements—the balance sheet, income statement, and statement of cash flows. (The latter is not required in all countries but is in the United States.)

Measurement issues are concerned with how financial statements should be prepared, which generally accepted accounting principles (GAAP) to employ, and how assets and liabilities are to be valued. Several substantive international accounting measurement issues are discussed in Chapter 2. *Disclosure* issues, on the other hand, relate to the information in an annual report that supplements the financial statements.

If you obtain the annual report of a U.S. company, you typically find a number of supplemental disclosures:

    1. A letter from the company president or chairman of the board explaining the major events affecting the firm, significant operating and financing activities, and perhaps, prospects for the future.

    2. A description of the major products or services of the company, what markets are served, where facilities are located, and a list of major subsidiary companies.

    3. A narrative review of the operations for the past year. This may be broken down by product line or geographic area. This review is much more in-depth than the president's letter and is designed to help the annual report

user more easily interpret the financial statements by expanding on the information they contain.

4. A statement of accounting policies. There are often several alternative ways to measure assets, liabilities, revenues, and expenses; and companies may choose the particular GAAP they wish to use. The description of accounting policies can be useful for a user of financial statements, especially if financial statements of several companies using different principles are being compared. This is especially important in an international context, since the differences in accounting worldwide are even more extensive than they are domestically.

5. Notes (or footnotes) to the financial statements. These elaborate on the amounts in the financial statements. Most companies like to keep their financial statements as lean and uncluttered as possible. Extra details and disclosures that do not fit conveniently in the financial statements are then placed in the footnotes.

FINANCIAL AND NONFINANCIAL DISCLOSURE

Disclosures in financial reports are often classified as either financial or nonfinancial. *Financial* disclosures consist of those items of information quantifiable in monetary amounts (dollars, for U.S. companies). For example, companies often report one figure for inventory on the balance sheet but show in a footnote how much of that is finished goods, how much is raw materials, and so on. A company may show one amount for property in the balance sheet and reveal in a footnote how much is located in the United States, how much in Europe, and so forth. When a company signs a long-term contract obligating it to rent property for a number of years, that obligation does not fit the definition of a liability and therefore will not appear on the balance sheet. However, because cash has been committed for future years, much like the commitments that are considered liabilities, companies generally show lease obligations in footnotes. Similarly, if a company is a defendant in a lawsuit, it wants shareholders to know the amounts of potential damages it may be liable for. The case may not have progressed far enough in the courts for the defendant to know whether it will actually have to pay damages. And so, in the meantime, it reveals in a footnote the general circumstances surrounding the lawsuit. These are all types of financial disclosures seen in financial statements. For various reasons, the related monetary amounts do not appear in the financial statements themselves. They are disclosed in footnotes (or elsewhere in the annual report) to more fully inform the reader about the company's financial well-being.

Nonfinancial disclosures are either (1) narrative descriptions, facts, or opinions that do not readily lend themselves to quantification in monetary terms or (2) items of information quantified in something other than money. An example of the former is the statement of accounting policies referred to above. An example of the latter is data about the number of employees located in each country. (Labor *costs* per country are a financial disclosure, but *number* of employees is nonfinancial.) Nonfinancial disclosures may be just another way to express things that are already expressed monetarily in the financial statements. Most of the information that accountants provide is financial—financial statements and financial disclosures. However, not everything can be expressed monetarily, and nonfinancial disclosures can be very important, too.

SOME OBSERVATIONS ABOUT DISCLOSURE

Disclosures can also be distinguished based on whether they are required or suggested, or whether they are voluntary. While most countries *require* certain disclosures to be made by companies operating within their borders, the amount of disclosure required varies by country. Often the GAAP of a particular country will also *suggest* items to be disclosed in companies' annual reports. Many companies, though, disclose information that is neither required nor suggested; that is, some disclosures are completely *voluntary*. Disclosures that are required or suggested in one country may be voluntary in another, and vice versa.

The fact that companies sometimes disclose more than they have to suggests that they perceive some advantages in doing so. In particular, it appears that the worldwide competition for investment funds is the most important force propelling increased levels of disclosure by multinational corporations. MNCs significantly increase disclosure whenever they seek major amounts of new funds.

Disclosure can also enlarge the scope of interest in a company by expanding the annual report's audience. After all, the annual report is the major vehicle for getting people interested in what the company is doing. Chapter 1 explained how companies orient their annual reports to a primary audience group—investors, creditors, the government, and so on. Disclosure enables the firm to maintain the primary orientation of its financial statements and provide information of interest to other parties as well. Continental European companies are especially effective and innovative in doing this.

Disclosure can overcome differences in generally accepted accounting principles. The problems associated with transnational financial reporting for financial statement users and multinational corporations are discussed in Chapters 3 and 4. Until a worldwide harmonization of accounting practices is achieved, disclosure can be an effective mechanism for overcoming these problems.

Deciding what and what not to disclose is not always an easy decision for corporate managements to make. If they decide not to disclose an item of information, in a very real sense, they have chosen to keep something secret from financial statement users. Many things, of course, are simply irrelevant to users of financial statements—the size of the company president's waistline, for example. But for many items of information, managements must use judgment to decide on their usefulness to financial statement readers. If too much information is disclosed, a reader can easily get lost in all of the clutter (i.e., suffer from "information overload''). So managements need a way to pare down the amount of information revealed in financial statements.

Disclosure is a substantive issue, since information *revealed* can potentially affect people's decisions and actions. Unrevealed information does not have that potential. When GAAP require a disclosure, this is tantamount to saying that the information is potentially significant enough to affect decisions and, therefore, ought to be revealed. A suggested disclosure or a voluntary disclosure should be made whenever knowledge of that information has the potential to influence the decisions of financial statement users.

EXAMPLES OF DISCLOSURE

This chapter examines disclosure from an international perspective. It also illustrates certain disclosures made by European multinational corporations that are not typically made by U.S. firms. Some disclosures have a longer tradition and are better developed in Europe than in the United States. This is one area where U.S. accountants can learn from their European cousins. Indeed, a recent survey of annual reports from around the world concludes that U.S. companies have not kept up with a worldwide trend toward providing informative and innovative disclosures to the public.[1]

What, how much, and how a company discloses supplemental information varies depending on (1) the requirements of generally accepted accounting principles, (2) the needs of users, (3) the influence of users, and (4) the philosophy of management. This chapter specifically looks at:

1. Geographic area and product line disclosures.

2. Financial forecast disclosures.

3. Information about shares and shareholders.

4. The value added statement.

5. Employee disclosures.

6. Environmental disclosures.

Geographic Area and Product Line Disclosures

Consolidated financial statements combine the separate financial statements of a parent company and its subsidiaries so that a single set of financial statements is issued for the entire economic entity. This subject is discussed in Chapter 6, where the argument is made that for a multinational corporation operating in a number of different countries and perhaps having several different product lines, consolidated financial statements may in fact hide some important information. If

---

[1] *World Survey of Published Accounts* (London: Lafferty Publications, 1989).

a company's continued profitability depends heavily on a certain region of the world or on a particular product, knowledge of that may be useful to investors, creditors, employees, and other financial statement users. After all, not all areas of the world have equally risky business environments or present equal business opportunities. Products vary in terms of risks and returns as well. Thus, in addition to consolidated financial statements, perhaps companies should provide, supplementally, more details about where and how total profits are derived.

The purpose of *disaggregated* geographic and product line disclosure is to aid the financial statement user to identify a company's *dependency* on a country, area of the world, or product line. Accounting researchers have determined that investors can improve their predictions about a company's future prospects when they are given financial information disaggregated by geographic region and "line of business" in addition to consolidated financial information.

Large U.S. multinationals are required to observe *FASB Statement 14*, "Financial Reporting for Segments of a Business Enterprise." This standard gives guidance for disclosures by both geographic area and product line, but the guidelines are fairly vague. Exhibit 5–1 (pp. 74–75) shows how Coca-Cola Company complies with this standard. Note that Coca-Cola defines two product line segments—soft drinks and foods. The company also defines five geographic areas—the United States, Latin America, the European Community, Northeast Europe and Africa, and Pacific and Canada. Coca-Cola separately discloses the following by line of business and by geographic area: net operating revenues, operating income, identifiable operating assets, capital expenditures, and depreciation and amortization. The soft drinks information is further split between United States and international. In addition, Coca-Cola includes a more detailed discussion (not reproduced here) of its operations by geographic area.

Certain disaggregated disclosures by the British firm Cadbury Schweppes are reproduced in Exhibit 5–2 (p. 76). Cadbury Schweppes uses a matrix format to disclose sales, trading profit, and operating assets by product line and geographic area. The company defines two product lines—confectionery (candies) and beverages. It also defines five geographic regions—the United Kingdom, (Continental) Europe, the Americas, the Pacific Rim, and Africa & Other. Cadbury Schweppes also provides an in-depth analysis of its operations by product line (not reproduced here). A matrix presentation provides more detail than separate product line and geographic area disclosures. However, the approach is not very common.

Presenting disaggregated data is now common among large multinational corporations, with the notable exception of Japanese MNCs. Several countries require it, the International Accounting Standards Committee has issued *Standard 14*, "Reflecting Financial Information by Segments," and both the United Nations and the Organization for Economic Cooperation and Development (discussed in Chapter 3) suggest such disclosures by multinationals. There is, however, a wide variety in the disclosure practices of multinationals. Clearly, defining product lines is easier than defining meaningful geographic segments. Countries and regions vary in terms of (1) stage of development, (2) political risk, (3) cur-

---

EXHIBIT 5–1   Coca-Cola Company, Product Line and Geographic Area Disclosure

---

Notes to Consolidated Financial Statements *The Coca-Cola Company and Subsidiaries*

18 Lines of Business

The Company operates in two major lines of business: soft drinks and foods (principally juice and juice-drink products). Information concerning operations in these businesses at December 31, 1991, 1990 and 1989, and for the years then ended, is presented below (in millions):

	Soft Drinks				
1991	United States	International	Foods	Corporate	Consolidated
Net operating revenues	$2,645.2	$7,244.8	$1,635.7	$ 45.9	$11,571.6
Operating income	468.7	2,141.1	103.7	(394.5)	2,319.0
Identifiable operating assets	1,447.0	4,742.3	755.0	1,124.1[3]	8,068.4
Equity income				40.0[1]	40.0
Investments (principally bottling companies)				2,154.0	2,154.0
Capital expenditures	131.1	546.3	57.1	57.2	791.7
Depreciation and amortization	81.9	111.9	30.8	36.8	261.4

	Soft Drinks				
1990	United States	International	Foods	Corporate	Consolidated
Net operating revenues	$2,461.3	$6,125.4	$1,604.9	$ 44.8	$10,236.4
Operating income	358.1[2]	1,801.4	93.5	(301.4)	1,951.6
Identifiable operating assets	1,691.0	3,672.2	759.2	1,131.2[3]	7,253.6
Equity income				110.1	110.1
Investments (principally bottling companies)				2,024.6	2,024.6
Capital expenditures	138.4	321.4	68.2	65.0	593.0
Depreciation and amortization	88.5	94.4	28.3	32.7	243.9

	Soft Drinks				
1989	United States	International	Foods	Corporate	Consolidated
Net operating revenues	$2,222.2	$4,759.2	$1,583.3	$ 57.6	$ 8,622.3
Operating income	390.6	1,517.6	87.4	(269.8)	1,725.8
Identifiable operating assets	1,814.4	2,806.0	695.3	1,036.4[3]	6,352.1
Equity income				75.5	75.5
Investments (principally bottling companies)				1,930.4	1,930.4
Capital expenditures	136.3	215.6	61.6	49.0	462.5
Depreciation and amortization	73.9	48.4	30.7	30.8	183.8

Intercompany transfers between sectors are not material.

[1] *Reduced by $44 million related to restructuring charges recorded by CCE.*
[2] *Includes nonrecurring charges of $49 million.*
[3] *Corporate identifiable operating assets are composed principally of marketable securities and fixed assets.*

EXHIBIT 5–1   *(concluded)*

Notes to Consolidated Financial Statements *The Coca-Cola Company and Subsidiaries*

▽19 Operations in Geographic Areas

Information about the Company's operations in different geographic areas at December 31, 1991, 1990 and 1989, and for the years then ended, is presented below (in millions):

1991	United States	Latin America	European Community	Northeast Europe/ Africa	Pacific and Canada	Corporate	Consolidated
Net operating revenues	$4,124.8	$1,103.2	$3,338.3	$613.6	$2,345.8	$ 45.9	$11,571.6
Operating income	560.2	404.6	767.3	204.1	777.3	(394.5)	2,319.0
Identifiable operating assets	2,160.9	814.6	2,558.0	423.5	987.3	1,124.1³	8,068.4
Equity income						40.0¹	40.0
Investments (principally bottling companies)						2,154.0	2,154.0
Capital expenditures	184.8	105.5	330.6	61.3	52.3	57.2	791.7
Depreciation and amortization	111.3	23.3	65.8	9.7	14.5	36.8	261.4

1990	United States	Latin America	European Community	Northeast Europe/ Africa	Pacific and Canada	Corporate	Consolidated
Net operating revenues	$3,931.0	$ 813.0	$2,804.8	$562.8	$2,080.0	$ 44.8	$10,236.4
Operating income	440.4²	300.2	666.5	174.2	671.7	(301.4)	1,951.6
Identifiable operating assets	2,414.2	640.3	1,818.8	400.1	849.0	1,131.2³	7,253.6
Equity income						110.1	110.1
Investments (principally bottling companies)						2,024.6	2,024.6
Capital expenditures	204.0	59.7	203.5	38.8	22.0	65.0	593.0
Depreciation and amortization	115.6	18.0	54.5	7.6	15.5	32.7	243.9

1989	United States	Latin America	European Community	Northeast Europe/ Africa	Pacific and Canada	Corporate	Consolidated
Net operating revenues	$3,678.7	$ 646.2	$1,855.1	$425.2	$1,959.5	$ 57.6	$ 8,622.3
Operating income	468.2	226.7	540.6	147.3	612.8	(269.8)	1,725.8
Identifiable operating assets	2,476.0	515.4	1,342.8	328.8	652.7	1,036.4³	6,352.1
Equity income						75.5	75.5
Investments (principally bottling companies)						1,930.4	1,930.4
Capital expenditures	196.4	30.7	133.9	24.6	27.9	49.0	462.5
Depreciation and amortization	103.5	11.8	18.0	4.9	14.8	30.8	183.8

Intercompany transfers between geographic areas are not material.
Identifiable liabilities of operations outside the United States amounted to approximately $1.7 billion, $1.5 billion and $1.1 billion at December 31, 1991, 1990 and 1989, respectively.

¹ *Reduced by $44 million related to restructuring charges recorded by CCE.*
² *Includes nonrecurring charges of $49 million.*
³ *Corporate identifiable operating assets are composed principally of marketable securities and fixed assets.*

Operating Income by Geographic Area
(In millions)

Net Operating Revenues by Geographic Area
(In millions)

■ United States
■ Latin America   ■ Northeast Europe/Africa
European Community   Pacific & Canada

■ United States
■ Latin America   ■ Northeast Europe/Africa
European Community   Pacific & Canada

EXHIBIT 5–2   Cadbury Schweppes—Product Line and Geographic Area Disclosure

---

SALES, TRADING PROFIT AND OPERATING ASSETS ANALYSIS

1991		Total £m	United Kingdom £m	Europe £m	Americas £m	Pacific Rim £m	Africa & Others £m
Sales							
	Confectionery	1,387.3	767.0	207.1	30.9	284.7	97.6
	Beverages	1,845.0	739.0	448.7	407.4	206.5	43.4
		3,232.3	1,506.0	655.8	438.3	491.2	141.0
Trading Profit							
	Confectionery	170.2	85.4	21.7	9.2	43.9	10.0
	Beverages	192.3	76.8	54.5	33.6	20.6	6.8
		362.5	162.2	76.2	42.8	64.5	16.8
Operating Assets*							
	Confectionery	576.0	337.5	94.7	5.9	119.1	18.8
	Beverages	590.8	245.0	196.3	48.8	70.2	30.5
		1,166.8	582.5	291.0	54.7	189.3	49.3
1990	**Sales**						
	Confectionery	1,322.7	715.4	195.6	30.2	290.3	91.2
	Beverages	1,823.4	760.6	442.4	373.5	205.2	41.7
		3,146.1	1,476.0	638.0	403.7	495.5	132.9
Trading Profit							
	Confectionery	163.0	83.3	19.3	8.9	42.3	9.2
	Beverages	170.9	65.2	48.7	34.4	16.3	6.3
		333.9	148.5	68.0	43.3	58.6	15.5
Operating Assets*							
	Confectionery	547.7	320.4	81.1	5.9	102.1	38.2
	Beverages	565.3	259.9	167.1	51.1	77.8	9.4
		1,113.0	580.3	248.2	57.0	179.9	47.6
		%	%	%	%	%	%
Return on Assets (Average)							
	1991	31.8	27.9	28.3	76.6	34.9	34.7
	1990	31.6	27.5	32.3	66.7	30.2	34.0

*Operating assets represent tangible fixed assets, stock, debtors and creditors after excluding restructuring provisions, borrowings, taxation, dividends and deferred share purchase consideration.

rency strength, and (4) economic stability. The risks associated with these varia-bles somehow need to be conveyed. This represents a significant challenge for accountants.

Financial Forecast Disclosures

Given that a primary concern of investors is assessing a company's future profitability and cash flows, it is reasonable to ask whether companies provide their own internal forecasts of such financial information. Financial forecasts would seem to be relevant information for investors. In practice, few MNCs pro-vide them. One reason is that forecasts can be unreliable because they incorporate (often highly) subjective estimates of uncertain future events. In addition, there can be legal repercussions for managements if the forecasts are not met. In liti-gious countries such as the United States, the potential for lawsuits is a major de-terrent to providing financial forecasts.

Though unusual by international norms, some forecast disclosures can be ob-served, notably by some larger Swedish MNCs. For example, the 1991 annual report of Astra, the Swedish pharmaceutical company, projected ''group sales and pretax earnings are expected to increase by 20–25 percent in 1992.''

Information about Shares and Shareholders

A number of continental European companies have recently begun disclosing rather extensive information about their shares and shareholders. Exhibit 5-3 (pp. 78–79) is an example of such a disclosure provided by the Swedish telecommuni-cations company Ericsson in its annual report. Share information disclosed by Ericsson includes the following: (1) a description of Ericsson's class A and B shares, (2) the stock exchanges where Ericsson's shares are traded and the approx-imate percentage of total trading on the exchanges, (3) information about Erics-son's stockholders, and (4) selected other data, such as the year-end price and the yearly high and low price per share for five years. Ericsson also discloses the over-all distribution of its stockholdings and the identity and number of shares owned by its 11 largest stockholders.

What is the value of such information? It is aimed primarily at current and prospective shareholders. Past trend data can be useful in predicting future pat-terns, and it is also useful when making comparisons with the trends of other com-panies. Shares are more marketable when they are traded on several exchanges and when the volume of trading is high. Information about shareholders is useful for judging how concentrated the ownership of the company is. Widely scattered ownership tends to provide ready sales opportunities when present shareholders wish to dispose of some or all of their share holdings. Management may be con-strained if a large block of shares is owned by relatively few individuals or groups. For example, notice that two groups, with a combined ownership of 84.7 (42.9 and 41.8) percent of the voting rights, dominate Ericsson's stockholder owner-

EXHIBIT 5-3   Ericsson, Information about Shares and Shareholders

Capital stock

The capital stock of the Parent Company, Telefonaktiebolaget LM Ericsson, amounted at December 31, 1991 to SEK 2,059,864,550, represented by 205,986,455 shares, each with a par value of SEK 10. Of the total number of shares outstanding, 12,398,420 are restricted A shares and 6,244,155 are unrestricted A shares, each carrying one vote, and 187,343,880 are unrestricted B shares, each carrying one thousandth of a vote.

The Articles of Association of the Parent Company stipulate that not more than 35 percent of the voting rights in the company may be represented by unrestricted shares, which may be owned by foreign citizens as well as citizens of Sweden. At year-end 1991, the maximum voting rights accruing to unrestricted shares amounted to 34.2 percent of the total voting rights and the actual voting rights of foreign-owned unrestricted shares represented 0.3 percent of the total.

During 1991 the number of shares increased by 257,372 through conversion of debentures. During the period between January 1 and February 15, 1992 additional debentures were converted to 4,775 B shares, increasing to 205,991,230 the total number of shares entitled to dividends as of the record date.

Employee ownership of Ericsson shares

Ericsson employees are able to purchase the company's shares via bank loans arranged by the company. Since 1973, slightly more than 6,700 employees have taken advantage of this opportunity, purchasing a total of approximately 2.4 million shares.

Ericsson's Share Savings Fund was started in 1981, and Ericsson's General Savings Fund in 1984. There are 1,430 participants in the Share Savings Fund and 2,429 in the General Savings Fund. The funds have invested in Ericsson shares and in Ericsson's convertible debenture certificates. At year-end, combined holdings of the two funds amounted to 393,500 shares, or approximately 0.2 percent of the total number of shares, and the funds held debentures convertible to 394,250 shares.

The debenture certificates may be converted to B shares up to and including March 15, 1993. To date, SEK 42.1 m. of the SEK 626.4 m. loan has been converted to 795,299 B shares. Slightly more than 10,000 Ericsson employees hold Company debentures.

Stock exchange trading

LM Ericsson A and B shares are listed on the Stockholm Stock Exchange. The B shares are listed on the exchanges in Basel, Düsseldorf, Frankfurt am Main, Geneva, Hamburg, London, Oslo, Paris and Zürich and are also traded in the U.S. in the form of ADR's (American Depository Receipts) via the NASDAQ electronic quotation system.

Each ADR represents one B share. The most active trading occurs in Stockholm, London and New York.

Approximately 264 million shares were traded during 1991. The turnover was distributed as follows (approximate percentages): 43 percent on the London Stock Exchange, 31 percent on NASDAQ, 25 percent on the Stockholm Stock Exchange, and one percent on other exchanges.

Stockholders

Dominant interest is shared by the so-called Svenska Handelsbanken interests, with 42.9 percent of the voting rights, and the Wallenberg and Skandinaviska Enskilda Banken interests, with 41.8 percent.

Approximately 75 percent of Ericsson's shares are owned by institutions in Sweden and other countries.

At year-end 1991, about 25 percent of the company's shares were held by stockholders outside Sweden.

Trading on the Stockholm Stock Exchange

∎ Ericsson unrestricted B shares   — General index   © Findata

EXHIBIT 5-3 (concluded)

Share data	1991	1990*	1989	1988	1987
Exports of shares from Sweden (SEK m.)	2,310	777	499	585	401
Imports of shares to Sweden (SEK m.)	1,218	1,873	1,384	635	1,233
Net imports of shares to Sweden	1,092	1,096	885	50	832
P/E ratio I, "B" shares 1)	29.3	12.0	15.1	13.6	8.5
P/E ratio II, "B" shares 2)	25.1	12.4	16.4	11.8	7.9
Share prices, December 31, Stockholm Stock Exchange (SEK)					
–"A" restricted	140	245	1,000	470	300
–"A" unrestricted	145	245	950	470	300
–"B" unrestricted	108	184	880	368	153
–"B" unrestricted High for year	225	280	940	369	304
–"B" unrestricted Low for year	88.5	175	356	155	149

1) P/E ratio I = Price per share divided by profit per share after actual taxes paid.
2) P/E ratio II = Price per share divided by profit per share after actual and estimated deferred taxes.
* After 5-for-1 stock split

Changes in capital stock		Number of shares	Capital stock
1976	January 1	15,380,117	769,005,850
	1-for-4 stock dividend	3,845,029	192,251,450
	1-for-6 new issue, SEK 75	2,563,352	128,167,600
1982	1-for-2 stock dividend	10,894,248	544,712,400
1983	Special new issue, USD 62.5	4,000,000	200,000,000
	Conversions	181,677	9,083,850
1984	Conversions	39,049	1,952,450
1985	Conversions	47,789	2,389,450
1986	Conversions	1,211,121	60,556,050
1988	Conversions	52,242	2,612,100
1989	Conversions	2,760,310	138,015,500
1990	Conversions	854,413	8,544,130
1990	5-for-1 stock split	163,899,736	–
1991	Conversions	257,372	2,573,720
1991	December 31	205,986,455	2,059,864,550

Distribution of shares, year-end 1991 Stockholder's holding	Stockholders Number	%	Number of shares	%	Number of shares/ stockholder
1 – 500	78,761	78,5	12,947,430	6,3	164
501 – 5 000	19,909	19,8	28,333,463	13,8	1,423
5 001 – 20 000	1,245	1,2	12,148,987	5,9	9,758
20 000 –	483	0,5	152,556,575	74,0	315,852
	100,398	100,0	205,986,455	100,0	2,051

The largest stockholders, ranked by voting rights, were as follows at December 31, 1991	Number of shares	Voting rights percent
AB Industrivärden	6,459 035	26.5
Knut och Alice Wallenbergs stiftelse	2,651 480	14.0
AB Investor	1,970 000	10.4
Oktogonen, Stiftelsen	1,310 000	5.9
Svenska Handelsbankens Pensionsstiftelse	116 000	5.6
Livförsäkrings AB Skandia	7,467 240	3.8
Pensionskassan SHB Försäkringsförening	90 000	3.1
EB-stiftelsen, SE Bankens Pensionsstiftelse	508 440	2.6
Wallanders o Hedelius' stiftelse	450 000	2.4
Wallenbergs stiftelse, Marianne och Marcus	450 000	2.3
Svenska Handelsbankens personalstiftelse	280 000	1.5

ship. The identities of the largest shareholders might also be of interest to current and potential shareholders for the same reason.

Information such as that in Exhibit 5–3 is provided voluntarily. There are no standards, such as from the organizations discussed in Chapter 3, that require companies to provide information about shares and shareholders. Although the practice seems to be growing, it is still not very widespread.

The Value Added Statement

The value added statement originated in Europe and is now occasionally provided by companies from outside Europe (for example, Australia and South Africa). To our knowledge, no country's GAAP require value added statements. Thus, they are provided on a completely voluntary basis.

The statement produced by the British firm Imperial Chemical Industries is reproduced in Exhibit 5–4. This statement shows that, net of materials and services used in producing its chemical products, ICI added £4,352 million to the world economy in 1991. This contribution went to the following groups:

1. Employees, in the form of salaries, pensions, etc.

2. Governments, in the form of taxes.

3. Providers of capital, in the form of interest to creditors and dividends to shareholders.

4. ICI itself—amounts reinvested in the business.

The value added statement presents the view that a corporation is a provider of wealth to society—that its presence is a positive force. Because the corporation exists, people are employed, governments receive more taxes, and investors and creditors are rewarded for risking their funds in the business. The value added statement reflects the philosophy that a business enterprise should, and actually *does*, do more than just make a profit. It is consistent with the notion that creating employment and making other contributions to society at large are also legitimate objectives of business. This is not the prevailing attitude in the United States, but it is in most other countries of the world. One can see that the environmental variables discussed in Chapter 1 affect not only measurement practices but also disclosure practices.

Employee Disclosures

Exhibit 5–5 (pp. 82–83) is reproduced from the annual report of the French drinks company Pernod Ricard. Notice that Exhibit 5–5 shows information about age and seniority, training, fringe benefits, and absenteeism. Employee disclosures reflect the viewpoint that a company's continued success depends in part on its employees, or human resources. Exhibit 5–5 also demonstrates the influence of organized labor in Europe, where it is relatively more powerful than in the United States.

This type of disclosure developed in Europe and is now finding its way into

EXHIBIT 5–4   Imperial Chemical Industries—Value Added Statement

SOURCES AND DISPOSAL
OF VALUE ADDED

For the year ended 31 December	Notes	1991 £m	1990* £m	Change %
SOURCES OF INCOME				
Sales turnover		12,488	12,906	–3%
Royalties and other trading income		119	150	–21%
Less materials and services used		(8,285)	(8,764)	
Value added by manufacturing and trading activities		4,322	4,292	+1%
Share of profits less losses of associated undertakings		30	113	–73%
Total value added		4,352	4,405	–1%
DISPOSAL OF TOTAL VALUE ADDED				
Employees	1			
Pay, plus national insurance contributions, pension costs and severance payments		2,892	2,735	
Profit-sharing bonus	2	31	39	
Total employee costs		2,923	2,774	+5%
Severance payments and other employment costs relating to extraordinary items	3	(166)	(6)	
	4	2,757	2,768	–
Governments				
Corporate taxes	5	279	336	
Less grants		(17)	(30)	
		262	306	–14%
Providers of capital				
Interest cost of net borrowings		220	206	
Dividends to shareholders		391	389	
Minority shareholders in subsidiary undertakings		22	22	
		633	617	+3%
Re-investment in the business				
Depreciation		549	525	
Extraordinary items		–	(92)	
Profit retained		151	281	
		700	714	–2%
Total disposal		4,352	4,405	–1%

* Restated, see note 2 on page 38.

Notes
1   The average number of employees in the Group worldwide decreased by 3 per cent.
    The average number employed in the UK decreased by 4 per cent.
2   The 1991 UK bonus rate was 3.5p per £1 of remuneration (1990 4.7p).
3   See note 31 on page 54.
4   Employee costs charged in arriving at trading profit (see note 31).
5   Does not include tax deducted from the pay of employees. Income tax deducted from
    the pay of UK employees under PAYE amounted to £201m in 1991 (1990 £185m).

This table, which is used for calculating the bonus under the Employees' Profit-Sharing Scheme, is based on the audited accounts; it shows the total value added to the cost of materials and services purchased from outside the Group and indicates the ways this increase in value has been disposed.

EXHIBIT 5-5   Pernod Ricard—Employee Disclosure

PERSONNEL PROFILE 1991

At December 31, 1991, the Group's Human Resources totalled 11,082 people:

– 185 work In non-consolidated companies (Sacca SNC, Cusenier SAIC),

– 135 work with companies included in the financial reports of the Group but not in its personnel profile (Casella Far East, Pernod Ricard Japan, Lizas & Lizas, BC Trading).

The Group's total payroll in 1991 therefore involves 10,762 employees from new companies:

■ **In France: Renault Bisquit, merger of Castillon Renault and Bisquit,**

■ **Abroad:•** SIAS Korea, ■ **SIAS Mexico and Caxton, a Campbell subsidiary.**

HUMAN RESOURCES

At December 31, 1991, companies deemed consolidated for the personnel profile employed 10,762 individuals (of whom 4,248 worked abroad and 6,514 in France), a slight decrease compared with 1990 (-2.4%), when the Group employed 11,025.

The number of permanent employees in1991 remained virtually stable (10,231 at year- end 1991, and 10,296 at year-end in 1990).

This drop in employee numbers stems from the substantial decrease in the number of fixed-term contracts at December 31 (- 28% from 1990), notable among plant workers (-30%), particularly at Orangina, Orlando Wyndham and SVF.

The Group hired 1,304 people on permanent contracts, 722 of whom were in France.

Compared with total personnel, the proportion of the sales force continues to rise and increased from 21% in 1989 to 23% in 1991.

AGE AND SENIORITY

The average age of Group personnel has increased slightly and is now 39 years 5 months, as opposed to 39 years last year. The proportion of employees under 25 decreased (from 9.1% in 1990 to 8.3% in 1991), which can be explained by the reduced number of fixed-term contracts, which are usually awarded to younger workers.

Average seniority reached 11 years 4 months in 1991, as opposed to 11 years even in 1990. Percentage of employees with less than five years seniority has increased appreciably: 31.9% in 1990 versus 33.8% in 1991.

PAYROLL

The payroll figures listed involve French companies only. It would not be logical to report the salaries from other countries due to differences in factors such as parity, cost of living or taxation.

Average salaries increased 3.05%

Payroll changes in certain categories can be explained as follows:

– classification updates (for example, SVF and Orangina, where certain employees were promoted to line supervisor).

– a youth trend in the population concerned (the average age of internal managers decreased from 42.5 in 1990 to 42.2 in 1991).

TRAINING

In 1991, professional development programs were maintained. Nearly 119,000 hours of training were given to 3,885 people, representing a training effort of 2.27% of payroll (2.08% in 1990, and 1.9% in 1989).

Emphasis was placed on training of the sales force with Ricard, CSR, Crus et Domaines de Frances, and Orangina.

An extensive general training operation intended for the professional development of employees is being conducted by SIAS-MPA for the second year in a row.

BREAKDOWN OF PERSONNEL BY CATEGORY

1990: Total 11,025 of which sales force 2,484
1991: Total 10,762 of which sales force 2,474

AGE

SENIORITY

AVERAGE ANNUAL SALARY (in FF)

	1990	1991
Workers	107,671	110,833
Employees	119,080	123,491
Line supervisors	160,207	163,361
Internal managers	353,002	354,395
Sales people	125,535	128,884
Sales representatives	187,906	191,896
Sales managers and supervisors	243,243	251,714

EXHIBIT 5–5   *(concluded)*

TRAINING

	1990	1991
Number of hours	110,899	118,657
% of work time	0.64%	0.69%
Number of trainees	3,854	3,885
% of total employees	39.7%	36.1%
Number of hours per trainee	28 h 48	30 h 30
Cost (in FF)	30,989,736	
% of payroll	2.08%	

ABSENTEEISM

Absentee rate
Number of accidents
1,000,000 work hours

90	42.17
91	39.98

Seriousness index
Number of days lost
1,000 work hours

90	0.91
91	0.86

Both Ricard and Pampyrl are maintaining their language and communications training programs.

Training expense at Orlando-Wyndham, for its part, went from 0.75 to 1.17 % of payroll from 1992 to 1991, which is in keeping with Australian legislation compelling companies to devote at least one percent of their payroll to professional development.

FRINGE BENEFITS AND WORKING CONDITIONS

At the Group level, the "Human Resources Management" operation launched in 1990 was extended to our principal foreign subsidiaries in 1991.

For each of the Group's companies, the ultimate purpose is to project different growth scenarios for principal managers and future personnel needs. Such information is then compared and processed at Group level to balance potential against needs and develop some mobility among companies.

In 1991, more than 70 people changed companies within the Group, as opposed to 30 or so in 1990.

In our subsidiaries, fringe benefits are constantly improving, as borne out by the following examples:

– renewal of profit-sharing agreements by Orangina, Ricard, Cusenier, Pernod, and SIAS France,

– an improvement of the benefits package by renegotiating pension and insurance benefits for CSR and Cusenier, which now offer a choice between a death benefit annuity and a limited death benefit accompanied by a college fund,

– an agreement allowing employees of Cooymans Kerstens and SIAS-MPA to open savings accounts with the business,

– an update of employee classifications at Orangina and SVF.

One example of the Group's concern for constant improvement of working conditions is the establishment of a steering committee on that topic at CSR. Other examples are:

– air conditioning systems (Austin Nichols, Irish Distillers, BWG Foods, Orlando Wyndham, SIAS, Cooymans Kerstens),

– renovations (Cusenier, Orlando, Pampyrl, Ricard and SVF).

ABSENTEEISM IN 1991

The absenteeism rate dropped by 2 % compared with 1990.

The Groups efforts in occupational safety resulted in a decrease in both the frequency and seriousness of work accidents.

In this respect, SIAS-France took the initiative of starting up a personnel incentive plan to reduce absenteeism and work accidents.

GROUP INFORMATION SESSIONS AND GET-TOGETHERS

Every year at the general employees' meeting the Group's general management presents the results of the fiscal year just ended. The Group's ranking in different markets and the principal results and objectives are outlined for each subsidiary. In addition to this communication effort by general management, one should also mention the internal communication of certain subsidiaries which, like Orangina, host a variety of conventions. Orangina is just one such example; in 1991, as it does every year, it organized conventions for the sales force and management. The management meeting decided to split up into work Groups, one commissioned to examine communication within the Group company, the other commissioned to define goals and orientations common to all of Orangina's personnel.

EXHIBIT 5-6   Ford Motor Company—Employee Disclosure

Employment Data

Ford Motor Company and Subsidiaries

Employment and Payrolls

In 1991, employment worldwide decreased 10% to 332,700 from 370,383 in 1990. Worldwide payrolls of $12.8 billion in 1991 decreased 9% from 1990. The decreases in average employment and in payroll for 1991 resulted primarily from the sale of Ford Aerospace Corporation in the fall of 1990 and the sale of Ford New Holland Inc. in the spring of 1991.

Average employment by geographic area, compared with 1990, follows:

	1991	1990
United States	156,802	180,940
Canada	14,907	16,491
Europe	117,689	126,261
Latin America	28,563	27,793
Asia-Pacific	14,739	18,898
Total	332,700	370,383

Retirement Plans

Virtually all Ford employees are covered by retirement plans. In 1991, in the United States, the plans paid $1.2 billion in retirement benefits to approximately 127,200 retired employees and surviving spouses. At year end, U.S. pension fund assets had a market value of $19.5 billion, $2.4 billion more than in 1990. Additional information on retirement plans appears in Note 2 of Notes to Financial Statements.

Employment of Minority-Group Personnel and Women at Year End

	Total U.S. Employment*		Minorities		Women	
	1991	1990	1991	1990	1991	1990
Hourly Employees	102,800	106,000	24.3%	24.1%	12.4%	12.2%
Salaried Employees	52,400	54,800	12.5	12.2	23.6	23.6
Total	155,200	160,800	20.3%	20.1%	16.2%	16.0%

* Includes Ford Motor Company, Ford Motor Credit Company, Ford Electronics and Refrigeration Corp., and Ford Microelectronics Inc.

Representation of Minority-Group Members and Women in EEO-1 Job Categories at Year End

Job Categories*	Blacks		Hispanics		Other Minorities**		Women	
	1991	1990	1991	1990	1991	1990	1991	1990
Officials & Managers	8.1%	8.2%	1.4%	1.3%	1.6%	1.5%	6.6%	6.2%
Professionals	6.9	6.8	1.8	1.7	3.5	3.3	20.6	20.4
Technicians	7.3	7.1	1.5	1.4	2.2	2.1	16.3	16.7
Office and Clerical	15.9	15.5	3.6	3.4	0.9	0.9	49.7	51.1
Craft Workers (skilled)	8.9	8.4	1.0	1.0	0.5	0.5	1.6	1.4
Operatives (semiskilled)	26.3	26.3	2.1	2.1	0.5	0.5	16.4	16.0
Laborers (nonskilled)	27.0	26.4	1.6	1.6	0.8	0.9	10.2	11.0
Service Workers	26.3	26.2	1.9	1.9	0.4	0.4	13.9	14.0
Percentage of Work Force	17.1%	17.0%	1.9%	1.8%	1.2%	1.2%	16.2%	16.0%

* Excludes Sales Workers (retail), a category that is not applicable to Ford.

** Includes Asians, Pacific Islanders, American Indians or Alaskan Natives only.

the annual reports of U.S. companies. For example, Exhibit 5-6 is the employee disclosure of Ford Motor Company. It includes information about the number of employees by geographic area and the number of minority group members and women employed.

Environmental Disclosures

The annual report of the German firm VEBA illustrates environmental disclosures. VEBA is an electricity generation and chemicals and oil company. It devotes five pages to the environmental protection measures it has taken. The following quote begins the discussion:

Environmental Protection—A Global Challenge

In view of global challenges like the growth of the world's population, the danger of climatic changes from the so-called greenhouse effect, the hole in the ozone layer, the consumption of resources, measures by individual states to protect the environment increasingly lose their significance.

The highly industrialized countries of this world, in particular, are called upon to reduce energy consumption while the economy is expanding and to make economic growth environmentally compatible. What is more, with the opening up of Eastern Europe and the emergence of sometimes catastrophic ecological conditions in those countries, the Western world is faced with new tasks.

In future, the mostly parochial view of environmental protection must cover a much wider area. The global responsibility for our actions must be seen as a task to be performed.

The VEBA Group is prepared to accept the global demands for the protection of our environment in all of its activities and to take the factor of nature into account even more than in the past. However, we must not disregard the basic principles of a free market economy. Only a sound and strong company can help to bear the increased burdens of protecting the environment and promote and support the protection of our environment.

In 1991, DM 354 million was spent on environmental protection equipment in the VEGA Group. Expenses related to environmental protection (operating costs and capital service) amounted to DM 1.6 billion. The following table shows the development in recent years.

The two items reproduced in Exhibit 5–7 (p. 86) are included in VEBA's environmental disclosure. These show the five-year pattern of VEBA's expenses for environmental protection and the trend in CO_2 emissions since 1965.

Such disclosures can be found in the annual reports of large continental European companies, particularly those from Germany, Switzerland, and Scandinavia. In addition, one might also find extensive discussions of safety measures adopted by the company and how the company's products and services benefit the community at large.

Environmental disclosures reflect the point of view mentioned earlier: that contributing to society at large is a legitimate aim of business. We see these disclosures as an attempt to provide information to more than just the traditional financial statement users. These disclosures are directed to the consumers of the company's products and to the citizens in general who coexist with the firm. Relevant disclosures by European firms are also a reaction to environmental political parties that have some strength there.

Green accounting, as it is sometimes referred to, is just emerging, and the Europeans are leading the way. The 1990s have been dubbed the "environmental decade," and the enhanced awareness of the environment has created demands for more information on corporate environmental performance. At the present time, there is little comparability of the information provided and most of it is provided on a voluntary basis. Nevertheless, environmental disclosures are beginning to draw the attention of accounting standard setting bodies in a number of countries. We believe that these developments bear watching.

EXHIBIT 5–7   VEBA, Environmental Disclosure

Expenses for Environmental Protection (DM million)

	1987	1988	1989	1990	1991
Capital spending	655	698	638	497	354
Operating costs and capital service	1,252	1,554	1,531	1,541	1,610

Specific Emissions of CO_2 from VEBA Power Stations (kg CO_2/kwh)   (11)

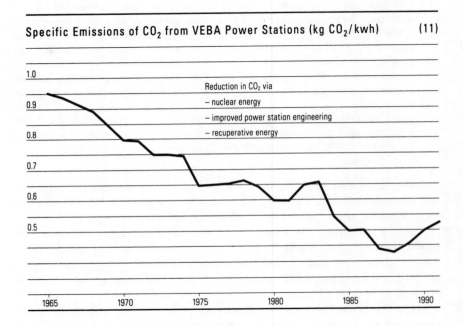

CONCLUSION

During the 1960s and 1970s a disclosure explosion took place in most indus-
trially developed countries, mandated by new national laws. Companies began
revealing information about themselves that they had never revealed before. A
major motivation for such laws seemed to be a low level of investor confidence.
Beyond that, companies themselves began to realize that secrecy is self-defeating.
Failure to make reasonable disclosures in response to user needs can severely limit
the pool of funds available to a corporation. Potential providers of capital, when
kept in the dark, will simply put their money elsewhere.

Studies by accountants have shown that firms significantly increase disclosure levels when they seek new sources of investment funds, that differences in disclosure levels among nations are rapidly narrowing, and that increased disclosure can lead to lower costs of capital for business enterprises. These findings are consistent with the arguments made in this and earlier chapters.

Disclosure is a way for the world's multinationals to reach out to investors and creditors in other countries without abandoning their own financial accounting practices. Exhibit 4–5 illustrates how the Swedish multinational Electrolux accomplishes this. Until the differences in generally accepted accounting principles observed by the world's multinationals can be reconciled and harmonized, disclosure can be a way around the transnational financial reporting problems discussed in Chapter 4.

Most accountants agree that the basic financial statements (balance sheet and income statement) have primacy over disclosures. In other words, such issues as valuing assets and determining net income—the so-called measurement issues— are, for the most part, more important than disclosure issues. Thus, disclosure issues are less controversial, and disclosure requirements tend to be easier to change than accounting measurement rules. Increased disclosure should not be a substitute for improving accounting measurements. Nevertheless, disclosure is an effective way to communicate information that does not fit what is required in financial statements by generally accepted accounting principles. Disclosures need not be constrained by financial reporting rules and are limited only by the imagination of accountants and corporate managements.

KEY POINTS

1. American companies have not kept up with the worldwide trend toward providing informative and innovative disclosures in corporate annual reports.

2. U.S. companies comply with FASB *Statement 14* in providing geographic area and product line disclosure. Presenting this information in a matrix format is a European innovation.

3. Some European companies provide financial forecasts and detailed information about shares and shareholders.

4. Innovative social disclosures coming from Europe are the value added statement and disclosures about the environment and employees.

CASES

Bellhaven Ltd.

Transform the following traditional income statement of Bellhaven Ltd. into a value added statement:

BELLHAVEN LTD.
Statement of Income
For the Year Ended December 31, 1993

	£000s	
Sales	2,450	
Cost of goods sold	1,660	
Gross profit		790
Salaries and retirement benefits	340	
Rent expense	45	
Outside services used	18	
Interest expense	30	433
Income before taxes		357
Provision before income taxes		140
Net income		217

NOTES: 1. All goods sold were purchased from outsiders.
2. Dividends declared and paid during 1993 amounted to £145 thousand.

The Controller Gets a Suggestion

Cathie Hawthorne works for the corporate reporting section of a U.S. multinational corporation. Cathie has just been called into a conference by the corporate controller, who is obviously irritated about something.

"Cathie, I just got a letter from my new hotshot division controller in Europe. I want you to look at this. He's got all kinds of goofy suggestions about how we can 'improve' our company's annual report by disclosing a bunch of stuff that some of the European companies do.

"Frankly, European accountants haven't had a good idea since the Italians invented double-entry bookkeeping 500 years ago. What is this value added statement? And why should I put in a bunch of junk about protecting the environment and how nice we are to our employees?

"Our job is to make a profit, and that's all our investors care about. Why, they'd probably *complain* if I put in a lot of useless information like that."

Questions

1. If you were Cathie, how would you answer the controller's protests?
2. What is the purpose of the value added statement? Environmental disclosures? Employee disclosures?
3. How does the controller's attitude differ from that found in Europe?
4. What might the multinational corporation gain by including in its annual report some of the "hotshot" European division controller's "goofy suggestions"?

Reporting about the Environment

Harlan Davis works in the financial reporting section of a large U.S. chemical company. He has been examining the annual reports of some of the company's European competitors and has noticed that many of them have extensive disclosures about what they are doing to protect the environment. Harlan is intrigued by these disclosures, since his company only discloses information about the costs of complying with environmental regulations. His mind is set in motion: "I wonder if we should include environmental disclosures in our annual report, like our European competitors do?"

Questions

1. What kinds of information might Harlan's company include in an environmental disclosure section of its annual report?
2. To whom would this type of information be valuable, and in what way?
3. Should Harlan recommend that environmental disclosures be added to his company's annual report? Why or why not?

Singleton Ltd.

Prepare a traditional income statement for Singleton Ltd. based on the following value added statement:

	1993 £ million
SINGLETON LTD. Sources and Disposal of Value Added	
Sources of income	
Sales	5,300
Royalties	340
Less: Materials and services used in manufacturing	(4,170)
Total value added	1,470
Disposal of total value added	
Employees (pay, plus pension contributions)	840
Governments (corporate income taxes)	160
Providers of capital:	325
Interest on borrowings	125
Dividends to stockholders	200
Reinvested in business	145
	1,470

NOTE: 1. Manufacturing labor costs amounted to £310 million while all other labor costs were £530 million.

ADDITIONAL READINGS

Ahadiat, N., and B. R. Stewart. "International Geographic Segment Reporting Standards: A Case of the Harmonization of Accounting Reporting Practices." *International Journal of Accounting* 27, no. 1 (1992), pp. 45–56.

Gray, R.; D. Owen; and K. T. Maunders. *Corporate Social Reporting*. Englewood Cliffs, N.J.: Prentice Hall, 1987.

Gray, S. J.; L. H. Radebaugh; and C. B. Roberts. "International Perceptions of Cost Constraints on Voluntary Information Disclosures: A Comparative Study of U.K. and U.S. Multinationals." *Journal of International Business Studies* (Fourth Quarter 1990), pp. 597–622.

Hawkshaw, A. "Accounting and the Environment: Status Quo Vadis?" *CA Magazine* (March 1991), pp. 22–27.

Meek, G. K., and S. J. Gray. "The Impact of Stock Market and Corporate Globalization on Disclosure Trends in International Financial Reporting." In *The Changing International Financial Markets and Their Impact on Accounting*, ed. V. K. Zimmerman. Urbana,

Ill.: Center for International Education and Research in Accounting, University of Illinois, 1992, pp. 43–66.

_____. "The Value Added Statement: An Innovation for U.S. Companies?" *Accounting Horizons* (June 1988), pp. 73–81.

Roberts, C. B. *International Trends in Social and Employee Reporting*. London, England: Chartered Association of Certified Accountants, 1990.

6

MULTINATIONAL CONSOLIDATIONS AND FOREIGN CURRENCY TRANSLATION

This chapter deals with the preparation of consolidated (group) financial statements by multinational corporations. We first cover consolidation practices around the world and then examine a related issue unique to multinational corporations—foreign currency translation. These topics are complicated and advanced, so our coverage necessarily touches only the basic ideas. Nevertheless, we feel that some knowledge of these topics is important to an initial exposure to international accounting.

THE BASIC IDEA

Consolidated financial statements combine the separate financial statements of two or more companies to yield a single set of financial statements *as if* the individual companies were really one. What is the rationale for preparing consolidated financial statements? Often, a business finds it advantageous to organize itself as a set of separate (legal) corporate entities rather than as one large corporate entity. For example, tax savings sometimes occur because of the way corporate income tax rates are structured. Or a company may separately incorporate the components of its business to limit legal liability. Multinationals are often required by the countries in which they do business to set up a separate corporation in each country. The point is that a *legal* entity is not necessarily the same as an *economic* entity. From an economic point of view, the activities of these various legal entities are centrally administered from corporate headquarters. Thus, the intent of consolidated financial statements is to provide financial accounting information about the group of companies from an overall perspective.

Transactions among the members of a corporate family are not included on consolidated financial statements; only assets, liabilities, revenues, and expenses with external third parties are shown. By law, however, the separate corporate entities are required to keep their own accounting records and to prepare individual financial statements. This means that transactions with other members of the group must be identified so they can be *excluded* when the consolidated statements are prepared. The situation is analogous to preparing combined financial statements for a family. Even though a child may owe a parent some money, from the perspective of the family entity, the liability on the child's personal balance sheet and the receivable on the parent's offset one another. When the child is given his or her weekly allowance, there is a transfer of funds on an individual basis. However, the family unit is no better or worse off as a result. The family's wealth is affected only when that money is given to someone outside the family. Thus, transactions that are all in the family affect individual members but not the family as a whole. The same holds true for corporate "families."

The process of preparing consolidated financial statements involves adding up the individual assets, liabilities, revenues, and expenses reported on the separate financial statements and then *eliminating* the intracompany ones. One company—the *parent*—normally dominates the other *subsidiary* companies. Taking a simple example, assume the following selected items from the individual financial statements of the parent and one subsidiary company:

	Parent	*Subsidiary*
Cash	$ 100	$ 75
Receivables	360*	280
Payables	90	100*
Revenues	2,000†	2,300
Expenses	1,600	1,900†

*Subsidiary owes Parent $50.
†Subsidiary rented some machinery from Parent for $400.

The $50 receivable that Parent includes on its financial statements and the $50 payable included on Subsidiary's statements represent an intracompany item. Since the purpose of consolidated financial statements is to treat the separate entities as if they were one, it would be incorrect to include this item on the consolidated financial statements. After all, the company cannot owe itself. Similarly, from a consolidated perspective, revenues and expenses would each be overstated by $400 if the rental transaction were included on the consolidated financial statements. Accountants handle these kinds of things by preparing a *consolidation worksheet*, as illustrated by the following:

| | Parent | Subsidiary | Eliminations | | Consolidated |
			Debit	Credit	
Cash	$ 100	$ 75			$ 175
Receivables	360	280		50*	590
Payables	90	100	50*		140
Revenues	2,000	2,300	400†		3,900
Expenses	1,600	1,900		400†	3,100

*Intracompany receivable/payable.
†Intracompany revenue/expense.

Thus, on a consolidated basis, receivables are $590; payables are $140; revenues are $3,900; and expenses total $3,100.

To reiterate, the purpose of consolidated financial statements is to present information from an overall perspective about a group of companies under common control and operating as an economic unit.

AN INTERNATIONAL PERSPECTIVE ON CONSOLIDATED FINANCIAL STATEMENTS

Consolidated financial statements first appeared around the turn of the 20th century in the United States. This was a time of great economic expansion during which a number of corporations grew into giants. The era witnessed a wave of corporate mergers. It is said that J. P. Morgan was so proud of his U.S. Steel Company (the first billion-dollar company in the world) that he insisted on preparing and disseminating consolidated financial statements since the company's inception in 1901. Since *holding companies* first became important in the United States, it is not surprising that U.S. accountants were the first to experiment with consolidated financial statements. These statements are now a part of U.S. generally accepted accounting principles.

Holding companies became important in Great Britain and the Netherlands in the 1920s, so consolidated financial statements appeared there somewhat later than in the United States. Today, they are required in both countries. The practice moved much more slowly in the other European countries: German law began requiring consolidations in the 1960s, although for domestic German subsidiaries only. The requirement was extended to all subsidiaries—German and non-German—effective 1990. French law requiring consolidated financial statements was enacted in the late 1980s. In Italy, only companies whose shares are listed on the stock exchange must prepare consolidated statements. In Switzerland, there are no legal requirements for consolidated statements, but a growing number of major companies prepare them anyway. At the moment, Europe represents a rather "mixed bag." Japan's requirement dates from 1977.

The observance or nonobservance of consolidated financial statements in a country can be related to several of the variables shaping accounting development discussed in Chapter 1.

1. The Legalistic/Nonlegalistic Orientation of Accounting.

Countries with a legalistic approach to accounting tend to focus on the legal entity as the object to be accounted for. In nonlegalistic countries, accounting emphasizes the economic entity. Therefore, consolidated financial statements are less common in legalistic countries, but are the norm in nonlegalistic countries. Nevertheless, the effect of this factor in legalistic countries is being ameliorated by the two factors discussed next.

2. The Relationship between Business and Capital Providers.

Group financial statements were first accepted in the Netherlands, Great Britain, and the United States—countries where financial accounting is oriented toward the decision needs of a diverse set of investors and creditors for whom the annual report is an important source of information about the company. Consolidated financial statements are also often used by multinational corporations— regardless of home country—that have global financing strategies. When a company secures funds on a worldwide basis, it probably prepares consolidated financial statements. Thus, the worldwide competition for funds seems to be propelling this practice (a point that is discussed in relation to disclosure issues in Chapter 5).

3. Political and Economic Ties.

Finally, political and economic ties affect this practice. Accounting technology is imported and exported, which is why consolidations are customary in Mexico and the Philippines, countries heavily influenced by the United States. As a result of U.K. influence, such statements are also widespread among British Commonwealth countries such as Australia, Malaysia, and South Africa. One of the most dramatic examples today is occurring within the European Community (EC). The *Seventh Company Law Directive* requiring consolidated accounts was adopted in 1983, and full implementation by EC member countries is expected during the 1990s. Once this happens, consolidated statements will become common in EC countries. (The recent changes in German and French laws discussed above are the direct result of the *Seventh Directive*. Refer to Chapter 3 for more details about this organization.) Indeed the effect of EC *Directives* extends to other European countries as well. Some companies from non-EC countries voluntarily comply with EC *Directives* in anticipation of their countries joining the EC.

Preparing consolidated financial statements is becoming the norm for the world's multinational corporations. Investors realize that without consolidated financial statements, companies can conceal losses in unconsolidated subsidiaries and thus hide the economic status of the entire group. To illustrate, consider the consolidations example discussed earlier. Suppose that the parent company is operating at below-normal profits. It could increase its reported profits by increasing the rental charge to the subsidiary above the current $400 amount. From a consolidated perspective, raising the rent has no effect on group profits since the rent is intracompany and gets eliminated in the consolidation process. But as far as the parent's own financial statements are concerned, an increased rental charge to the subsidiary "drops right down into income." The parent could accomplish the same result by shifting some of its employees to the subsidiary's payroll. Again, this would not affect consolidated profits, but it directly increases the parent's profits by reducing expenses. A third possibility is to sell some inventory to the subsidiary at inflated prices.

Firms that do not publish consolidated statements typically publish parent-only financial statements. Since they do not publish the subsidiaries' separate financial statements, they have an opportunity to control their profits using methods like those described above. For example, such practices were widespread in Japan before the 1977 requirement for consolidated financial statements. We are not suggesting that all multinational companies preparing parent-only statements engage in such practices. However, knowledge of these *possibilities* casts a long shadow over such financial statements. And corporations that think they are fooling the resource providers probably are not.

The trend toward consolidated financial statements is unmistakable. *Standard 27*, "Consolidated Financial Statements and Accounting for Investments in Subsidiaries," issued by the International Accounting Standards Committee (IASC), reinforces this trend. *Standard 27* modifies (and supercedes) the earlier *Standard* issued in 1976.

Having argued in favor of consolidated financial statements, we should also point out that they have their limitations. If a company is heavily dependent on a particular product line or on a certain area of the world for its profits, consolidated financial statements can mask such dependencies without additional disclosures. Also, the existence of specific unprofitable operations may be somewhat hidden when blended with the rest of the company. And, changing product mixes are harder to detect unless the company provides additional information. For these reasons corporations are increasingly disclosing—on a supplemental basis— detailed accounting information by product line and geographic area. (This subject was explored in Chapter 5.)

FOREIGN CURRENCY TRANSLATION

The foreign subsidiaries of multinational corporations normally keep their accounting records and prepare their financial statements in the currency of the country in which they are located. They do this because it would be too inconvenient to transact business in anything other than the local currency and too impractical to record these transactions in accounting records using another country's currency. As a result, the individual financial statements of a multinational's foreign subsidiaries are expressed in many different currencies. For example, a U.S. multinational corporation may have separate foreign subsidiary financial statements expressed in pounds, pesos, francs, yen, marks, and lire. Yet in order for worldwide consolidated financial statements to be prepared, the subsidiaries' financial statements must all be expressed in a single currency (the U.S. dollar for U.S. multinationals). It is not possible to add up assets, liabilities, revenues, and expenses when they are expressed in different currencies. Therefore, whenever multinational corporations prepare their consolidated financial statements, the financial statements from individual foreign subsidiaries must be *translated* from the currency of the foreign country into the currency of the country where the multinational is headquartered. Foreign currency translation is accomplished using exchange rates.

Exchange Rates

The major currencies of the world are traded in many places and in many ways. An *exchange rate* is the price of one currency relative to another; that is, how much of one currency it takes to buy so much of another currency. (Those of you who have traveled outside the United States probably exchanged your U.S. dollar traveler's checks for some foreign currency. You may recall seeing quoted exchange rates in bank windows or stores.)

Exchange rates are not stable over time; they fluctuate just like the price of nearly everything else does. Exchange rates change for the following reasons:

1. *Trade balance of payments surpluses or deficits*. When a country exports more than it imports, it is said to run a trade balance of payments surplus. Surpluses cause the nation's currency to appreciate in value (i.e., to strengthen). The opposite condition—trade deficits—causes a currency to command less of other nations' currencies.

2. *Relative rates of inflation*. Currencies of countries with higher rates of inflation depreciate relative to the currencies of countries with lower levels of inflation. Generally speaking, inflation means that one is able to buy less and less of everything (including another country's currency) for a fixed amount of one's own currency.

3. *Relative interest rates*. Whenever one nation has higher interest rates relative to other nations, its currency appreciates in value. (Foreigners purchase more of its currency in order to invest in and earn the higher interest.)

4. *Political factors and government intervention*. For international transactions, the currencies of countries considered politically stable tend to be favored over the currencies of unstable countries. Governments also buy and sell currencies when they want to change exchange rates.

The Problem with the Current Rate Method

Given that exchange rates change, a question arises as to which exchange rate should be used to translate the financial statements of a foreign subsidiary. The exchange rate at balance sheet date (this is called the *current rate method*) may seem a logical choice, but the problem with translating all balance sheet and income statement items using the rate existing at balance sheet date is that the procedure is incompatible with historical cost, which is, of course, the basis for current generally accepted accounting principles.

You can see why in the following example. Suppose a U.S. parent invests $30,000 in a foreign subsidiary and the subsidiary converts the money to its local currency when the exchange rate is 1 LC (local currency) = $1.25. The foreign subsidiary takes its LC24,000 ($30,000 ÷ 1.25) and buys land. On a historical cost basis, the land has a value of LC24,000 or $30,000. If by year-end the exchange rate changes to 1 LC = $1.50 and is used to translate the LC24,000 piece of land, it will appear on the consolidated U.S.-dollar financial statements at $36,000 [LC24,000 × (1 LC = $1.50)]. The piece of land appears to have magically increased in value! An alternative exchange rate to use is the one existing when the land was bought (i.e., 1 LC = $1.25). Accountants call this the "historical" exchange rate. In this way, the land would always appear on the consolidated financial statements at $30,000.

The Problem with the Temporal Method

Unfortunately, another problem arises when historical exchange rates are used (the *temporal* method of translation). Since the various assets are acquired at different times, different exchange rates have to be used to translate them. When this happens, the translated balance sheet no longer balances. What to do with the difference between debits and credits is a highly controversial subject among accountants. The amount of the imbalance arises mechanically as a result of the translation process and does not fit the definition of asset, liability, or owners' equity. Yet it has to go somewhere to preserve the accounting equation.

The following example illustrates the point. Assume that on January 1, U.S. Multinational, Inc. (USMI), forms a foreign subsidiary named Foreign Sub. USMI converts $100,000 into Foreign Sub's local currency (LC) at a time when the exchange rate is 1 LC = $1.25. The initial investment, therefore, is LC80,000. Foreign Sub's opening balance sheet (in local currency and dollars) looks like this:

FOREIGN SUB
Balance Sheet
January 1

Cash	LC 80,000 × (1 LC = $1.25) = $100,000
Owners' equity	LC 80,000 × (1 LC = $1.25) = $100,000

Now, assume that on February 1, when the exchange rate is 1 LC = $1.30, Foreign Sub buys LC40,000 worth of inventory. On February 28, when the exchange rate is 1 LC = $1.40, Foreign Sub buys a fixed asset for LC40,000. The March 1 balance sheet will look like this:

FOREIGN SUB
Balance Sheet
March 1

Inventory	LC 40,000 × (1 LC = $1.30) =	$ 52,000
Fixed asset	LC 40,000 × (1 LC = $1.40) =	$ 56,000
	LC 80,000	$108,000
Owners' equity	LC 80,000 × (1 LC = $1.25) =	$100,000
	LC 80,000	$100,000

While the balance sheet before translation (in local currency) balances, it does not balance after translation into U.S. dollars. In the translated balance sheet, debits exceed credits by $8,000. What to do with the nonexistent credit is a good question, and accountants disagree on the answer.

A conclusion may be apparent to you. Preserving the historical cost basis of accounting by translating foreign financial statements at different historical exchange rates introduces a dangling debit or credit whose nature is difficult to define. That problem can be solved by translating financial statements using a single exchange rate (the so-called current rate method), but the procedure is inconsistent with the historical cost basis of accounting. Either choice involves some undesirable side effects.

Translation Methods Used

U.S. multinational corporations must follow the requirements of *Statement 52*, "Foreign Currency Translation," issued by the Financial Accounting Standards Board (FASB) in 1981. Its provisions will be discussed in a moment. Prior to *Statement 52*, however, U.S. multinational corporations translated the financial statements of their foreign subsidiaries under the terms of *Statement 8*, issued by the FASB in 1975. *Statement 8* required the temporal method just described, with the "dangling debit or credit" treated as a loss or gain on the consolidated income statement. To illustrate, USMI in the example above would show a translation gain of $8,000 in its consolidated income statement as a result of translating Foreign Sub's financial statements on March 1. (An $8,000 credit is required to bring Foreign Sub's translated balance sheet into balance.)

During the years that *Statement 8* was in effect, exchange rates were highly volatile, and because the translation imbalance was required to increase or de-

---

EXHIBIT 6-1   Illustration of Modified Current Rate Method

Assume that the following trial balance, expressed in local currency (LC), is received from a foreign subsidiary. The year-end exchange rate is 1 LC = \$1.40, and the average exchange rate for the year is 1 LC = \$1.20. Translating the trial balance into U.S. dollars would be performed as shown below. (Note that when employing the modified rate method, owners' equity stated in U.S. dollars is a "balancing" amount.)

| | Local Currency | | Exchange | U.S. Dollars | |
	Debit	Credit	Rate	Debit	Credit
Cash	LC 15,000		(1 LC = \$1.40)	\$ 21,000	
Inventory	70,000		"	98,000	
Fixed assets	35,000		"	49,000	
Payables		LC 30,000	"		\$ 42,000
Owners' equity (beginning)		70,000	to balance		102,000
Sales		200,000	(1 LC = \$1.20)		240,000
Cost of goods sold	120,000		"	144,000	
Depreciation expense	5,000		"	6,000	
Other expenses	55,000		"	66,000	
	LC300,000	LC300,000		\$384,000	\$384,000

---

crease reported income or loss, corporations experienced more volatility in their reported earnings than managements desired. A volatile earnings pattern normally indicates riskiness, yet managements alleged that translation gains and losses were on paper only—that they had little or no direct effect on actual cash flows. A large number of accountants cried "foul!" and it is fair to say that *Statement 8* was probably the most unpopular Statement ever issued by the FASB. For this reason *Statement 8* was replaced by *Statement 52*.

Under the provisions of *Statement 52*, a foreign subsidiary is classified as either (1) self-sustaining and autonomous or (2) integral to the activities of the parent company. A *self-sustaining, autonomous* subsidiary is one that operates relatively independently from the parent company. Revenues and expenses respond mostly to local conditions, few of the subsidiary's cash flows impact the parent's cash flows, and there are few intracompany transactions with the parent. The local (foreign) currency is said to be its "functional" currency. The balance sheet for a self-sustaining subsidiary is translated at the year-end exchange rate and the income statement at the average-for-the-year exchange rate. There is no effect on reported consolidated earnings from translating the financial statements of autonomous foreign subsidiaries. This so-called modified current rate method preserves the balance sheet and income statement financial ratios in U.S. dollars as in the local currency. Exhibit 6-1 illustrates this method.

On the other hand, an *integral* foreign subsidiary operates as an extension of and is dependent on the parent. Revenues and expenses are largely influenced by the parent, the subsidiary's cash flows directly impact the parent's cash flows, and

---

EXHIBIT 6–2   Illustration of Temporal Method

Under the temporal method, the trial balance in Exhibit 6–1 is translated as follows:

1. Inventory and cost of goods sold, at the exchange rate when the inventory was purchased. Assume this is 1 LC = $1.25.
2. Fixed assets and depreciation expense, at the exchange rate when the fixed assets were purchased. Assume this is 1 LC = $0.90.
3. Other balance sheet items, at the year-end exchange rate (1 LC = $1.40).
4. Revenues and expenses that are incurred evenly throughout the year (sales and other expenses) at the average exchange rate (1 LC = $1.20).
5. Beginning owners' equity in dollars equals last year's ending owners' equity (translated) in dollars. Assume this is $81,000.
6. A "translation" gain or loss is created to balance the dollar-denominated trial balance.

Thus, the temporal method translation looks like this:

	Local Currency		Exchange	U.S. Dollars	
	Debit	Credit	Rate	Debit	Credit
Cash	LC 15,000		(1 LC = $1.40)	$ 21,000	
Inventory	70,000		(1 LC = $1.25)	87,500	
Fixed assets	35,000		(1 LC = $0.90)	31,500	
Payables		LC 30,000	(1 LC = $1.40)		$ 42,000
Owners' equity					
(beginning)		70,000	—		81,000
Sales		200,000	(1 LC = $1.20)		240,000
Cost of goods sold	120,000		(1 LC = $1.25)	150,000	
Depreciation expense	5,000		(1 LC = $0.90)	4,500	
Other expenses	55,000		(1 LC = $1.20)	66,000	
Translation loss				2,500	
	LC300,000	LC300,000		$363,000	$363,000

---

there are frequent intracompany transactions with the parent. For this type of subsidiary, the U.S. dollar is said to be its "functional" currency. The financial statements of such subsidiaries are translated at various historical rates, and the dangling debit or credit decreases or increases consolidated earnings for the period. This method has the effect of translating subsidiaries' financial statements as if their transactions originally occurred in U.S. dollars. In other words, the same temporal method used under *Statement 8* continues to be used under *Statement 52* for integral subsidiaries. However, because the financial statements of fewer foreign subsidiaries are now translated using the temporal method, the overall impact of fluctuating exchange rates on reported earnings of U.S. multinational corporations is less. Exhibit 6–2 illustrates the temporal method.

The Australian, British, and Canadian standards on foreign currency translation basically recommend treatment similar to the above, as does *International Accounting Standard 21*, "Accounting for the Effects of Foreign Exchange

Rates.'' (Recently proposed modifications to *IAS 21* leave the translation requirements of *IAS 21* essentially unchanged.)

The requirements for foreign currency translation are generally flexible in most other nations. For example, many Japanese MNCs use the year-end exchange rate to translate current assets and liabilities, historical rates for noncurrent assets and liabilities, and defer any resulting imbalance as an asset or liability. The EC *Seventh Company Directive* (on consolidations), referred to earlier, does not specify how to translate the financial statements of foreign subsidiaries. Thus, foreign currency translation is an unresolved issue in the European Community. Overall, it is an area with significant diversity of practice and little hope for a quick resolution. International comparability is likely to be a problem for some time to come.

In Chapter 1 we argued that inflation can strain the historical cost model of accounting. Inflation is related to foreign currency translation, since exchange rates change in response to different levels of inflation among countries. The fact that the problems of inflation and fluctuating exchange rates are related suggests that accounting solutions are also related. Hence, the use of the current rate method is another source of stress on historical cost accounting.

CONCLUSION

Consolidated financial statements are intended to present an overall look at a company's operations and financial position. Unfortunately, for multinational corporations, existing accounting tools are not always up to the task. Measuring accounting earnings is an imperfect process anyway, but when fluctuating foreign exchange rates are introduced into that process, it gets even more jumbled. In our opinion, foreign currency translation is one of the most conceptually difficult tasks facing accountants today, and potential solutions do not fit neatly into the traditional accounting framework.

When examining the financial statements of companies from different countries, special care should be taken to understand the companies' consolidation policies and how they translate the financial statements of their foreign operations. The variety of possible methods makes comparing the statements very difficult.

KEY POINTS

1. Consolidated financial statements are becoming the norm internationally.

2. The temporal foreign currency translation method was the basis of FASB *Statement 8*, which was highly unpopular in the United States.

3. The current rate foreign currency translation method is the basis for FASB *Statement 52* as well as *International Accounting Standard 21* and standards in Australia, Britain, and Canada. Subsidiary financial statements are translated based on their relationship with the parent company. This method of translation is inconsistent with historical cost.

4. Significant diversity of practice exists in foreign currency translation and consolidation.

CASES

Parent and Subsidiary

The following selected amounts are from the separate financial statements of Parent Company (unconsolidated) and Subsidiary Company:

	Parent	Subsidiary
Cash	$ 200	$ 70
Receivables	400	190
Accounts payable	265	100
Retained earnings	810	670
Revenues	5,000	3,510
Rent income	0	220
Dividend income	270	0
Expenses	4,180	2,950

Additional information:

a. Parent owes Subsidiary $85.

b. Parent owns 100 percent of Subsidiary. During the year, Subsidiary paid Parent a dividend of $270.

c. Subsidiary owns the building that Parent rents for $220.

d. During the year, Parent sold some inventory to Subsidiary for $2,100. It had cost Parent $1,600. Subsidiary, in turn, sold the inventory to an unrelated party for $3,050.

Questions

1. What is Parent's (unconsolidated) net income?
2. What is Subsidiary's net income?
3. What is the consolidated profit on the inventory that Parent originally sold to Subsidiary?
4. What are the amounts of the following, on a consolidated basis?
   a. Cash.
   b. Receivables.
   c. Accounts payable.
   d. Revenues.
   e. Expenses.
   f. Dividend income.

   g. Rent income.
   h. Retained earnings.
5. If, instead of consolidated financial statements, Parent presented only its own unconsolidated statements, what kinds of transactions could it engage in with Subsidiary to improve the appearance of its own profitability?

Égalité S.A. (A)

Huge Multinational, Inc., received the following trial balance from its French subsidiary, Égalité S.A. It is expressed in French francs (FF).

	Debit	Credit
Cash	15,000	
Inventory	82,000	
Fixed assets (net)	46,000	
Payables		20,000
Capital stock		42,000
Retained earnings (beginning)		48,000
Sales		330,000
Cost of goods sold	240,000	
Salaries	28,000	
Depreciation expense	5,000	
Other expenses	24,000	
	440,000	440,000

NOTES: 1. When Égalité was formed, the exchange rate was 1 FF = $0.24. The fixed asset was purchased by Égalité immediately after formation.
   2. At year-end the exchange rate was 1 FF = $0.16. The average-for-the-year exchange rate was 1 FF = $0.18.

Questions

1. Assume that Égalité is an autonomous subsidiary. Translate Égalité's trial balance into U.S. dollars using the modified current rate method required by *FASB Statement 52.*
2. What is Égalité's net income expressed in French francs?
3. What is Égalité's net income expressed in U.S. dollars?

Égalité S.A. (B)

Assume the same information as in Égalité S.A. (A), except that the year-end exchange rate is 1 FF = $0.16, and the average-for-the-year exchange rate is 1 FF = $0.14.

Questions

1. Translate Égalité's trial balance into U.S. dollars using the modified current rate method required by *FASB Statement 52*.

2. What is Égalité's net income expressed in French francs? How does this compare to the answer you determined in (A)?

3. What is Égalité's net income expressed in U.S. dollars? How does this compare to the answer you determined in (A)?

Égalité S.A. (C)

Refer to the information provided in Égalité S.A. (A). If Égalité is deemed an integral subsidiary, Huge Multinational translates Égalité's trial balance according to the temporal method, as follows:

a. Cash and payables at the year-end exchange rate.

b. Sales, salaries, and other expenses at the average exchange rate.

c. Fixed assets and depreciation expense at the rate in effect when the fixed asset was purchased.

d. Inventory at the rate in effect when purchased. Cost of goods sold at a weighted average rate based on beginning and ending inventory and purchases.

e. Capital stock at the rate in effect when Égalité was formed.

f. Beginning retained earnings is the translated (U.S.-dollar) balance of the prior year's ending retained earnings.

g. A translation gain (loss) is credited (debited) to bring the dollar-denominated trial balance into balance.

Questions

1. Translate Égalité's trial balance according to the technique described above. Assume that the relevant exchange rates for inventory and cost of goods sold are 1 FF = $0.17 and 1 FF = $0.19 respectively. (Other exchange rates are given in Égalité S.A. [A].) Assume that the translated U.S.-dollar balance of beginning retained earnings is $7,700.

2. What is Égalité's net income expressed in French francs?

3. What is Égalité's net income expressed in U.S. dollars?

ADDITIONAL READINGS

Demirag, I. S. "A Review of the Objectives of Foreign Currency Translation." *International Journal of Accounting* (Spring 1987), pp. 69–85.

Gray, S. J., and A. G. Coenenberg. *International Group Accounting*. London, England: Croom Helm, 1988.

Houston, C. O. "Foreign Currency Translation Research: Review and Synthesis." *Journal of Accounting Literature* 8, (1989), pp. 25–48.

Lowe, H. D. "Shortcomings of Japanese Consolidated Financial Statements." *Accounting Horizons* (September 1990), pp. 1–9.

Organization for Economic Cooperation and Development. *Consolidation Policies in OECD Countries*. Paris: OECD, 1987.

Revsine, L. "The Rationale Underlying the Functional Currency Choice." *The Accounting Review* (July 1984), pp. 505–14.

Rosenfield, P. "Accounting for Foreign Operations." *Journal of Accountancy* (August 1987), pp. 103–12.

7

INTERNATIONAL FINANCIAL STATEMENT ANALYSIS

Suppose you have just been recently hired as a financial analyst for a major U.S. multinational corporation. Your boss is extremely interested in expanding operations in the Pacific Rim. She has given you a set of financial statements from a Japanese corporation, one with a solid reputation for sustained growth and profitability, which comes highly recommended as an investment opportunity. You sharpen your pencils, get out your calculator, and proceed to apply the ratio analysis techniques you learned as a student. As the company comes so highly recommended, you assume it will be a routine exercise to generate the supporting numbers to back up the purchase decision.

Imagine your surprise when you finish your analysis and discover that the Japanese company is a financial disaster, apparently on the verge of bankruptcy. Its debt-to-asset ratio is almost three times as large as that of U.S. firms. Contributing to your worries is current debt nearly double that of U.S. firms. The equity base is approximately half of what U.S. firms usually have. You are wondering who in the world would recommend this company as an acquisition prospect.

This chapter explores what is wrong with this picture. A *framework* is developed that uses the information from the previous chapters to analyze a foreign-based corporation's financial position in light of the environment in which it operates.

FINANCIAL ACCOUNTING REFLECTS THE ENVIRONMENT IT SERVES

One of the biggest problems in the Japanese scenario described above is the analyst's assumption that U.S. ratio analysis expectations can be "exported" for analyzing foreign financial statements. This is effective only if the foreign financial accounting system and the operating environment closely parallel that of the United States. Chapters 1 through 6 showed that this is rarely the case. Each country's national financial accounting system evolved to serve the needs of its domestic environment and, in particular, the needs of the users of accounting information in that country. Therefore, each country's national financial accounting and reporting requirements are different. The best way to properly analyze financial statements from another country is to understand the domestic accounting system and business practices in that country.

Becoming familiar with each country's accounting and business practices is a monumental task. However, we have the necessary tools. We need to develop an approach—a framework—that we can use with any country.

A FRAMEWORK FOR FINANCIAL STATEMENT ANALYSIS

Environmental Variables

Chapter 1 discussed how an accounting system is shaped by the environment in which it operates. The many variables discussed include the relationship between business and the providers of capital, political and economic ties with other countries, the legal system, levels of inflation, the size and complexity of business enterprises, sophistication of management and the financial community, and general levels of education. Exhibit 7–1 compares the U.S. and Japanese environments using these variables. It shows that the two countries differ on two critical dimensions, the providers of capital and the legal system. This analysis begins with an awareness of these differences.

Cultural Values

The accounting system is also influenced by culture and the values that a society shares. Knowing something about a people's values can help us understand

EXHIBIT 7–1 Environmental Variables

Variable	United States	Japan
Business and providers of capital	Investors	Banks
Political and economic ties with other countries	Influenced by U.K.	Influenced by Germany; later by U.S. after WWII
Legal system	Common law	Code law
Levels of inflation	Low	Low
Size and complexity of business enterprises	Large and complex	Large and complex
Sophistication of management and the financial community	High	High
General levels of education	High	High

their accounting system. Values are defined as a tendency to prefer a certain state of affairs over another. For instance, people in the United States value the concept of individualism whereas in Japan it is not the individual who is important but how the individual relates to the group. Japanese culture maintains a strong degree of interdependence among individuals, and group norms are far more important than a single individual's opinion or professional judgment.

The Japanese society accepts that there is a natural hierarchical order in which each person has a role that is not questioned. In the United States, we do not accept the notion that power is distributed unequally. In fact, we demand that people have equality.

One final cultural dimension will be discussed here—how a society feels about uncertainty and ambiguity. A culture that prefers less uncertainty depends on institutions to maintain conformity, and deviating from the norm or the rule is discouraged, as in Japan. Rules make people comfortable because the rule prescribes what to do in any circumstance, thus removing the uncertainty and need for judgment. The opposite is a society that values practice more than principles and allows for the exception to the rule, as in the United States and the United Kingdom.

Cultural values can be linked to *accounting values,* which gives us some insight into a country's accounting system and its measurement and disclosure practices. Exhibit 7–2 diagrams this link. This concept is explored more fully in the following section.

Accounting Values[1]

The following accounting values are not meant to be exhaustive, but are offered as representative of values that influence the development of national accounting systems and measurement and disclosure practices:

> Professionalism versus statutory control.
> Uniformity versus flexibility.
> Conservatism versus optimism.
> Secrecy versus transparency.

Knowing something about a country's accounting values helps to interpret and understand the financial reports of companies operating in that environment. The goal is to be able to realistically analyze the financial reports of any multinational corporation, given the national accounting and business practices that evolved from the operating environment.

Accounting values include a preference for independent *professional judgment* as opposed to *statutory control.* A preference for exercising professional

---

[1]This section is based on S. J. Gray, "Towards a Theory of Cultural Influence on the Development of Accounting Systems Internationally," *Abacus* 24, no. 1 (1988), pp. 1–15.

EXHIBIT 7–2   Culture, Accounting Values, and Accounting Systems—A Framework
for Analysis

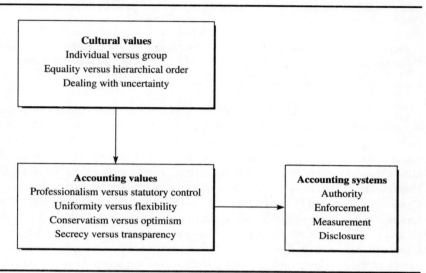

SOURCE: Adapted from S. J. Gray, "Towards a Theory of Cultural Influence on the Development of Accounting Systems Internationally," *Abacus* 24, no. 1 (1988), p. 7.

judgment is consistent with a preference for individualism and subjectivity, which
we find in the accounting systems of countries listed in the British-American
model from Chapter 1. The United Kingdom values the concept of presenting a
"true and fair view" of a company's financial reports, and the auditor is given the
right to use professional judgment to accomplish this goal. Statutory control, or
compliance with prescriptive legal requirements, is an accounting value of both
the Continental and the South American models. In Japan, France, and Germany,
accountants follow legal rules and exercise much less judgment than in the United
Kingdom.

A second set of accounting values that influence financial reporting systems is
uniformity versus flexibility. A society that values uniformity shows a preference
for the enforcement of uniform accounting practices, whereas a society that values
flexibility takes into account the circumstances of individual companies. There is
a link between this accounting value and the cultural value of dealing with uncertainty that we discussed in the prior section. Uniformity is found in the accounting
practices of the code law Continental and South American models. Flexibility is
exhibited by the countries in the common law British-American model. Once
again, we see a difference between Japan and the United States; Japan's accounting system is influenced by uniformity, while flexibility prevails in the United
States.

EXHIBIT 7–3   Accounting Models and Accounting Values

British-American	Continental	South American	Mixed Economy
Professionalism	Statutory control	Statutory control	Statutory control
Flexibility	Uniformity	Uniformity	Uniformity, flexibility
Optimism	Conservatism	Conservatism	Optimism, conservatism
Transparency	Secrecy	Secrecy	Secrecy, transparency

The accounting value of *conservatism* relates to the measurement of accounting information and manifests itself in a preference for a cautious approach to measurement as a way to cope with the uncertainty of future events. *Optimism* tolerates more uncertainty in measurement practices. To illustrate, many expenditures made by a company are expected to benefit future periods. Of course, the benefits are uncertain. Should these expenditures be expensed immediately, or should they be shown as an asset and charged to expenses in future periods? Conservatism calls for the former, while optimism would allow the latter in certain situations. The diversity of measurement practices was the topic of Chapter 2. Countries in the British-American model take a more optimistic approach to measurement than do those countries of the Continental and South American models. The difference in approach has been attributed to different providers of capital and the demands of different users as well as the influence of tax laws. For example, Japanese financial accounting is strongly influenced by the tax law, which leads to more conservative measurement practices in order to minimize taxes.

The last set of accounting values we discuss here is *secrecy* versus *transparency* in regard to disclosure practices, which was the topic of Chapter 5. The countries of the Continental and South American models show a preference for confidentiality and tend to restrict disclosure of information to management and those who provide the business financing. Secrecy and conservatism are related in that both result in a more cautious approach to reporting, as is seen in Japan. The British-American model countries disclose more information and take a more publicly accountable approach to financial reporting, which is their response to the providers of capital being private investors. Exhibit 7–3 offers a matching of accounting values with the four accounting models discussed in Chapter 1.

ANALYSIS OF FINANCIAL INFORMATION

Timeliness, Language, Terminology, and Format

In the United States, corporate annual reports are received in a timely fashion, which adds relevance to the information's usefulness. In fact, this is more or less taken for granted. Companies must file their financial statements with the Securities and Exchange Commission within 90 days after their year-end. However, users may experience delays in the receipt of foreign financial information. Exhibit 7–4

EXHIBIT 7–4   Average Delay between Year-End Date and Date of Auditor's Report

Number of Days	Countries
1–30	None
31–60	Brazil
	Canada
	United States
61–90	Australia
	Denmark
	Finland
	Netherlands
	Norway
	Sweden
91–120	Belgium
	France
	Germany
	India
	Malaysia
	South Africa
	Switzerland
	United Kingdom
121 and over	Austria
	Italy

SOURCE: F.D.S. Choi and G. G. Mueller, *International Accounting* (Englewood Cliffs, N.J.: Prentice Hall, 1992), p. 413.

provides insight into the number of days that elapse between a company's year-end and the date of the auditor's report.

For English-speaking users, a second barrier to usefulness may be that the report is not in English. Companies will naturally publish their reports in the national language of their country and then consider translating to second and perhaps third languages. Chapter 4 discussed convenience translations. Exhibit 7–5 provides a listing of countries whose companies provide English language translations of all or part of their annual reports. It appears that English is becoming the accepted language of business and that the language barrier is no longer an insurmountable problem.

Differences in accounting terminology still present a communication problem. Several terms in a U.K. annual report could confuse the American user. Stocks refer to inventory, receivables are called debtors, and payables are called creditors. Fixed assets refer to all assets retained for continuous use, not just property, plant, and equipment. The profit and loss account refers to the income statement and turnover means sales. Reserves usually refers to retained earnings.

The format of the British balance sheet is the opposite of a U.S. balance sheet

---

EXHIBIT 7–5   Language of Financial Statements of Leading Non-U.S. Industrial Companies

Predominately English-language (0–10%) of reports Non-English)	Considerable percentage of Non-English (10%–50%)	Predominately Non-English (50% or more)
Australia	Belgium	Austria
Canada	Brazil	France
Denmark	Italy	Mexico
Finland	Germany	South Korea
India		Spain
Ireland		
Japan		
Malaysia		
Netherlands		
Norway		
South Africa		
Sweden		
Switzerland		
United Kingdom		

SOURCE: F.D.S. Choi and G. G. Mueller, *International Accounting* (Englewood Cliffs, N.J.: Prentice Hall, 1992), p. 414.

with assets and liabilities running from lowest to highest liquidity. Fixed assets appear above current assets. The user of foreign financial statements must be observant and a little suspicious because things that appear familiar may in fact be quite different.

Convenience translations were discussed in Chapter 4. In this case, the user must be careful to notice that both the language and the monetary amounts have been translated for the user; however, the statements are still in foreign generally accepted accounting principles (GAAP) and cannot be directly compared to those of the user's home country. Chapter 4 also discussed the fact that some multinationals provide limited restatements or secondary financial statements based on another set of GAAP, such as that of the International Accounting Standards Committee. Even if readers get financial statements in a language, currency unit, and based on accounting principles that they understand, they must still consider one additional point. Financial practices (as opposed to accounting practices) and business decision making differ around the world, and readers of foreign financial statements must understand how the business environment in a corporation's home country affects the firm's financial reports. This is especially critical if the user is comparing the accounting numbers of companies from different cultures. One device used to analyze financial reports is ratio analysis, which is the topic of the following section.

Ratio Analysis

Ratios of key items on the financial statements are calculated to determine such things as rate of return, riskiness, and the ability to pay debts (liquidity).

Indicators of Return.   Two popular ratios that provide the investor with information as to the rates of return on a particular investment are earnings per share and return on investment. Earnings per share gives the investor an indication of the earnings attributable to each share of stock and is calculated as follows:

$$\text{Earnings per share} = \frac{\text{Net income accruing to common stock}}{\text{Total shares of common stock outstanding}}$$

Return on investment indicates how efficiently capital has been employed by the company during a period of time, usually one year. Investment may be defined as average total assets or as average owners' equity. The asset base is used to indicate the return that the company generates on its asset commitment. Investors use return on equity when they are interested in the return that accrues to them on their contributed capital as common shareholders. The ratios are calculated as follows:

$$\text{Return on assets} = \frac{\text{Net income}}{\text{Average total assets}}$$

$$\text{Return on equity} = \frac{\text{Net income}}{\text{Average owners' equity}}$$

Indicators of Risk and Liquidity.   The ratios used to indicate risk and liquidity are the current ratio and the debt-to-asset ratio. The current ratio indicates the company's ability to pay its short-term creditors with its most liquid assets, the current assets. It is calculated as follows:

$$\text{Current ratio} = \frac{\text{Current assets}}{\text{Current liabilities}}$$

The debt-to-asset ratio provides the investor with another indicator of the relative risk of this investment. As the name implies, this ratio relates debt (investment provided by creditors) to the resources (assets) employed by the firm. Since liabilities must be paid off with company assets, the lower this ratio is, the greater the company's ability to pay off its debts, and therefore, the safer the company is perceived to be. Generally speaking, creditors should be more willing to lend money to, and investors should be more willing to invest money in, companies with lower debt-to-asset ratios. The reader should note that this is a very U.S. interpretation of the debt-to-asset ratio. More is said about this later. This ratio is computed as follows:

$$\text{Debt-to-asset} = \frac{\text{Total liabilities}}{\text{Total assets}}$$

EXHIBIT 7–6 Nippon Yusen Kabushiki Kaisha and Subsidiaries, Five-Year Summary (Consolidated), for Years Ended March 31

	US$ Thousand				
	1992	1991	1990	1989	1988
For the year:					
Revenues	$6,689,549	$6,341,605	$5,685,128	$4,888,653	$4,828,200
Cost and expenses	5,709,997	5,480,508	4,970,853	4,294,234	4,338,583
Selling, general and administrative expenses	725,424	641,696	538,117	421,221	389,726
Operating income	254,129	219,400	176,158	173,199	99,890
Other (income) and expenses	154,649	103,534	16,085	70,360	37,221
Income before income taxes and special items	99,480	115,867	160,073	102,838	62,669
Special items (loss).............................	(16,699)	7,557	15,144	2,235	(6,165)
Income before income taxes	82,781	123,424	175,217	105,074	56,504
Income taxes	57,792	89,013	98,316	84,751	47,352
Net income (loss)............................	49,194	47,251	79,725	21,827	6,578
At year's end:					
Current assets	$3,360,083	$3,994,789	$3,661,279	$2,914,719	$2,391,444
Current liabilities.............................	2,961,581	3,607,268	3,028,037	2,673,825	2,139,091
Vessels, property and equipment, net of depreciation	3,438,320	2,877,242	2,236,002	2,073,309	1,953,688
Total assets	9,555,275	9,574,485	8,611,892	7,384,839	6,489,273
Long-term debt	4,583,634	3,992,231	3,613,400	2,827,770	2,672,349
Stockholders' equity...........................	1,730,351	1,714,220	1,723,830	1,660,037	1,432,985
Retained earnings	563,193	505,527	525,412	485,334	493,689
Per 100 shares of common stock (US$):					
Income before income taxes and special items	$8.59	$10.10	$13.98	$9.23	$5.94
Net income	4.26	4.12	6.96	1.96	0.63
Stockholders' equity...........................	149.46	149.34	150.44	145.58	135.08
Dividends	3.01	3.01	3.01	3.01	3.01

Earnings per 100 shares are calculated on a weighted average basis, but not adjusted for free distribution of common stock.
The amounts previously reported for 1988, 1989, 1990 and 1991 are restated to reflect the same calculation and the same exchange rate used in the current year.

Nippon Yusen Kabushiki Kaisha 1992

Let's use the consolidated five-year summary of financial statements of Nippon Yusen (Exhibit 7–6) to practice our financial statement analysis skills in the Japanese environment. The first and second footnotes to the financial statements (Exhibit 7–7) alert us to the fact that the statements have been translated to English and to U.S. dollars, but the GAAP remain Japanese. Our first step is to calculate the ratios; and then we will interpret them. (While the ratios are calculated in U.S. dollars below, they would be the same in Japanese yen.) Earnings per share is taken directly from the consolidated statements of income and retained earnings and is reported to be $0.042.

$$\text{Return on assets} = \frac{\$49,194}{(\$9,574,485 + 9,555,275)/2} = 0.51\%$$

$$\text{Return on equity} = \frac{\$49,194}{(\$1,714,220 + 1,730,351)/2} = 2.86\%$$

$$\text{Current ratio} = \frac{\$3,360,083}{\$2,961,581} = 1.13$$

EXHIBIT 7–7   Nippon Yusen Kabushiki Kaisha and Subsidiaries, Notes to Consolidated Financial Statements

1. Basis of Presenting Consolidated Financial Statements:

The accompanying consolidated financial statements are an English translation of the consolidated financial statements prepared in accordance with generally accepted accounting principles in Japan, for filing with the Ministry of Finance and the Stock Exchanges in Japan.

In the English translation, certain account reclassifications are made and additional information is provided in order to present the consolidated financial statements in a format familiar to the international readers. The results of these reclassifications do not affect the financial position or results of operation of the consolidated companies as reported in the original consolidated financial statements.

2. United States Dollar Amounts:

The accompanying consolidated financial statements are stated in Japanese yen, and the dollar amounts represent the arithmetical results of translating yen to dollars on a basis of Y132.85 to US$1, the rate of exchange at 31st March, 1992. The inclusion of such dollar amounts is

solely for convenience and is not intended to imply that the yen amounts have been or could be readily converted, realized or settled in dollars at Y132.85 to US$1 or at any other rate.

Total debt is taken from the consolidated balance sheet for 1992 and is reported to be $7,824,924.

$$\text{Debt to assets} = \frac{\$7,824,924}{\$9,555,275} = 81.89\%$$

Indicators of return or profitability for Japanese companies are often lower, as they are for Nippon Yusen, than for U.S. companies because Japanese managers do not focus on short-term profit. Japanese managers have more job security because stockholders are more focused on building long-term strength and less on the infamous "bottom line." Recall too, that Japanese accounting is more conservative than U.S. accounting.

The current ratio is lower than what a U.S. investor in a U.S. company would hope to see (about 1.9 to 1 in the United States). However, a Japanese investor would not find it low at all because in Japan short-term borrowing is actually preferred to long-term debt. This allows for a more frequent adjustment of interest rates on the debt and a lower interest expense as short-term rates are usually lower than long-term. The short-term debt is continuously renewed and so serves the purpose of long-term debt and substitutes for longer-term borrowing.

The debt-to-asset ratio is high for average U.S. manufacturing companies (47 percent in the United States), but it is a sign of good health in Japan. In Japan, this ratio is an indication of how much confidence the banks have in a company. Companies have low debt-to-asset ratios because they are unable to get any more credit from the banks. Rather than demonstrating a risky company, in Japan, the reverse is true—companies with high debt-to-asset ratios are generally safer.

What this analysis tells us is that comparability between U.S. and Japanese from the banks. Rather than demonstrating a risky company, in Japan, the reverse is true—companies with high debt-to-asset ratios are generally safer.

What this analysis tells us is that comparability between U.S. and Japanese financial statements does not exist. For one thing, as discussed in Chapter 2, there is a great deal of diversity in financial accounting practices. In addition, many business practices are culturally based and are bound to have an impact on companies' financial statements. One must know something about the business environment of a company's home country in order to fully understand the company's financial statements. When analyzing the financial statements of *any* foreign corporation, it is important not to take the numbers out of context, out of the business and cultural environment in which the transactions underlying the financial statements actually transpired.

CONCLUSION

This chapter develops a *framework* for international financial statement analysis that can be used to analyze the financial reports of foreign multinational corporations. Once again, the analysis begins with a review of the environmental variables that shape a country's accounting system. Then the analysis includes attention to culture and the specific societal values that influence accounting values and, ultimately, accounting systems and measurement and disclosure practices. Analysts must pay attention to the timeliness, language, terminology, and format of foreign financial reports. In addition, they must always be wary of the fact that the foreign statements probably represent foreign GAAP. When analysts interpret the financial ratios, they must keep in mind that business practices are culturally based and can have a significant impact on a company's financial statements.

KEY POINTS

1. Financial statement amounts and ratios vary because of differences in accounting practices, ways of doing business, and even deep-rooted cultural values.

2. Barriers that must often be overcome in international financial statement analysis concern the timeliness of accounting reports, and differences in language, terminology, and format.

3. Cultural values impact accounting values which, in turn, impact accounting measurement and disclosure practices.

4. U.S. financial statement ratio analysis norms should not be inferred when analyzing foreign financial statements. Even if differences in GAAP are explained, and even after other barriers are overcome, differences in the business and cultural environment remain. Therefore, financial statements cannot be taken out of context: they must be analyzed within the business and cultural environment in which the transactions underlying the financial statements actually occurred.

CASES

United Biscuits

United Biscuits (UB) is a leading food manufacturer with operations in 19 countries worldwide. In North America, UB operates under the brand of Keebler, a household name that you probably recognize. We will use the consolidated profit and loss account and the consolidated balance sheet of UB to help us, as prospective investors, interpret and understand UB's financial results.

Questions

1. Comment on the differences in terminology and format between British- and American-style balance sheets and income statements.
2. Prepare a balance sheet for UB that follows the American-style format.
3. Select some financial ratios that are of interest to you in your analysis. Why have you selected these particular ratios? What do the results of your ratio analysis tell you about the financial health of UB?
4. What will you need to do if you want to compare your results for UB to those of Nabisco?

Consolidated profit and loss account   For the 52 weeks ended 28th December 1991

	Notes	1991 £m	1990 £m
Turnover		2,979.1	2,723.6
Trade discounts		318.6	295.3
Turnover after trade discounts		2,660.5	2,428.3
Cost of sales		1,490.8	1,434.1
Gross profit		1,169.7	994.2
Distribution, selling and marketing costs		786.1	655.9
Administrative expenses		141.4	122.2
Other income		(2.7)	(2.0)
Trading profit	2	244.9	218.1
Interest	3	31.7	21.3
Profit before profit sharing		213.2	196.8
Profit sharing	4	1.9	1.7
Profit on ordinary activities before tax		211.3	195.1
Tax on profit on ordinary activities	5	65.5	64.3
Profit on ordinary activities after tax		145.8	130.8
Minority interests	6	2.3	2.7
Profit attributable to shareholders		143.5	128.1
Extraordinary charges	7	13.4	11.8
Profit for the financial year		130.1	116.3
Dividends	8	71.7	64.0
Balance to reserves	21	58.4	52.3
Earnings per share – undiluted	9	30.8p	28.9p
– fully diluted	9	29.5p	27.1p

28th December 1991   **Consolidated balance sheet**

	Notes	1991 £m	1990 £m
Fixed assets			
Intangible-assets	10	**146.7**	155.4
Tangible assets	11	**780.9**	704.1
Investments	13	**12.3**	3.9
		939.9	863.4
Current assets			
Stocks	14	**214.2**	220.5
Debtors	15	**394.2**	348.7
Taxation	16	**17.3**	18.6
Short-term deposits and loans		**35.3**	9.3
Cash at bank and in hand		**43.2**	61.8
		704.2	658.9
Creditors: amounts falling due within one year			
Trade and other creditors	17	**376.4**	364.5
Loans, overdrafts and finance lease obligations	18	**71.5**	139.3
Taxation		**44.3**	49.4
Dividends		**73.3**	65.4
		565.5	618.6
Net current assets		**138.7**	40.3
Total assets less current liabilities		**1,078.6**	903.7
Creditors: amounts falling due after more than one year			
Loans and finance lease obligations	18	**255.5**	173.7
Other creditors		**13.9**	17.6
Taxation		**6.8**	2.1
		276.2	193.4
Provisions for liabilities and charges	19	**68.9**	78.8
		733.5	631.5
Capital and reserves			
Called up share capital	20	**120.5**	111.1
Share premium account	20	**144.3**	52.8
Revaluation and other reserves	21	**141.1**	144.4
Goodwill reserve	21	**(295.3)**	(273.7)
Profit and loss account	21	**579.8**	510.8
		690.4	545.4
Called up preference share capital issued by a subsidiary		**35.1**	80.4
Minority interests		**8.0**	5.7
		733.5	631.5

Approved by the board and signed on its behalf on 27th March 1992

Robert Clarke

John Warren

UB or NY?

You have some extra money to invest and are trying to decide between buying stock in United Biscuits (UB) or Nippon Yusen (NY). Suppose that the exchange rate from British pounds to U.S. dollars is £1 = $.70 on December 31, 1991. Earnings per share (1991) for Nippon Yusen were $0.041 and total debt was approximately the same as reported in 1992.

Questions

1. Outline the steps that you would follow to compare the financial results of UB to NY.
2. How will you analyze the operating environment of each multinational?
3. Compare the rates of return, riskiness, and liquidity of the two companies.
4. Which company will you invest in? You must choose one or the other.

Parlez-Vous Francais?

Let's turn our attention to France, the home of Peugeot, Renault, L'Oreal, and Pernod Ricard. Go to your library and find a recent annual report for a French multinational. (Alternatively, you may wish to request a copy directly from the company.) Prepare an analysis of the report and the French operating environment. Remember that France is an important player in the world economy and in the European Community.

Questions

1. Discuss the French environment (e.g., business practices, legal system, providers of capital), the cultural variables influencing business practices and financial reporting, and the accounting values of the French system.
2. Analyze the financial statements using the same framework that we used with Nippon Yusen.
3. Comment on the differences in terminology and format between French- and American-style balance sheets and income statements.
4. How do the French financial statements illustrate the characteristics that you described in your answer to question 1?

ADDITIONAL READINGS

Aaron, P. "Japanese P/E Multiples: The Tradition Continues." *Daiwa Securities America, Inc., Report #35* (October 23, 1989), pp. 1–23.

Choi, D. S., and R. M. Levich. "Behavioral Effects of International Accounting Diversity." *Accounting Horizons* (June 1991), pp. 1–13.

Lowe, H. D. "Shortcomings of Japanese Consolidated Financial Statements." *Accounting Horizons* (September 1990), pp. 1–9.

Nobes, C. *Interpreting European Financial Statements: Towards 1992.* London, England: Butterworth & Co. Ltd., 1989.

Schieneman, G. S. "The Effect of Accounting Differences on Cross Border Comparisons." *International Accounting and Investment Review* (April 29, 1988), pp. 1–14.

Weetman, P., and S. J. Gray. "A Comparative International Analysis of the Impact of Accounting Principles on Profits: The USA versus the U.K., Sweden, and the Netherlands." *Accounting and Business Research* (Autumn 1991), pp. 363–79.

_____. "International Financial Analysis and Comparative Corporate Performance: The Impact of U.K. versus U.S. Accounting Principles on Earnings." *Journal of International Financial Management and Accounting* (Summer/Autumn 1990), pp. 111–30.

8

ACCOUNTING INFORMATION SYSTEMS FOR MULTINATIONAL CORPORATIONS

The accounting information system provides the information that the multinational corporation (MNC) needs to plan, control, evaluate, and coordinate all of its business activities, including its international operations. It is senior management's responsibility to maximize the economic well-being of the MNC as an international entity, which normally translates to maximizing long-run profits globally.

This is not as easy as it sounds. The profit strategies of Japanese managers are more long-run than those of U.S. managers. Germans often base profit goals on costs incurred, the Swiss are more oriented to "what the market will bear," and Italians usually like to negotiate. Scandinavian countries control MNCs based there rather tightly, whereas Holland does not. Thus, accounting information needs vary not only from country to country and culture to culture, but also between central management (headquarters) and individual country managements.

Earlier chapters dealt with reporting information to users *external* to the MNC (stockholders, creditors, employees, and customers). Much of the information reported externally is required in the form of annual reports. Our attention now turns to the information needs of *internal* users—MNC management.

Management uses internal information to plan, control, and evaluate in both the short and long run. For example, short-run budgets are determined for the operating year and then used to determine how well managers have run their business unit, say, a subsidiary company located in another country. Long-run budgets may be developed for five years—thus the short-range annual budgeting process is turned into a long-range strategic plan for the MNC and all of its subsidiaries.

Managers at all levels in the MNC need internally developed and reported information to monitor and improve their decision making. An MNC's accounting information system must incorporate and report changes in the economic and political environments, legal constraints, cultural differences and fads, and sociological differences in each country of operation. This information is generally provided by the subsidiary managers and includes notice of anticipated changes in the exchange rates, in political ideology (for example, the downfall of Communism), or even in teenage buying habits (from heavy-metal rock groups to rappers to "grunge"). Such external conditions need not be considered when designing an accounting information system for a single-country situation, but they are important inputs for decision making in the MNC.

The information processed in an accounting information system comes from sources internal and external to the MNC and is used by all levels of management to make decisions that in turn affect the MNC both internally and externally. Externally, the MNC affects the operating environments of its subsidiaries; hence, the process is mutual. The accounting information system is pervasive, since all subsidiaries generate data and all managers use information. The system must be responsive to the changing needs of managers, and it must respond to changes internal and external to the subsidiaries. The quality and quantity of information received by management is critical to achieving the goals of the entire multinational organization. Exhibit 8–1 models the various flows of information that are part of the MNC accounting information system.

MNC ORGANIZATION AFFECTS THE ACCOUNTING INFORMATION SYSTEM

An MNC has various levels of managers with varying degrees of authority and responsibility. The distribution of these management levels constitutes the MNC *organizational structure* and determines what information each level needs to plan and control its operations. The information needs define how the data are collected and processed within the accounting information system. Therefore, the structure of data collecting, processing, and reporting within an accounting information system ought to parallel and complement the organizational structure of the MNC.

Forms of Organization

Five common forms of organization used by MNCs are: (1) the international division or international department, (2) a grouping by product line, (3) a grouping by function, (4) a grouping by geographic area, and (5) the global matrix organization. The *international division* separates foreign operations from domestic operations. This international division is usually evaluated as an independent operation and compared with domestic divisions. Hercules, Inc., Quaker Oats, 3M Company, and Allied Chemical International are examples of corporations that originally used this form to organize their international operations.

Organization by product line results in the integration of domestic and foreign operations and the evaluation of product lines based on worldwide results. DuPont

EXHIBIT 8–1   How Information Flows through an MNC Accounting Information
System

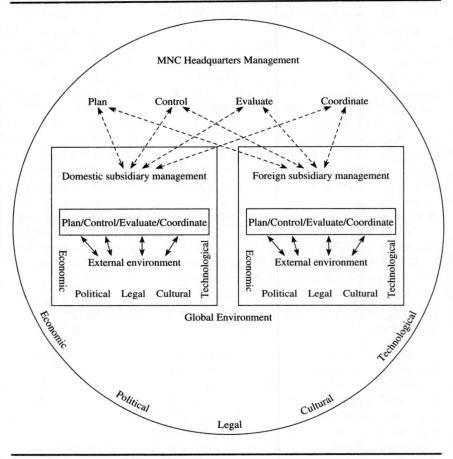

NOTE: Arrows indicate information flows.

and Motorola have highly diverse product groups, a situation that lends itself to
using product line organization.

A company grouped by specialty (such as marketing, manufacturing, or accounting) is called a *functional organization*, and management maintains centralized control over the functions. In a U.S.-based MNC, the vice president for marketing at headquarters would be responsible for the marketing function
worldwide. The VP for manufacturing or production would be responsible for this
function in all subsidiaries. Organizing by function is not as common as the other
forms, but is popular among extractive companies (for example, oil and coal),
whose products are quite homogeneous. Exxon uses this form because methods

used to produce and market oil do not vary much from one country to another and are therefore easily centralized at headquarters.

Geographic organization separates operations into geographic areas (North America, Europe, etc). A company would use this form when it has substantial foreign operations that are not dominated by a particular country or area of the world. U.S. MNCs are often dominated by their U.S. domestic market and, therefore, do not use this form as often as European and Japanese MNCs do. Nestlé, the Swiss chocolate company, is an example of an MNC organized by geographic area. This structure is appropriate for Nestlé because no one geographic region dominates its operations.

The *global matrix organization* blends two or more of the forms just discussed (e.g., the general manager of a French subsidiary will report to the vice president for worldwide product lines and to the vice president for Europe). Union Carbide's international operations are organized as area companies (geographic) reporting to the highest management levels in the company (function). The area companies are viewed as separate, profit-responsible entities, not as extensions of domestic divisions. Dow Chemical uses the matrix organization to avoid the problems inherent in either integrating or separating foreign operations. Exhibit 8–2 provides a diagram of each MNC organization form.

How do these various forms of organization affect the MNC accounting information system? The form of organization affects the direction of the information *flow*, not the information itself, that is reported by the accounting information system. In all cases, information about foreign operations is collected, processed, and reported within the overall MNC system.

With the international division, information flows from subsidiaries to the VP of the international division. In MNCs organized by product line, information flows from subsidiaries to the VP of the product line. In an MNC organized by function, information flows from subsidiary to headquarters according to specialty—marketing, manufacturing, accounting, and so on. When MNCs are geographically organized, the subsidiary information is collected within a geographic area and then sent to headquarters. With the matrix form, information flows in two directions; for example, from the subsidiary to the geographic location headquarters, say, Asia, and also by product line to MNC headquarters.

The organizational structure of the MNC evolves over time as multinational business opportunities present themselves and as multinational sales become more important. Each form has certain advantages and disadvantages and most MNCs organize their activities using a mixed structure, blending certain elements of two or more forms. Structures are dynamic in nature, but their flexibility is limited by the constraint of a company's cultural heritage.

Attitudes, Organization, and Control

The organizational structure and control functions of the MNC differ depending on the attitude of headquarters management toward multinational business. These attitudes, which are reflected in the MNC's business policies, can be classified as: (1) ethnocentric (home-country oriented), (2) polycentric (host-country oriented), and (3) geocentric (world oriented).

EXHIBIT 8–2   Diagrams of Various Forms of MNC Organization

---

1. International division

2. Product line

3. Function

4. Geographic area

5. Gobal matrix

An *ethnocentric* MNC thinks that home-country standards are superior and therefore applies them worldwide. A *polycentric* MNC assumes that host-country cultures are different and, therefore, allows local affiliates to operate quite autonomously (i.e., evaluation and control functions are determined locally). The goal of the *geocentric* approach is to focus on worldwide objectives and to consider foreign subsidiaries as part of a whole. To accomplish this goal, corporate managers try to establish standards for evaluation and control that are both universal and local. The organizational structure of this MNC must facilitate the global coordination of decisions, while at the same time being able to respond to the demands of host governments and the local consumer. Operating with a geocentric attitude is an ideal model not achieved by many MNCs.

Automakers have typically been ethnocentric. Home-country attitudes have prevailed for Fiat from Italy; for Citroen and Renault from France; for Mercedes-Benz and BMW from Germany; for Saab from Sweden; for Toyota and Nissan from Japan; and for General Motors, Ford, and Chrysler from the United States. But, as U.S. automakers try to break into the Japanese market, Japanese perceptions about U.S. cars have taken on an added importance and U.S. managers have taken on more of a polycentric attitude, recognizing the Japanese consumer's resistance to buying a standardized homogenized global product.

Pharmaceutical companies generally exhibit polycentric business strategies. Bayer of Germany wants all consumers from all cultures to think of its aspirin as a local product, just as Hoffman-LaRoche of Switzerland does with Valium. U.S. pharmaceuticals have established quite a successful presence in Japan and are known as "kakujitsu na kaisha," or reliable company. They have made a long-term commitment to doing business in the Japanese local economy and have built the necessary relationships between customer and supplier. At the same time, they have made an attempt to understand the culture while being open to learning from the Japanese.

Dutch/U.K. multinationals like N. V. Philips and Unilever come close to being geocentric. People of many different nationalities serve on their boards of directors and senior management teams. It is companies like these that are able to gain firm strategic control of their worldwide operations and manage them in a globally coordinated manner that will succeed in the emerging international economy.

The attitude of headquarters management also affects the location of decision making. If an MNC headquarters allows foreign subsidiaries to make important decisions, the corporation is considered *decentralized*. This attitude is currently the most prevalent among MNC managers who strive for global diversity. Many European and American multinationals have well-established networks of fairly independent and self-sufficient national subsidiaries. Foreign subsidiaries are granted a great deal of autonomy, and therefore subsidiary managers must have information to plan, control, and evaluate their own operations at the local level. These information needs must be built into each subsidiary's accounting information system. At the same time, headquarters management also needs information about the subsidiaries to plan, control, evaluate, and coordinate on a global level. This strategy, and the organizational structure that supports it, makes it difficult to design a system that is able to coordinate and control these worldwide operations, while still responding to global forces.

If decision-making authority rests with headquarters, an MNC is said to be *centralized*. MNCs generally do not make all decisions at one location but aim for a collaborative approach between headquarters and other levels. Many Japanese companies centralize operations in Japan, which allows them to respond to opportunities presented by changing global forces (e.g., movements in exchange rates). An MNC may centralize functions considered critical for success and decentralize those that are less critical. For example, IBM and Nestlé centralize their research and development activities, because headquarters feels R&D is critical to the company's long-run success and wants to maintain tight control over it. However, these companies take a more decentralized approach to their foreign operating subsidiaries, because the success of each one is not as critical to the long-run success of the MNC as a whole.

EXPORTING THE DOMESTIC ACCOUNTING INFORMATION SYSTEM

For years, U.S. companies have used basically the same accounting information system to collect and process data from foreign and domestic operations. This is true for several reasons. It is much less expensive to export an already established system than to design a new one. For control purposes, the headquarters accounting group may require all domestic and international subsidiaries to use similar reporting forms. In addition, because top management is already familiar with the domestic system, it is easier to use it internationally.

However, exported versions of the domestic control system are seldom as successful or effective internationally as they are domestically. A domestic system is designed to operate within the parent company's external environment. It incorporates political, economic, cultural, technological, and legal factors of the home country. Exporting such a system ignores the foreign subsidiary's operating environment and may result in a breakdown of communication. Obviously, communicating with a subsidiary manager who does not speak your language can present some formidable hurdles. Financial terminology often poses additional challenges. For example, in Spanish there is no equivalent for terms like leveraged buy-out, short sales, or insider trading. Successful multilingual communication requires companies to be more culturally aware and sensitive to the importance of effective translation and idea processing. Exhibit 8-3 can be used to visualize the pervasiveness of the impact of environmental diversity on an MNC's system of financial control. It illustrates that the four financial control functions—measurement, communication, evaluation, and motivation—must accommodate the environmental variables and constraints of every country in which the MNC operates. The same is true for an MNC's other control systems, such as those for manufacturing and marketing.

Example.   An MNC is based in the United States, and all domestic subsidiaries operate as decentralized units with the objective of maximizing after-tax profits in U.S. dollars. The foreign subsidiaries are not allowed as much autonomy in decision making. They primarily supply partially manufactured materials

EXHIBIT 8–3   Framework for Multinational Financial Control

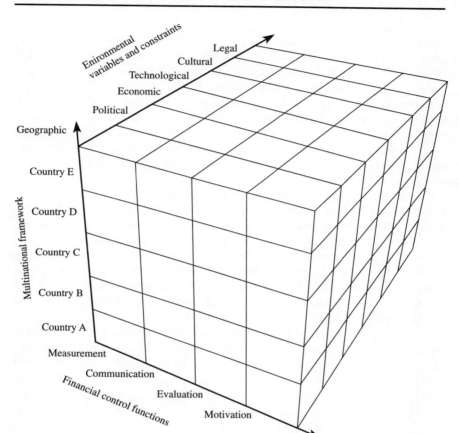

SOURCE: Frederick D.S. Choi and Gerhard G. Mueller, *International Accounting* (Englewood Cliffs, N.J.: Prentice Hall, 1992), p. 475.

to the U.S. subsidiaries. The parent needs information on changes in foreign exchange rates, export controls, import controls, tax rates in various countries, and so on, to effectively plan and control foreign operations. This information is not necessary when dealing with domestic subsidiaries.

The foreign subsidiaries of this MNC should not be evaluated on the same basis as domestic subsidiaries, because maximizing after-tax profit in U.S. dollars is not the foreign subsidiary's objective. Instead, each foreign subsidiary should be evaluated based on its service as a supplier. To make this evaluation, headquarters needs different accounting information from the foreign subsidiaries than it does from U.S. subsidiaries.

MNC CHARACTERISTICS AFFECT THE ACCOUNTING INFORMATION SYSTEM

To repeat, a major responsibility of the accounting information system is to provide the information necessary for planning, controlling, and evaluating an organization's operations. An MNC divides itself into organizational units when it selects an organizational structure. The information required by a particular unit depends on its assigned goals and functions. The designer of an MNC's accounting information system must understand the nature and purpose of the MNC, the subtleties of its organizational structure, the degree of centralization/decentralization, the levels of decision making, and the needs of each decision maker.

The size of the organization is another factor affecting informational requirements. A larger, more sophisticated MNC needs more complex information than a smaller MNC or domestic corporation.

Size also corresponds to the number of management levels. Depending on organization and management philosophy, each level may have a different responsibility and decision-making authority. Therefore, the accounting information system may have to supply various levels with information that differs in detail, timing, and scope. For example, a large MNC may be more centralized than a smaller MNC and prefer to control worldwide decision making at headquarters. A smaller, less sophisticated MNC may allow the foreign subsidiary managers more control over their operations; therefore the information used for decision making would be gathered and used at the subsidiary level.

Size may also affect the flow of information from foreign operations to headquarters. For example, a large MNC organized by international division may have all of the subsidiaries operating in Europe report to a manager for Europe, who in turn reports to the international division manager. A smaller MNC may have each European subsidiary manager report directly to the international division manager.

In summary, the designer of an accounting information system for an MNC must be aware of (1) the organization's nature and purpose, (2) the organizational structure, (3) the degree of centralization/decentralization, (4) the size of the MNC, and (5) management's basic philosophy and attitude toward foreign operations.

Each of these factors should be identified, studied, and evaluated. They should then be incorporated into the basic accounting information system design, which provides the needed framework for long-range planning, controlling, and evaluating operations. A system developed in this way theoretically ensures that expectations have been realistically determined. Only then can management expect congruence between its goals, the structure of the organization, and available information. Congruence is discussed further in Chapter 9.

TRANSNATIONAL ORGANIZATIONAL CAPABILITY

The classic *multinational* company has operated as a decentralized unit with the ability to respond to national and local differences and opportunities. The traditional *global* company has managed operations by tightly controlling its worldwide subsidiaries through centralization. Today's international business environment is becoming increasingly complex and competitive. Transnational strategies, organizational structures, and attitudes that allow a company to think globally and act locally are necessary for survival. The *transnational* company of tomorrow must operate efficiently and economically through global-scale operations. It must be able to respond to both national and local differences, retaining local flexibility while achieving global integration. The innovative company that can transfer knowledge quickly and efficiently by linking operations to each other will survive. Never before has the design of the accounting information system been so critical to the success of the transnational company. Information processing and technology transfer systems between parent and subsidiary and among the subsidiaries must be flexible and shared. Companies that can develop this transnational organizational capability will have the key to long-term success.

CONCLUSION

In this chapter, we discussed the information that managers need to plan, control, evaluate, and coordinate worldwide operations. In the following chapters, we discuss (1) planning and control, (2) performance evaluation, and (3) transfer pricing and international taxation. Managers depend on the accounting information system to provide the information they need to improve decisions about each of these topics. Without information, it is impossible to effectively plan, control, or evaluate multinational operations.

KEY POINTS

1. The organizational structure of a multinational corporation determines how the accounting information system collects, processes, and reports data for decision making. Common forms of multinational organization are the international division; groupings by product line, function or geographic area; and the global matrix.

2. Organizational structures vary depending on the attitude toward multinational business—ethnocentric, polycentric, or geocentric—and the degree of centralization versus decentralization that exists.

3. Most U.S. MNCs use the same accounting information system for foreign and domestic operations. However, exported versions of the domestic system are seldom very successful.

4. Multinational and global companies are giving way to transnational companies that think globally and act locally.

CASES

Ouch! Change Hurts

World, Inc., is not a new corporation, although it has only been operating internationally for five years. Prior to entering the international marketplace, it was called U.S. World, and the 20 domestic subsidiaries were organized as decentralized profit centers reporting directly to headquarters.

The five foreign subsidiaries currently report to an international division manager, who reports directly to headquarters. Each subsidiary is labeled a decentralized profit center; however, the international division manager maintains control over each foreign subsidiary manager, and decision making is centralized at headquarters. The foreign subsidiary managers have requested more authority and decision-making responsibility.

Headquarters has decided to reorganize worldwide operations by product line. Its goal is to develop a transnational approach to controlling all subsidiaries, both domestic and foreign. You have been hired to design and implement the new system.

Questions

1. Why were the foreign subsidiaries labeled decentralized profit centers when they were not allowed to act as such? What are the potential problems with a situation like this?

2. As the consultant, what information about this MNC will you need to develop a working accounting information system?

3. Diagram the information flows that will exist for this MNC after the reorganization by product line and the move to "transnationalize."

Why Is Change a Good Thing?

Domestic, Inc. operated its 20 U.S. subsidiaries for 30 years. Over time, a very effective accounting information system was developed to accommodate decentralized decision making by subsidiary managers. The economic, political, legal, cultural, and technological characteristics of the United States have quite naturally affected the system's development.

Now that the company is International, Inc., it has to have an accounting information system to coordinate worldwide operations. An international division manager will be responsible for reporting this information from the foreign subsidiaries to headquarters management.

During the planning stages of the foreign expansion, the designated international division manager makes the following suggestion:

It has taken us 30 years to develop an effective accounting information system that all the subsidiary managers understand and that provides what headquarters needs for decision making. Let's use the same system with all of our subsidiaries in Asia and South America. Why is change a good thing?

Questions

1. What type of attitude toward foreign operations is this manager exhibiting? Why does management have this attitude?
2. Are the manager's justifications valid? What are the dangers in exporting a domestic system to foreign operations?
3. What changes would you suggest for the accounting information system if you were the international division manager?

The Sky's the Limit

You are the Chief Executive Officer of a U.S.-based "would-be" multinational corporation. You have lots of cash because you have had five very successful years. You have decided to expand your operations and are able to invest anywhere in the world. The sky's the limit.

Questions

1. Pick a country in which you would like to establish operations and decide what organizational form these operations should take. (Hint: Refer to Exhibit 8–2 and think about why you would choose one of these organizational forms.)
2. What does your accounting information system look like after the expansion abroad?

ADDITIONAL READINGS

Baliga, B. R., and A. M. Jaeger. "Multinational Corporations: Control Systems and Delegation Issues." *The Journal of International Business Studies* (Fall 1989), pp. 25–40.

Bartlett, C. A. "Building and Managing the Transnational: The New Organizational Challenge." *Competition in Global Industries*, ed., Michael E. Porter. Harvard Business School, 1986.

Egelhoff, W. G. "Information-Processing Theory and the Multinational Enterprise." *The Journal of International Business Studies* 22, no. 3 (1991), pp. 341–68.

Elliott, R. K. "The Third Wave Breaks on the Shores of Accounting." *Accounting Horizons* (June 1992), pp. 61–85.

Karimi, J., and B. R. Konsynski. "Globalization and Information Management Strategies." *Journal of Management Information Systems* (Spring 1991), pp. 7–26.

Kelly, L.; A. Whatley; and R. Worthley. "Assessing the Effects of Culture on Managerial

Attitudes: A Three-Culture Test.'' *The Journal of International Business Studies* (Summer 1987), pp. 17–31.

Porter, M. E. "Changing Patterns of International Competition." *California Management Review* (Winter 1986), pp. 9–40.

9

STRATEGIC PLANNING AND CONTROL IN THE INTERNATIONAL ENVIRONMENT

Strategic planning and control are not new—domestic corporations have been doing them for years. The development of comprehensive MNC international planning and control systems with long-range strategic focus is new.

Before acquiring Pan American's Pacific routes in 1986, United Airlines (UAL) spent several years studying Pacific trade patterns. UAL also ran a single Seattle–Tokyo route of its own in order to acquire important firsthand experience in the Pacific travel market. Convinced of double-digit growth in the Pacific, UAL management believed that traffic from Asian cities would feed well into its domestic U.S. flights. Since most Pacific routes are assigned by strict treaties, assembling a network such as Pan Am's would have taken UAL decades. When Pan American found itself strapped for cash, UAL was ready with an offer to purchase Pan Am's Pacific Division. As a result, the acquisition was handled quickly and efficiently.[1]

The corporate planning process involves deciding: (1) the corporation's objectives, (2) how these objectives will change over time, (3) the resources needed to attain these objectives, and (4) the policies that govern acquisition, use, and disposition of the resources. For a multinational corporation (MNC), planning involves incorporating the economic, cultural, technological, legal, and political characteristics of each operating environment into the MNC's worldwide master (strategic) plan.

The job of the management control system is to ensure that the objectives of

---

[1]"Everyone Booed—But This Deal Was the Best Airline Bargain," *Business Week*, January 15, 1990, p. 55.

the strategic plan are accomplished. Thus, the control system regulates the MNC's activities so as to achieve its goals. As shown in Exhibit 8–1, the processes of planning, control, and evaluation are interrelated. Planning and control are the subjects of Chapter 9 and performance evaluation is discussed in Chapter 10.

COMPONENTS OF THE MNC PLANNING AND CONTROL SYSTEMS

There are six phases in the MNC planning and control systems:

1. Environmental assessment—identifying the relevant cultural, legal, political, and economic variables.
2. Subsidiary assessment—defining each subsidiary's strengths and weaknesses in relation to its environment.
3. Objective setting—setting priorities for the subsidiary.
4. Formulation of standards—developing budgets or other operating standards based on expectations.
5. Operational—measuring the actual output.
6. Evaluation—providing feedback.

Environmental Assessment Phase

A corporation involved in moving goods, people, capital, and ideas across national boundaries encounters unique environmental factors. The dominant environmental factor is different national currencies. Unexpected currency depreciation or appreciation and price-level fluctuations make currency exchange rates hard to predict. Varying rates of interest, multiple systems of taxation, and the influence of cultural differences also have significant implications for those involved in the planning and control process. Headquarters must assess the political, operating, and financial risk inherent in a foreign country. Government control of imports and exports is quite common throughout the world. Government expropriation of operations, with or without compensation, and political instability certainly have an adverse effect on business. Unfamiliar operating restrictions and increased regulations can make responding to opportunities or danger more difficult. For example, take the case of Ford Motor Company. It once had an operation in Hungary that was taken over by the government, one in France that was later bombed, and one in Mexico that was given very different operating requirements from other dealers.

Assessing risk is not easy because of the variety of environments an MNC confronts, so communication from local managers is critical. MNCs can hire outside organizations to assess the risks in foreign countries. Financial institutions and CPA firms also provide helpful information.

Subsidiary Assessment Phase

In this phase, headquarters management assesses the strengths and weaknesses of each subsidiary by country—its financial, human, and product resources. Financial resources include current and future cash flows and the ability to transfer these cash flows in and out of the operating environment, the availability of capital, and a subsidiary's borrowing capacity. Assessing human resources includes evaluating the specific and general skills of the work force and how readily employees can be transferred among various units. Headquarters must recognize and respond to the national attitude toward alien managers. Investigating product resources includes determining production capacity, whether or not the product must be adapted to foreign markets, transportation considerations, and so on. Once again, effectively communicating information from the manager of the foreign subsidiary to headquarters is critically important to success.

Objective-Setting Phase

After assessing the environments and the operating strengths and weaknesses of each subsidiary, top management must then select which products to produce (product strategy) and where (geographic strategy).

The objective-setting phase involves reviewing the available alternatives and setting priorities. In this way, the strategic plan can be altered as changes occur in the subsidiary's environment or resources. An MNC needs flexibility. The long-range strategic plan developed by headquarters management should allow for future changes.

Formulation-of-Standards Phase

This phase is similar to what occurs in a domestic corporation. After management decides where and what to produce, budgets are formalized for each operating subsidiary. The process involves estimating costs of production and setting selling prices.

The budget for each foreign subsidiary must be developed in the local currency. The MNC must then translate each subsidiary's budget to the parent corporation's currency (e.g., U.S. dollars). Therefore, foreign exchange rates are part of the budgeting process (see Chapter 10). MNC headquarters must also consider the possibility of changes in inflation and borrowing rates within a certain country, exchange controls, productivity, political changes, and so on, when developing budgets for foreign subsidiaries.

Operational Phase

In this phase, subsidiaries are actually conducting business operations to carry out headquarters' plans. Operations must be measured. Whether an organization is a domestic corporation or an MNC, it should be careful to measure actual operations according to the same rules it used for setting budgets. (More is said about this in Chapter 10).

Evaluation Phase

Two types of feedback are provided by the evaluation phase. One deals with past operations by comparing budgeted results to actual. The second deals with future plans; based on the information provided by the budget-to-actual comparison, management may institute corrective actions, make changes, and reevaluate priorities.

The MNC strategic planning process generally ranges from intermediate to long (i.e., from one to five years). The purpose is to define the company's current and future objectives and to formulate a way to achieve the company's overall goals. The plan is a synthesis of immediate objectives, anticipated world changes, and input from managers all over the world. It results in both long- and short-term strategies that will affect the MNC's operating results and growth.

INTEGRATION OF THE PHASES OF THE PLANNING AND CONTROL SYSTEMS

As mentioned previously, the management control system functions to ensure that the objectives of the strategic plan are accomplished. An effective management control system should (1) enhance corporate goal congruence across all domestic and foreign subsidiaries, (2) make certain that projections have been fully communicated, (3) communicate results, and (4) provide useful information to headquarters and subsidiary managers so that the plan can be implemented, evaluated, and changed.

Goal congruence is a buzz word frequently found in management and control literature. It means that everyone in an organization is "operating on the same wavelength" (i.e., individual managers accept, support, and work toward generally agreed on corporate goals, even if their personal goals for their own subsidiary differ).

The management control system and the strategic planning process should be completely integrated. The management control system ensures that headquarters resource allocation decisions are tracked and measured, and thus the system works to accomplish management's objectives.

The management control system is generally made up of several subsystems developed for use in foreign subsidiaries, domestic subsidiaries, and headquarters. Company standards have been formulated as part of the strategic planning process. Hence, the control process compares actual with budgeted performance specified in the individual subsystem for each subsidiary. Exhibit 9–1 shows how the components and phases in the MNC planning and control systems are integrated.

EXHIBIT 9–1 Basic Components of MNC Planning and Control Systems

SOURCE: Adapted from H. Itami, *Adaptive Behavior: Management Control and Information Analysis* (Sarasota, Fla.: American Accounting Association, 1977), p. 9.

THE FINANCIAL COMMUNICATION PROBLEM

Differences in Measurement and Disclosure Practices

As discussed in Chapters 1 through 7, accounting measurement, disclosure, and reporting practices vary a great deal across geographic boundaries. In many countries accounting systems are not well developed, and reporting practices are not as defined as those in the United States. However, for effective control an MNC needs an internal reporting system with standardized, consistent, and uniform accounting principles and practices. Ideally, all subsidiaries should use comparable accounting practices. Assets and liabilities should be valued and reported according to a common plan. Expense recognition should be consistent from year to year (e.g., each subsidiary should use the same depreciation method from year to year). All domestic and foreign managers should understand how headquarters defines the word *profit*. All domestic and foreign subsidiaries of U.S.-based MNCs should use

U.S. generally accepted accounting principles for reporting back to corporate head-quarters. Consistency and uniformity are particularly important when the information is used to compare one subsidiary's performance to another's.

Differences in cultural, technological, legal, political, and economic heritage pose barriers to communicating uniform information from subsidiaries to the parent company. Simply requiring uniformity does not make these barriers disappear, and simply requiring that certain information be reported on a regular and consistent basis does not guarantee that a subsidiary manager can or will comply. Japanese managers, by nature, are far more secretive and less comfortable with disclosing information than are U.S. managers. German managers are far more conservative when reporting results than are the British. Then there is the problem of businesses in developing countries not having the technical ability to maintain extensive records or formal accounting reports. For example, it is probably more difficult to acquire standardized information from, say, a subsidiary in Indonesia than from one in Australia. While uniformity is necessary, the system must remain adaptive and flexible to the information needs of both corporate headquarters and the operating subsidiaries. Nevertheless, adaptability is an obstacle to uniformity, and vice versa.

Ease of Communication

Geographic proximity is also a consideration in terms of facilitating the flows of information back and forth between the subsidiaries and headquarters. For example, a U.S.-based MNC would probably find it easier to communicate to a subsidiary in Mexico than one in Chile, simply because the Mexican subsidiary is physically closer. In addition, the availability and quality of telecommunication equipment can affect the frequency of contact with a foreign subsidiary. Developments in electronic transmission networks are making instantaneous communication between a parent and a distant subsidiary possible, or, at least they are reducing the lag in communication. A U.S. parent would find better communications capabilities with a subsidiary in Hong Kong than a subsidiary located in Shanghai or Beijing. These variables are extremely important to the control system, since the costs of implementing control systems in MNCs are higher than in domestic companies.

Financial and Operating Information for Internal Reporting

Many firms equate volumes of reports with good financial control. However, subsidiaries' local management may complain that the volume of required reporting hampers its ability to cope with daily operating problems. In fact, local management is responsible for reporting financial data to the parent *and* operating the subsidiary successfully.

Therefore, the problem is to identify the relevant information that top management needs to maintain the strategic planning and management control systems. This is difficult to achieve. In fact, several studies have shown that MNC headquarters may require a single subsidiary to submit over 200 different financial reports annually. Exhibit 9–2 indicates the kinds of reports required by the various functional areas of a U.S.-based MNC. Notice the number of reports required—106! Even with this many reports, there is no assurance that the MNC is well managed.

Goal Congruence

Most major companies in the United States use the profit center or investment center concept for domestic control systems.[2] This approach works relatively well domestically, because profit center managers make the major decisions affecting their center's performance. Good decision making ensures good performance evaluation, and good performance evaluation ensures good decision making. The goals are congruent because authority and responsibility are delegated to the same people. Managers are evaluated based on the performance that results from their decisions. Manager performance and profit center performance are linked.

International operations do not lend themselves to management control systems based on a profit center concept. As Chapter 11 explains, foreign subsidiary profits are often somewhat manipulated to facilitate paying the smallest possible amount of income taxes on a worldwide basis. Or, by manipulating the prices at which goods are transferred into a country, an MNC can minimize the import duties paid. Each scenario affects a subsidiary's reported profit. Therefore, using the strict profit center concept is inappropriate. In addition, headquarters management must juggle many other environmental variables (e.g., fluctuating exchange rates, inflation, and government controls).

For the profit center idea to work effectively, subsidiary managers must have the authority to make all decisions affecting their profits. Yet many MNCs maintain centralized control over subsidiaries, and most decisions are made at headquarters. Foreign managers may have responsibility for operations, but they do not have the authority to make major decisions affecting their profitability. Such a situation does not enhance goal congruence. Regardless of the situation, some degree of responsibility and authority should be provided to subsidiary managers so that they remain responsive to their local environments. These issues are discussed further in Chapter 10.

CONCLUSION

Strategic plans define a company's objectives and formulate a way to achieve them. Such plans involve a management control system and a system of performance evaluation. A management control system should complement the strategic

---

[2]For discussion see Charles T. Horngren and Gary L. Sundem, *Introduction to Management Accounting*, 8th ed. (Englewood Cliffs, N.J.: Prentice Hall, 1990), chapters 9 and 10.

EXHIBIT 9–2   Reports to Headquarters

	Number of Reports
I. Corporate controller	12
A. Management reports such as:	
1. Accounts receivable aging	
2. Consolidated income and sales (a flash report)	
B. Consolidation—not tabulated	
C. Government reports, such as:	
1. Department of Treasury	4
a. Foreign Currency Forms FC–3/3a and FC–4	
b. Foreign Exchange Form C–3	
2. Department of Commerce	8
a. Foreign units—data partly for Dept. of Comm. Merchandise, Forms F–1 and F–2	2
b. Domestic units—data partly for Dept. of Comm. Merchandise, Forms D–1, 2, and 3	3
c. Proxy questionnaire	2
II. Corporate treasurer	
A. Corporate finance such as:	12
1. Cash forecast for month	
2. Debt calendar	
3. Calculation of cash excess (deficit) for month (ahead)	
B. Tax	8
C. Pensions	10
D. Payroll	7
E. Risk management	8
F. Shareholders' records	2
III. Industrial relations such as:	13
A. Pension plan history cards, for new entrants only	
B. Employee stock purchase plan	
IV. Investor relations such as:	9
A. Dividend reinvestment plan	
B. Investor relations report	
V. Legal	3
VI. Systems and data processing	3
Total (excludes reports at the subsidiary level only)	106

SOURCE: George C. Watt, Richard M. Hammer, and Marianne Burge, *Accounting for the Multinational Corporation* (New York: Financial Executives Institute, 1977), p. 244.

plan, so that the goals of the international managers are congruent with the overall goals of the MNC.

KEY POINTS

1. Among the factors complicating planning and control by multinational corporations are foreign exchange risk, political risk, cultural differences, and legal restrictions on operations.

2. The planning and control phases that are significantly different for multinational (versus domestic) companies are those concerned with assessing the environment, defining the strengths and weaknesses of subsidiaries, and evaluating performance.

3. Communications within the multinational network are problematic because of the diversity of accounting practices worldwide, geographic distances, and cultural and technological barriers.

4. The accounting information system should support the strategic plan so that the goals of the international manager are consistent with the goals of the MNC.

CASES

So Much to Do, So Little Time

You are the new manager of the international division of a U.S.-based multinational corporation, and you report directly to the president of the MNC, as depicted in the organizational diagram below.

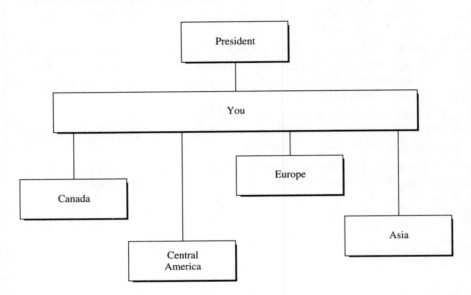

You are currently responsible for 6 subsidiaries operating in Canada, 3 in Central America, 11 in Europe, and 5 in Asia. Before being promoted to international division manager, you were in charge of European operations for five years, so you are quite familiar with the European managers and the environment. You have seen the Canadian and Central American operations but have not yet been to Asia.

In one month, all of your subsidiary managers will be in the United States to attend a planning meeting that you have organized. During this meeting, you hope to develop a strategic plan for the division's operations for next year.

In two months, you will be sitting in the boardroom with the president, the financial vice president, and the managers of domestic operations. The group's task will be to develop the strategic plan for the MNC's operations for next year.

Questions

1. What information will you request from your subsidiary managers in order to develop a strategic plan for the division?

2. What information will the president request from you in order to develop a strategic plan for the MNC?

3. How would your answers to questions 1 and 2 change if you had to develop a five-year plan rather than a one-year plan?

When in Brazil

You are the financial vice president of an MNC that has 15 foreign subsidiaries operating all over the world. Your president informs you that you are going to buy a plant in Brazil, your first one in that country.

You learn that the Brazilian operation is family owned, has no accountant, has no financial reporting system in place, and is generally unreceptive to complying with any outside request for information.

Your other 15 subsidiaries report to you in U.S. dollars and use U.S. generally accepted accounting principles when compiling information for headquarters. You require the following: (1) monthly financial statements, (2) quarterly reports with appropriate footnotes, (3) annual reports, (4) annual budgets, and (5) annual review of the next five-year strategic plan. You feel that your reporting system works very effectively in controlling operations, and you intend to institute your system in Brazil.

Questions

1. What problems do you anticipate when attempting to impose your financial control system on the Brazilian subsidiary?

2. How will you solve these problems?

3. How will you gain the Brazilian subsidiary's support and cooperation?

Zannah International

Zannah International is a U.K. multinational engineering company that has made recent acquisitions in Continental Europe and the United States. The company intends to continue to expand by acquiring already existing operations. Products are marketed worldwide and managed geographically by three divisions, but it is the Continental Europe–U.S.A. division that is of particular interest to us. Sales of this division have tripled in the past year and account for 25 percent of the company total. The management structure is diagrammed below. The company supports decentralized control. A uniform planning and control system is applied throughout the group, and a finance team at headquarters regularly monitors progress reports. (An organization chart is shown on the next page.)

Prior to being acquired by the company just over a year ago, the Netherlands operation was a family-owned business. Evert Slijper was annoyed when the company accounting system was imposed at the time of takeover, but he recognizes its usefulness. He has been told very little about company strategy and has had very little contact with company management. Little information about the other subsidiaries or the potential for joint actions has been given, and Evert has found himself competing for the same client's work as other group subsidiaries.

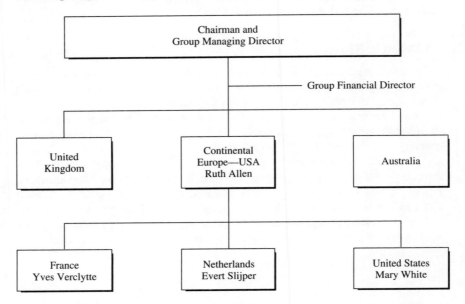

Yves Verclytte, manager of the French operation, has been on board for 18 months. Under the present arrangement, there are no opportunities for him to make presentations to headquarters management, a situation he finds unusual and frustrating. Quarterly meetings with the group finance director emphasize financial performance indicators, and discussions of strategy are confined. Yves has talked with potential target companies, not fully understanding the exact characteristics that headquarters is seeking. Interaction and cooperation with other subsidiaries, even in the same subgroup, are not encouraged.

Mary White's experience in the business spans some 20 years, although she only joined Zannah International's U.S. operation two years ago, after the takeover. Her subsidiary consistently meets the company's financial targets and therefore she has little communication with the company. She has little understanding of group strategy and cannot operate as a team player. No written feedback on performance is ever provided, but Ruth Allen, the Continental Europe–U.S.A. manager, does visit once in awhile and provides verbal feedback.

Questions

1. Describe the corporate strategy followed by Zannah International.
2. Critically evaluate the effectiveness of the management control system in promoting Zannah's strategy.

3. To what extent is the management style of Zannah top management creating problems or opportunities relevant to the future success of Zannah?

ADDITIONAL READINGS

Abdallah, W. M. "Change the Environment or Change the System." *Management Accounting* (October 1986), pp. 33–36.

Doerner, E., and J. Kloock. "A Survey of Management Accounting Research from a German View." In *European Contributions to Accounting Research*, eds. A. G. Hopwood and H. Schreuder. Amsterdam: Free University Press, 1984, pp. 83–102.

Eiteman, D. K. "Foreign Investment Analysis." In *Handbook of International Accounting*, ed. F. D. S. Choi. New York: John Wiley, 1991, pp. 27/1–19.

Hiromoto, T. "Another Hidden Edge—Japanese Management Accounting." *Harvard Business Review* (July–August 1988), pp. 22–26.

Macharinza, K. "Strategic Planning Systems." In *Handbook of International Accounting*, ed. F. D. S. Choi. New York: John Wiley, 1991, pp. 25/1–18.

Means, G. E. "The CFO, Information Flow, and Global Competition." *Financial Executive* (September–October 1989), pp. 26–31.

Sambharaya, R. B., and A. Phatak. "The Effect of Transborder Data Flow Restrictions on American Multinational Corporations." *Management International Review* 3 (1990), pp. 267–89.

Schweikart, J. A. "The Relevance of Managerial Accounting Information: A Multinational Analysis." *Accounting, Organizations, and Society* 6 (1986), pp. 541–54.

10

PERFORMANCE EVALUATION IN MULTINATIONAL CORPORATIONS

Performance evaluation is a critical issue in international accounting. The development of the multinational corporation (MNC) requires an accounting system that records and reports the results of worldwide operations. Now, headquarters must have information to evaluate the performance of subsidiaries all over the world.

This chapter begins with a definition of performance evaluation followed by a discussion of what MNCs currently employ as performance evaluation systems. The peculiarities of the MNC operating environment are then introduced. Finally, suggestions for developing an MNC performance evaluation system are presented and discussed.

PERFORMANCE EVALUATION DEFINED

Performance evaluation is the periodic review of operations to ensure that the objectives of the enterprise are being accomplished. A corporation's performance evaluation system is part of its financial control system. The MNC must have accounting information to evaluate domestic and foreign operations.

FINANCIAL MEASURES USED BY MNCs TO EVALUATE DOMESTIC AND FOREIGN SUBSIDIARIES

MNCs use various measures to evaluate the results of their operations at home and abroad. For the last 20 years, U.S.-based MNCs have consistently reported using three measures more frequently than any others: profit, budgeted profit compared to actual profit, and return on investment (ROI). Exhibit 10–1 compares the results of four similar surveys that report on U.S. MNC performance evaluation measures. Although the rankings change over time, the three most frequently used measures have remained the same.

A similar survey was conducted on U.K.-based MNCs and the rankings of performance measures are presented in Exhibit 10–2. The three most frequently used measures are reported to be budget compared with actual profits, return on investment, and budget compared with actual return on investment. Profit, which is reported by U.S. MNCs as the most frequently used measure, falls to fifth place when we look at the U.K. operating environment. Both return on investment and budgeted to actual return on investment are important to U.K. managers. A possible explanation for the reported differences is that U.K. managers maintain a more international focus (polycentric) as compared to the more domestic focus (ethnocentric) of U.S. managers. More will be said about these differences later in the chapter when we discuss using local currency information to assess manager performance.

Profit and Return on Investment

We have seen that one of the frequently reported tests of profitability is the relationship of profit to invested capital. As discussed in Chapter 7 on financial statement analysis, this relationship is expressed as the rate of return on investment (ROI). This statistic retains its appeal because it presents all of the profitability components in one ratio. However, it is not the only measure of profitability and should be used only in conjunction with other performance measures.

EXHIBIT 10–1   Financial Measures Used as Indicators of Subsidiary Performance Evaluation: U.S.-Based MNCs.

	Rankings			
Financial Measures	*1980[a]*	*1984[b]*	*1990[c]*	*1991[d]*
Profit	1	2	1	1
Budget versus actual profit	3	1	2	2
Return on investment	2	3	3	3

[a]SOURCE: Helen Gernon Morsicato, *Currency Translation and Performance Evaluation in Multinationals* (Ann Arbor, Mich.: UMI Research Press, 1980). MNCs surveyed: 70.

[b]SOURCE: Wagdy M. Abdallah, *Internal Accountability: An International Emphasis* (Ann Arbor, Mich.: UMI Research Press, 1984). MNCs surveyed: 64.

[c]SOURCE: Ahmad Hosseini and Zabihollah Rezaee, "Impact of SFAS No. 52 on Performance Measures of Multinationals," *The International Journal of Accounting* 25, no. 1 (1990), pp. 43–52. MNCs surveyed: 109.

[d]SOURCE: Orapin Duangploy and Dahli Gray, "An Empirical Analysis of Current U.S. Practice in Evaluating and Controlling Overseas Operations," *Accounting and Business Research* 21, no. 84 (1991), pp. 299–309. MNCs surveyed: 111.

EXHIBIT 10–2   Financial Measures Used as Indicators of Subsidiary Performance
Evaluation: U.K.-Based MNCs.

Financial Measures	Rankings 1988
Budget versus actual profit	1
Return on investment	2
Budget versus actual return on investment	3
Cash-flow potential from subsidiary	4
Profit	5

SOURCE: I. S. Demirag, "Assessing Foreign Subsidiary Performance: The Currency Choice of U.K. MNCs," *The Journal of International Business Studies* (Summer 1988), pp. 257–75. MNCs surveyed: 105.

Budgets as a Success Indicator

For some time, budgeting has been accepted as a management tool for controlling operations and forecasting future operations of domestic companies. One purpose of the budget is to clearly set out the objectives of the entity. A budget generally provides a forecast and a means of comparing the actual results of operations to the budget. This comparison produces variances that can be analyzed to evaluate performance and improve the efficiency of future operations.

When a budget is used for a foreign subsidiary, the budget should be developed by that subsidiary. The experience of the local manager is extremely important, in that it produces a very deep knowledge of the specific business situation. A budget developed on this level will help control the operations and make achievement of goals possible. This budget can be used by the local manager on a daily basis.

Budgeting gives local managers the opportunity to set their own performance standards. In international operations top management is not as familiar with what the standards should be. Headquarters must rely to a greater extent on good local or regional budgets, which help facilitate the strategic planning process.

Preparation of the budget at the local level is not always an easy task. Local managers have different degrees of budgeting expertise. Local customs and norms may affect the budgeting process and are likely to affect the degree of its acceptance and usefulness. Implementation of a system is also difficult due to a lack of familiarity with the technique on the part of local employees of foreign subsidiaries. Budgeting may be a more critical performance evaluation tool for international operations than for domestic ones.

Headquarters uses each foreign subsidiary's budget to develop a worldwide, companywide forecast. Headquarters analyses are based upon a wide spectrum of knowledge, including knowledge of possible environmental, objective, and strategy changes at the international level. At this headquarters level, profit and return on investment provide the information necessary to assess worldwide profitability and its success or failure. Budgeted information is used more frequently to assess the individual subsidiaries performances rather than the overall performance of the MNC.

The subsidiaries' budgets are approved at the parent-company level and often require the endorsement of the president and/or the board of directors. Presumably, headquarters uses the budget to consider the circumstances peculiar to each subsidiary. However, as noted above, executives repeatedly return to the ROI statistic. They may use the budget for *supplementary* information on subsidiary performance; but, they still select ROI as a key success indicator.

NONFINANCIAL MEASURES USED TO EVALUATE PERFORMANCE

Exhibit 10–3 lists several nonfinancial criteria that U.S.-based multinationals use in their performance evaluation systems. These criteria are considered important, despite the difficulty one might have in trying to measure them. For example, it is difficult to place a numerical value on "cooperation with parent company."

The data in Exhibit 10–3 indicate that market share is considered the most important nonfinancial measure. Other important items are productivity improvement, relationships with host governments, quality control, employee development, and safety. Community service and research and development are considered less important.

EXHIBIT 10–3   Nonfinancial Measures Used to Evaluate Performance of Subsidiaries and Their Managers

	Use in Performance Evaluation of U.S. MNCs— Average Importance*	
Nonfinancial Measures	*Subsidiary*	*Manager*
Increasing market share	1.8	1.5
Relationship with host country government	2.1	1.8
Quality control	2.2	1.9
Productivity improvement	2.2	2.1
Cooperation with parent company	2.4	2.0
Environment compliance	2.4	2.3
Employee development	2.4	2.0
Employee safety	2.4	2.2
Labor turnover	2.7	2.5
Community service	2.9	2.8
Research and development in foreign subsidiary	3.1	3.2

*1 = Very important; 2 = Important; 3 = Less important; 4 = Not important.

SOURCE: F.D.S. Choi and I. J. Czechowicz, "Assessing Foreign Subsidiary Performance: A Multinational Comparison," *Management International Review* 23 (1983), p. 17. MNCs surveyed: 64.

EXHIBIT 10–4   Financial Measures Used to Evaluate Foreign Subsidiaries and Their Managers

	Use in Performance Evaluation Ranking			
	Abdallah[a]		Hosseini/Rezaee[b]	
Financial Measures	*Subsidiary*	*Manager*	*Subsidiary*	*Manager*
Profit	2	2*	1	1
Budget versus actual profit	1	1	2	2
Return on investment	3	2*	3	3

*These are ranked equally because their scores are extremely close.

SOURCES: (a) Wagdy M. Abdallah, *Internal Accountability: An International Emphasis* (Ann Arbor, Mich.: UMI Research Press, 1984). MNCs surveyed: 64. (b) Ahmad Hosseini and Zabihollah Rezaee, "Impact of SFAS No. 52 on Performance Measures of Multinationals," *The International Journal of Accounting* 25, no. 1 (1990), pp. 43–52. MNCs surveyed: 109.

MAJOR FRUSTRATIONS IN AN MNC PERFORMANCE EVALUATION SYSTEM

Separating Manager Performance from Subsidiary Performance

Many managerial accountants advocate making a distinction between the performance of the subsidiary manager and that of the subsidiary itself. In practice, MNCs report that they do not make a distinction between the evaluation of the manager and the subsidiary. Exhibit 10–4 reveals that in two recent surveys, MNCs reported using the same financial measures to evaluate the performance of the manager as that of the subsidiary. The three most frequently used financial measures are profit, budget compared to actual profit, and return on investment.

Responsibility reporting as an accounting system traces costs, revenues, assets, and liabilities to the individual manager who is responsible for them. It follows that a manager who has the ability to control the results of operations should be evaluated on the basis of the results over which she or he has control. This system has been widely implemented in U.S. domestic operations and has proven to be generally effective as an evaluation tool. However, the very nature of international operations does not lend itself to effectively implementing a responsibility reporting system in MNCs.

MNC headquarters manages from a worldwide perspective and allocates costs and sets transfer prices to optimize companywide profits and to facilitate worldwide cash flows. (Chapter 11 focuses on transfer prices and taxation.) Therefore, it is very naive to evaluate the operating performance of foreign subsidiary managers without first considering all the possible uncontrollable costs that could be allocated to their operations (i.e., royalties, interest, taxes, and exchange gains and losses).

For these reasons, evaluating a manager's performance should be separate from judging the subsidiary as an investment. The manager's evaluation should involve a degree of subjectivity that considers the uniqueness of the subsidiary, environmental peculiarities, actions of the host government, and specific goals of the manager being evaluated. If managers are delegated responsibility for results that are beyond their control, it may lead to behavior that is not in line with head-quarters' goals.

Evaluating managers in their local currency before allocation of costs over which they have no direct control is ideal, although somewhat impractical because headquarters usually prefers information translated to the parent currency. Objective measures of performance, profit, and ROI may then be used effectively by headquarters to judge the subsidiary as an investment.

Treating Foreign Subsidiaries as Profit Centers

Profit centers located internationally do not operate in a uniform environment. They operate in environments with different inflation rates and different economic, political, cultural, and technological conditions. Top management is not likely to understand all of the peculiarities of each environment; therefore, it will have trouble evaluating the managers' performance. For these reasons, the profit center concept is less useful when applied to foreign subsidiaries than when applied to domestic subsidiaries. Therefore, it is less successful as a performance indicator.

MNCs also integrate and coordinate operations globally, and it becomes difficult under these circumstances to recognize a particular subsidiary's contribution. The subsidiary manager is not directly responsible for all of the subsidiary's activities. Subsidiaries of an MNC are not independent, and although some control may be decentralized, many major decisions affecting both worldwide profit and individual subsidiary profit are made at headquarters for worldwide efficiency in operations.

Transfer pricing policy (see Chapter 11) in the MNC is not compatible with the profit center concept. A transfer price is a charge for goods exchanged between subsidiaries of the same company. Transfer prices in domestic profit centers are usually set with the objective of maintaining equity between the independent subsidiaries. Transfer prices are set *internationally* for many reasons, which do not necessarily include equity among subsidiaries. These reasons include taxes, tariffs, fluctuating currencies, inflation, economic restrictions on fund transfers, and political instabilities.

Even so, local managers and subsidiaries of MNCs are often evaluated like profit centers. Yet central coordination of the MNC makes it difficult to evaluate the local managers' performance. These managers do not make many of the important decisions affecting their operations. It is also difficult to evaluate how effectively a subsidiary is using its resources.

The responsibility reporting concept implies that the manager and the local entity should be evaluated separately. Separating the two enables each to be judged according to its contribution to global optimization.

Translation

The accounting records and financial statements of a foreign subsidiary are generally maintained in the subsidiary's local currency. The U.S. parent company must be able to translate these foreign currency financial statements to U.S.-dollar terms. Translation is necessary for any of the following reasons:

1. To communicate to foreign subsidiary managers the parent company's objectives for the foreign subsidiary in terms of U.S.-dollar results and flows.
2. To judge the foreign subsidiary's profitability.
3. To evaluate the performance of the foreign subsidiary's managers.
4. To evaluate capital budgeting decisions.
5. To evaluate the return produced by the dollar investment of the U.S. company.
6. To determine the periodic gain or loss sustained by the U.S. parent company from movements in foreign exchange rates.
7. To consolidate foreign financial statements with domestic statements and present them to top management in a currency they are familiar with (see Chapter 6).

To prepare statements in U.S.-dollar terms, the amounts expressed in foreign currency must be changed to dollars. As discussed in Chapter 6, the process of changing the amounts from foreign currency to dollars is commonly referred to as *translation*. This is a measurement conversion process—it changes only the unit of measure, not the accounting principles used to prepare the statements. Translation satisfies the need to use a single unit of measure in the consolidated financial statements of domestic and foreign operations.

Management, investors, and other users of financial information need translated statements to judge the past, present, and future profitability of the foreign operations. The results of operations are more easily compared if presented in terms of a single currency (e.g., U.S. dollars).

The key issue that arises when translating financial statements is the selection of the exchange rate (method) to translate various accounts from one currency into another.

For external reporting purposes, the Financial Accounting Standards Board has issued *Statement 52*, "Foreign Currency Translation" (see Chapter 6). Assuming that we are dealing with *autonomous* subsidiaries, we use the year-end exchange rate (current rate) to translate the balance sheet and average-for-the-year rate to translate the income statement. The result is that operating relationships and income statement ratios remain intact throughout the translation process. Users of this information can then see in dollars the same relationships that existed in the currency where the revenues were earned and expenses were incurred. Notice in Exhibit 10–5, for example, that the ratio of total debt to total assets is the same in local currency (LC 1100 ÷ LC 1500 = 73 percent) as it is in U.S. dollars ($550 ÷ $750 = 73 percent).

EXHIBIT 10–5   Effect of Translation on Balance Sheet Accounts

	Local Currency	*Current Rate*	*U.S. Dollars*
Cash	LC300	1 LC = $0.50	$150
Inventory	400		200
Building and land	800		400
	LC1,500		$750
Current liabilities	LC300	1 LC = $0.50	$150
Long-term debt	800		400
Stockholder's equity	400		200
	LC1,500		$750

Studies have shown that most MNCs use the same method to translate for internal reporting purposes (managerial accounting) that they use for external reporting purposes (financial accounting). Therefore, with *FASB Statement 52* requiring use of the current rate for financial reporting, it can be assumed that information used to evaluate foreign subsidiaries and their managers is also translated at the current exchange rate in effect at the time of translation. This method provides translated financial statements that are similar to local currency financial statements.

POINTS TO CONSIDER WHEN DEVELOPING THE SYSTEM

Use of Local Currency Information

If a subsidiary operates in a country with a stable currency, an evaluation of the subsidiary's performance in either U.S. dollars or local currency should be meaningful. When the currency is unstable, a foreign subsidiary's performance is more clearly reflected by its *local* currency operating results.

Profit and ROI in U.S. dollars can be used to judge the *subsidiary's* value to the enterprise as a whole. These financial measures are less applicable when evaluating a subsidiary *manager*. As noted earlier, such managers should be evaluated on meeting primary *goals* in local currency (e.g., annual profits and sales forecasts, meeting projected production levels, managing the effects of inflation, and managing employees).

Comparisons of the past, present, and future operations of a subsidiary are far more meaningful and valid if calculated in local currency. Comparing either the U.S.-dollar or local currency results of subsidiaries operating in different environments is useless. The environmental peculiarities of each operating environment need to be isolated and weighed in order to achieve a meaningful comparison. Yet U.S. managers continue to use more U.S. dollar financial measures than local currency measures. U.K. managers report a preference for using budget compared with actual profit information in local currency. They say that the local currency provides information that relates to local environment conditions and avoids distortions that result from fluctuating exchange rates.

However, there is a problem with universally employing local currency information for evaluating foreign operations. Sometimes higher-echelon managers have difficulty interpreting subsidiary results reported in local currency. These managers also have difficulty understanding and interpreting the effect that foreign exchange gains and losses have on the overall enterprise results. Decision making by boards of directors and management headquarters is generally based on U.S.-dollar information. If one level of management bases decisions on U.S.-dollar information and another on local currency information, problems with goal congruency and optimization of resources may result. To minimize these problems, multinational corporations are requiring managers and directors to become familiar with foreign currency operating results in addition to U.S.-dollar information.

The local currency perspective recognizes that foreign subsidiaries function in different countries and economic environments and may have a different operating relationship with the parent than domestic subsidiaries. Therefore, local currency financial statements of a foreign subsidiary present a more meaningful picture of the subsidiary's activities.

Developing and Tracking the Operating Budget

Despite the arguments in favor of using a local currency perspective, many U.S. MNCs use a U.S.-dollar perspective for developing and tracking their budgets. Therefore, it is important to consider the exchange rate(s) used for these purposes. An MNC has alternatives when it comes to selecting an exchange rate to use in developing the budget and tracking results. The company may use the same rate to both develop and track the budget, or it may use one rate to develop and a different rate to track. MNCs report using the following alternatives:

Rate Used to Develop the Budget	Rate Used to Track the Budget
Actual at time of budget	Actual at end of period
Projected at time of budget	Projected at time of budget
Projected at time of budget	Actual at end of period

If the exchange rate used to develop the budget is the actual exchange rate at the beginning of the period and the rate used to track results is the actual rate at the end of the period (Alternative 1), the subsidiary manager will absorb the full impact of changes in the local environment and fluctuating currencies. This is true even though possible exchange fluctuations were not even considered in preparing the budget. The following diagram helps to explain this concept:

Develop Budget	Track Budget
Expected volume at	Actual volume at
Expected LC prices at	Actual LC prices at
Actual exchange rate	Actual exchange rate
(beginning of period)	(end of period)
Variance includes *both* {	Changes in local environment
	Fluctuating exchange rates

If the exchange rate used to develop the budget is the same rate used to track results (Alternative 2), then only the impact of changes in the local environment fall on the subsidiary manager. There is no difference from exchange rate change effects, because the same rate is used to develop and then to track the budget. This alternative introduces forecasting into the budgeting process while insulating the manager from exchange rate shifts. The following diagram presents this concept:

Develop Budget	Track Budget
Expected volume at	Actual volume at
Expected LC prices at	Actual LC prices at
Projected exchange rate	Projected exchange rate
(end of period)	(end of period)
Variance includes: Changes in local environment only	

Alternative 3 uses a projected (forecasted) rate to develop the budget and the actual rate at the end of the period to track a manager's results. This alternative holds the manager responsible for the unexpected portion of exchange rate fluctuations in addition to changes in the local environment. See the following diagram.

Develop Budget	Track Budget
Expected volume at	Actual volume at
Expected LC prices at	Actual LC prices at
Projected exchange rate	Actual exchange rate
(end of period)	(end of period)
Variance includes *both* {	Changes in local environment
	Unexpected exchange rate
	fluctuations

Example 1. Let's compute variances with this information:

Expected volume	500	Actual volume	500
Expected LC price	2	Actual LC price	2
Actual exchange rate (BOP)	1 LC = $0.50	Actual exchange rate (EOP)	1 LC = $0.25
Projected exchange rate (EOP)	1 LC = $0.25		

a. Expected volume × Expected LC price × Actual exchange rate (BOP) = $500
    (500)   ×   (2)   ×   1 LC = $0.50
  Actual volume × Actual LC price × Actual exchange rate (EOP) = $250
    (500)   ×   (2)   ×   1 LC = $0.25

Variance is $250 due to fluctuating exchange rates; a devaluation of the LC has occurred.

b. Expected volume × Expected LC price × Projected exchange rate (EOP) = $250
    (500)   ×   (2)   ×   1 LC = $0.25
  Actual volume × Actual LC price × Projected exchange rate (EOP) = $250
    (500)   ×   (2)   ×   1 LC = $0.25

Variance is zero because there were no unexpected changes in the local environment. This manager is not held responsible for exchange rate fluctuations.

Example 2. Now compute variances with slightly different information:

Expected volume	1,200	Actual volume	1,000
Expected LC price	2	Actual LC price	2
Actual exchange rate (BOP)	1 LC = $0.50	Actual exchange rate (EOP)	1 LC = $0.25
Projected exchange rate (EOP)	1 LC = $0.25		

a. Expected volume × Expected LC price × Actual exchange rate (BOP) = $1,200
    (1,200)   ×   (2)   ×   1 LC = $0.50
  Actual volume × Actual LC price × Actual exchange rate (EOP) = $500
    (1,000)   ×   (2)   ×   1 LC = $0.25

Total variance is $700. Fluctuating exchange rates contribute $600 of this amount while the remaining $100 is due to actual volume being less than expected $[(1,200-1,000) \times 2 \times 0.25 = \$100]$.

b. Expected volume × Expected LC price × Projected exchange rate (EOP) = $600
    (1,200)   ×   (2)   ×   1 LC = $0.25
  Actual volume × Actual LC price × Projected exchange rate (EOP) = $500
    (1,000)   ×   (2)   ×   1 LC = $0.25

Variance is $100 due to the difference in expected and actual volume. This manager may be held responsible for the volume variance while not being held responsible for exchange rate fluctuations.

Subsidiary managers should understand, accept, and contribute to the budget process. A good way to minimize undesirable behavior is to include managers in the preparation of any budget relevant to their own performance.

Budgets should be the key indicators of a foreign subsidiary manager's performance. Although it is best to develop and track budgets in the local currency, budgets translated to U.S. dollars provide more meaningful information than other financial indicators (e.g., return on investment and profit).

When managers participate in the preparation of their own budgets, they can incorporate any cultural, legal, political, and economic factors that might affect their operating performance during a budget period. An unexpected currency devaluation can eliminate a subsidiary's entire annual budgeted profit. The budget can reflect anticipated fluctuations in exchange rates and price levels and allow for all of the different tax rates applicable to a specific environment that either benefit or penalize operations. Employment practices and local regulations may affect operations and can be reflected in a subsidiary's budget. In fact, any of the following environmental differences may be incorporated into a budget: (1) the fluctuating exchange rates and price levels, (2) the cost and methods of borrowing money, (3) the tax system, (4) the customer payment terms, (5) the local regulations, (6) the employment practices, and (7) the accounting system. This is only a partial list.

CONCLUSION

Multinational corporations need flexible performance evaluation models capable of incorporating factors peculiar to an MNC for the separate evaluation of subsidiary and manager. This chapter has identified the financial measures currently being used in MNC performance evaluation systems. Explanations of why these measures are inappropriate in a multinational environment have led the authors to suggest more effective techniques. Because performance evaluation systems used by MNCs have international economic impact, these systems should be under constant examination, and improvements should be made continuously.

KEY POINTS

1. The financial measures most used in multinational performance evaluation are profit, budget versus actual profit, and return on investment.

2. Nonfinancial measures are also used to evaluate performance in multinational corporations; the most important of these is market share.

3. The performance of the manager should be evaluated separately from the performance of the subsidiary.

4. In MNCs, many decisions are centralized and beyond the control of the international manager. Thus, the profit center concept of performance evaluation is normally inappropriate for foreign operations.

5. Many U.S. MNCs use the U.S. dollar for setting the budget and, later, tracking results. The responsibility the international manager has over foreign exchange risk should be considered in choosing the combination of exchange rates used for these purposes.

CASES

Ciba-Geigy

Ciba-Geigy is a large diversified Swiss MNC that uses the matrix form of organization in order to pay attention to products and geographic areas. Headquarters management is responsible for the development and implementation of management principles and business policies, setting strategic targets for subsidiaries and the company as a whole, allocation of resources (money, people, and facilities), and organizational structure. Other responsibilities are delegated to the subsidiaries in a highly decentralized fashion. ROI is considered the most important financial indicator of success. The calculation of ROI is dependent upon the accounting rules used in the computation. Ciba-Geigy is able to choose its own set of accounting rules because Swiss MNCs are not required to publish consolidated financial statements, although the company has voluntarily done so since 1972. Ciba-Geigy uses current values for fixed assets and an operating income concept, (i.e., the only revenues and expenses appearing on the income statement of a subsidiary are those resulting from the direct operations of that unit). In general, the subsidiary managers are very happy with the performance evaluation system.

Questions

1. Can you identify any advantages to the Ciba-Geigy information and control system? Do you notice any disadvantages?
2. What influence has the Swiss operating environment had on the development of the information and control system?
3. Do you think it possible for a large U.S. MNC to adopt the Ciba-Geigy information and control system? Why or why not?

Global Enterprises, Inc.

Global Enterprises, Inc., is a large diversified U.S. MNC with operations all over the world. Headquarters takes a centralized approach to control and exhibits an ethnocentric attitude toward international business. Consequently, top management is rather suspicious of foreign nationals and attempts to use U.S. personnel throughout its foreign subsidiaries. The established control system holds managers accountable for exchange rate fluctuations, and this is incorporated in the budgeting process. Global requires that all budgets be prepared in U.S. dollars and that the actual rate at the beginning of the period be used to set the budget. The actual rate at the end of the period is then used to track results.

Questions

1. What effects might this approach have on the operating manager of a subsidiary?

2. Suggest an alternative approach that would not hold the local manager accountable for exchange rate fluctuations.

3. If you wanted to turn Global into a transnational MNC, what changes would you have to make to the strategic planning and control processes?

Hannaz International

Hannaz International is a U.S. multinational that uses a number of measures to evaluate the performance of its domestic and foreign operations, including ROI. Its Spanish subsidiary, El Torro, Inc., sells exclusively to an affiliated subsidiary at a price 30 percent below market. Annual sales are approximately $250,000, with cost of goods sold at $100,000 (without the labor component). Local labor laws result in the labor component of cost of goods sold being inflated by $25,000, after translation to U.S. dollars. Hannaz International allocates headquarters' administrative expenses across all subsidiaries and charges El Torro $15,000. Financing decisions, foreign exchange risk management, and tax planning are centralized at headquarters.

Questions

1. Identify and discuss which elements should be considered when judging the performance of El Torro as a unit of performance.

2. How does your discussion change if you are evaluating El Torro's operating manager instead?

3. Are there any nonfinancial measures that you can use in your evaluation?

ADDITIONAL READINGS

Abdallah, W. M., and D. E. Keller. "Measuring the Multinational's Performance." *Management Accounting* (October 1985), pp. 26–30, 56.

Choi, F. D. S., and I. J. Czechowicz. "Assessing Foreign Subsidiary Performance: A Multinational Comparison." *Management International Review* (1983), pp. 1–21.

Demirag, I. S. "Assessing Foreign Subsidiary Performance: The Currency Choice of U.K. MNCs." *The Journal of International Business Studies* (Summer 1988), pp. 257–75.

Duangploy, D., and D. Gray. "An Empirical Analysis of Current U.S. Practice in Evaluating and Controlling Overseas Operations." *Accounting and Business Research* 21, no. 84 (1991), pp. 299–309.

Hassel, L. G. "Performance Evaluation in a Multinational Environment." *Journal of International Financial Management and Accounting* 3, no. 2 (1991), pp. 17–38.

Hosseini, A., and Z. Rezaee. "Impact of SFAS No. 52 on Performance Measures of Multinationals." *The International Journal of Accounting* 25, no. 1 (1990), pp. 43–52.

Susumu, U., and U. Sekaran. "The Influence of Culture on Budget Control Practices in the USA and Japan: An Empirical Study." *The Journal of International Business Studies* 23, no. 4 (1992), pp. 659–74.

11

MULTINATIONAL TRANSFER PRICING AND INTERNATIONAL TAXATION

We have established that the purpose of a management control system is to accomplish the objectives of the strategic plan. The control system is designed to communicate information that enhances goal congruence and that provides the basis for decision making throughout all levels of the multinational corporation (MNC).

The MNC must deal with two additional complicating variables that do not affect domestic corporations. The first is setting transfer prices for goods and services in a worldwide arena. The second is dealing with international taxation and its pervasive influence on all aspects of MNC operations. This chapter discusses the objectives of MNC transfer pricing and then turns to a discussion of how MNCs attempt to minimize taxes on an international scale. As we shall see, the transfer price selected for transferring goods and services across national boundaries has a significant impact on the MNC's international tax liability, and vice versa.

OBJECTIVES OF TRANSFER PRICING

The need for determining a transfer price arises when goods or services are exchanged between organizational units of the same company. A transfer price is a substitute for a market price. It is used when one subsidiary of a corporation sells to another. The transfer pricing system places a monetary value on intracompany exchanges that occur between operating units. This price is recorded by the seller as revenue and by the buyer as cost of goods sold.

Example 1.   Subsidiary A sells 1,000 units of product X to subsidiary B for $7 per unit. The $7 selling price is the *transfer price*.

It is generally agreed that the transfer pricing system for a *domestic* corporation should accomplish certain objectives including (1) the communication of information resulting in desirable decision making by managers, (2) providing a report of divisional profits that reasonably measures the economic performance of the division, and (3) enhancing goal congruence.

Achieving these objectives may be difficult. If a manager makes a decision that increases the profit of his/her particular profit center, it may affect the profits of a competing profit center negatively. An example of such a decision is charging an inflated transfer price for goods transferred to a division. The first profit center will show increased sales and a higher profit; however, the second profit center will show increased cost of purchases and a lower profit.

Example 2.   Subsidiary A sells 1,000 units of product X to Subsidiary B for $8 per unit. The normal market price is $6 per unit. Subsidiary A shows increased sales of $2 per unit and a higher profit. Subsidiary B shows that cost of goods sold has increased by $2 per unit and therefore has a lower profit.

Those who develop domestic internal transfer pricing systems are aware of this potential dilemma and attempt to create a system that motivates managers not to make undesirable decisions. Ideally, a manager acts in the best interests of the company as a whole, even at the expense of the reported profits of his/her own division. To effect this ideal behavior, the system of performance evaluation must reward a manager who chooses companywide goal congruence over divisional performance.

OBJECTIVES OF INTERNATIONAL TRANSFER PRICING

Developing an MNC transfer pricing system is far more complex than developing a domestic system. As with the *domestic* corporation, an MNC pricing system should result in managers making desirable decisions that enhance goal congruence. Providing a reasonable measure of a subsidiary's economic performance is often an irrelevant transfer pricing objective when dealing with an MNC. An MNC pricing system must attempt to meet the objectives of the strategic plan, the management control system, and the system of performance evaluation. (See Chapters 9 and 10 for a discussion of these objectives). The international transfer pricing system must also attempt to accomplish objectives that are irrelevant in a purely domestic operation. These objectives include (1) worldwide income tax minimization, (2) minimization of worldwide import duties, (3) avoidance of financial restrictions, (4) managing currency fluctuations, and (5) winning host-country government approval.

It is unlikely that an MNC will be able to accomplish all objectives with a single transfer pricing strategy. Strategies may vary as environmental variables change. Exhibit 11–1 presents the results of two studies that investigated the im-

---

EXHIBIT 11–1   Environmental Influences on Transfer Prices

| | Burns Survey | | Kim and Miller Survey |
Rank	Variable	Rank	Variable
1	Market conditions in foreign country	1	Profit repatriation restrictions within host country
2	Competition in foreign country	2	Exchange controls
3	Reasonable profit for foreign affiliate	3	Joint-venture constraints within host country
4	U.S. federal income taxes	4	Tariffs/customs duties within host country
5	Economic conditions in foreign country	5	Income tax liability within host country
6	Import restrictions	6	Income tax liability within the U.S.
7	Customs duties	7	Quota restrictions within the U.S.
8	Price controls	8	Credit status of U.S. parent firm
9	Taxation in foreign country	9	Credit status of foreign affiliate
10	Exchange controls		
11	U.S. export incentives		
12	Floating exchange rates		
13	Management of cash flow		
14	Other U.S. federal taxes		

SOURCE: Jane O. Burns, "Transfer Pricing Decisions in U.S. Multinational Corporations," *Journal of International Business Studies* (Fall 1980), pp. 23–39; and Seung H. Kim and Stephen W. Miller, "Constituents of the International Transfer Pricing Decision," *Columbia Journal of World Business* (Spring 1979), pp. 69–77.

portance of environmental variables that influence transfer prices. Although these studies are nearly 15 years old, their results are still valid because the ranking of environmental variables is slow to change. The variables are ranked from those having the most importance to those having the least. Both studies surveyed U.S.-based MNCs; however, the Kim and Miller study focused on U.S. MNCs that have subsidiaries in developing countries rather than industrialized countries. It is easy to see why setting international transfer prices is such a complicated process. An MNC must prioritize the importance of environmental influences, but the rank of these influences may change as the country of operation changes.

Worldwide Income Tax Minimization

The transfer pricing system can be used to shift taxable profits from a country with a high tax rate to a country with a lower tax rate; the result is that after taxes the MNC retains more profits. Exhibit 11–2 reports the corporation income tax rates for a variety of countries throughout the world. The Cayman Islands have long been considered a tax haven for corporations due to the zero corporate in-

EXHIBIT 11–2   Corporate Income Tax Rates

Country	Rate
Australia	39%
Brazil	30
Cayman Islands	0
China, Peoples Republic of	33
Germany	50
Italy	36
Japan	38
Korea	34
Norway	28
Pakistan	50
Singapore	31
Switzerland	10
Taiwan	25
United Kingdom	33
United States	34

come tax rate. As you can see, corporate rates vary considerably. Unless the performance evaluation system is compatible with the transfer pricing system, undesirable decision making can result at the subsidiary manager level. If each subsidiary is evaluated as an independent profit center, the transfer pricing policies must be considered when evaluating the manager's performance, or else conflict between subsidiary and MNC goals may result.

Example 3.   Subsidiary X operates in Pakistan, where the tax rate is 50 percent. Subsidiary Y operates in Switzerland with a tax rate of 10 percent. X sells goods to Y at an inflated transfer price of $10 per item. The current market price is $7 per item. Subsidiary X shows a higher profit and is taxed at 50 percent. Subsidiary Y shows a higher cost of goods sold and a lower profit on future sales taxed at 10 percent. These subsidiaries are not practicing worldwide tax minimization.

Minimization of Worldwide Import Duties

Transfer prices can reduce tariffs. Import duties are normally applied to intracompany transfers as well as to sales to unaffiliated buyers. If the goods are transferred in at low prices, the resulting tariffs will be lower. This same pricing strategy may be used when a country places a ceiling on the value of goods that may be imported. By valuing at low transfer prices, a subsidiary may be able to import a larger *quantity* of goods and services. If a country had a low tariff on imports, a higher transfer price could be charged.

Tariffs interact with income taxes. Low import duties are often associated with a country with high income tax rates. The opposite may also be found—high import duties with low income tax rates. The MNC must deal with the customs officials and income tax administrators of the importing country and with the income tax administrators of the exporting country. A higher import tariff would result in a lower remaining profit for determining income taxes. The MNC has to evaluate the benefits of a lower (higher) income tax in the importing country against a higher (lower) import tariff as well as the potentially higher (lower) income tax paid by the MNC in the exporting country.

Avoidance of Financial Restrictions

When a foreign government places economic restrictions on MNC operations, transfer prices may mitigate the impact of these national controls. Suppose a country restricts the amount of cash that may leave its boundaries in the form of dividend payments. Setting a high transfer price on goods imported into the country may facilitate the desired movement of cash because the importing subsidiary must remit payment. However, cash transfers are not easily accomplished in a country that watches import and export prices closely.

Some countries allow a tax credit or subsidy based on the value of goods exported. In this case, a high transfer price on exported products is followed by a larger tax credit or higher subsidy. A tax credit of this nature reduces the corresponding tax liability to the host country dollar for dollar and more than offsets the higher taxable income. A subsidy is generally a payment from the government to the subsidiary.

Restrictions may be placed on an MNC by disallowing a foreign subsidiary to deduct certain expenses provided by the parent against taxable income. Common examples include research and development expenses, general and administrative expenses, and royalty fees. By inflating the transfer price of imports to the subsidiary, such expenses may be recovered.

If an MNC desires to show lower (higher) profitability, high (low) transfer prices on imports to subsidiaries may be used. An MNC may want to appear less profitable to discourage potential competitors from entering the market. Higher profits may cause the subsidiary's employees to demand higher wages or even to request some type of profit-sharing plan. Expropriation (takeover) of highly profitable foreign-owned subsidiaries may also be avoided if they appear less profitable.

Lower transfer prices on imports should improve the subsidiary's financial position. This may be desirable when the MNC wants to finance the foreign subsidiary with funds from a local lender rather than committing its own capital. In this instance, the lender would probably require that the subsidiary have a positive financial condition. Lower transfer prices may also allow the subsidiary to enjoy a competitive edge during its initial stages of growth.

Managing Currency Fluctuations

A country suffering from balance-of-payments problems may decide to devalue its national currency. Losses from such a devaluation may be avoided by using inflated transfer prices to transfer funds from the country to the parent or to some other affiliate.

Balance-of-payments problems often result from an inflationary environment. Inflation erodes the purchasing power of the MNC's monetary assets. Using inflated transfer prices on goods imported to such an environment may offer a timely cash removal method.

Winning Host-Country Government Approval

The manipulation of transfer prices has not gone unnoticed. Generally, there is increased government concern about intracorporate pricing and its effect on reported profits. In an era when an MNC must be concerned about justifying its existence, maintaining positive relations with the host government is a good idea. Continually changing and manipulating transfer prices is not good policy.

Most governments are becoming more sophisticated and aware of the results of using high or low transfer prices. Using unfavorable prices to a country's detriment may result in the loss of goodwill. It is beneficial in the long run to develop transfer pricing policies that satisfy the foreign authorities, even though it may mean sacrificing some profits.

In summary, we have discussed several transfer pricing objectives that MNCs must consider and that are not applicable to a purely domestic corporation. These objectives include worldwide income tax minimization, minimization of worldwide import duties, avoidance of financial restrictions, managing currency fluctuations, and winning host-country government approval. Exhibit 11–3 provides a summary of the conditions that make it advisable to use a particular transfer price. Conditions that were influential 20 years ago are still influential today. Unfortunately, an MNC is usually faced with conditions that appear in both columns of the exhibit.

MNCs may resort to maintaining a separate set of financial information for the foreign governments and another set for headquarters to use in the management control process and the performance evaluation system. Unfortunately, the information provided to the foreign government is often used to evaluate the performance of a subsidiary that has been told to produce a low profit to minimize income taxes. If headquarters overlooks the fact that low profits were due to an unfavorable transfer price, hard feelings between subsidiary managers and headquarters may result. It may also cause subsidiary managers to act undesirably. In the long run, morale problems could develop and destroy the short-run effect of tax minimization.

Ideally, the objectives of the management control process should be separated from those of MNC transfer pricing. Headquarters must realize that the performance evaluation system should provide information that discriminates between subsidiary performance and worldwide corporate performance.

SELECTING A TRANSFER PRICE

A headquarters management team takes a global perspective when considering the trade-offs between the costs and benefits of setting transfer prices for their

---

EXHIBIT 11-3   Conditions in Subsidiary's Country Inducing High and Low Transfer
Prices on Flows between Affiliates and Parent

Conditions Inducing Low Transfer Prices *on Flows from Parent and* High Transfer Prices *on Flows to Parent*	*Conditions Inducing* High Transfer Prices *on Flows from Parent and* Low Transfer Prices *on Flows to Parent*
High ad valorem tariffs	Local partners
Corporate income tax rate lower than in parent's country	Pressure from workers to obtain greater share of company profit
Significant competition	Political pressure to nationalize or expropriate high-profit foreign firms
Local loans based on financial appearance of subsidiary	Restrictions on profit or dividend remittances
Export subsidy or tax credit on value of exports	Political instability
Lower inflation rate than in parent's country	Substantial tie-in sales agreements
Restrictions (ceilings) in subsidiary's country on the *value* of products that can be imported	Price of final product controlled by government but based on production cost
	Desire to mask profitability of subsidiary operations to keep competitors out

---

SOURCE: Jeffrey S. Arpan, *Intracorporate Pricing: Non-American Systems and Views* (New York: Praeger Publishers, 1972).

---

operations throughout the world. Each pricing decision affects the entire multinational corporate system. It is extremely difficult to quantify the trade-offs, because each environment is different, and the variables are constantly changing. The decision makers must consider the tax rate, tariffs, inflation, foreign exchange controls, government price controls, government stability, and a whole host of other factors operating in each country. Transfer pricing decisions also affect individual subsidiaries and the multinational corporation system simultaneously. Transfer pricing choices and MNC characteristics that impact these choices are discussed next.

Transfer Pricing Choices

Most transfer pricing systems in use today are based on either external market prices or internal costs. The use of market prices is consistent with the concept of operating subsidiaries as decentralized profit centers. When transfers are recorded at market prices, divisional profitability approaches the real economic contribution of the subsidiary to the total MNC. Using market prices ideally creates the sense of competition that would normally be present if the subsidiaries were independent corporations transacting business at arm's-length market prices. If the transfer price does reflect market conditions, then the subsidiary may be fairly evaluated on its own performance. Market prices also appear less arbitrary to government tax authorities who are watching for manipulation of profits and, therefore, are usually less scrutinized.

Using market prices implies that subsidiaries are autonomous profit centers and that their managers have the authority to make autonomous decisions. However, this is rarely the case in multinational corporations. It may be difficult to establish a free competitive market price if no intermediate market exists for the transferred goods. Finally, using market prices does not afford the MNC much flexibility with which to manipulate profits and cash flows to accomplish the various objectives discussed earlier.

If market prices are either unavailable or cannot be reasonably estimated, then the transfer price will probably be based on the costs of the selling subsidiary. Cost may be the full cost, a variable cost, or a marginal cost with a markup added to allow the selling subsidiary some percentage of profit. Generally, cost-based transfer prices are conveniently determined, because the information on costs is available. Using cost plus markup is easily justified as reasonable when dealing with government authorities, which is another important consideration when administering transfer prices.

Cost-based systems have disadvantages just as market-based systems do. Using cost gives the selling party little incentive to control costs or to operate efficiently, since the inefficiencies may be passed along to the purchasing subsidiary. Undesirable behavior may result in the form of poor decision making.

MNC Characteristics and Current Practices

In addition to all of the objectives incorporated into a transfer pricing methodology, several variables characteristic of an MNC add to the selection process. How an MNC is organized affects the choice of a market- or cost-based transfer pricing system. A highly decentralized MNC would be expected to use market-based transfer prices; whereas a centralized MNC would not allow subsidiary managers to be autonomous decision makers, and therefore headquarters would control the setting of cost-based prices.

The size of the MNC has an influence on organizational structure and thus influences the transfer pricing system. Large firms are generally more centralized due to worldwide optimization of objectives, including income maneuvering for profit maximization. With increased size and involvement comes a need for flexibility and control. Cost-based systems afford a multinational both of these requirements. Smaller, more decentralized firms are not yet as involved or subject to as many risks or as concerned with flexibility or control. Therefore, they use market-based transfer pricing systems to achieve their objectives and to avoid foreign government scrutiny.

Studies have shown that the nationality of the parent company's management also affects whether the MNC uses market prices or costs in establishing a transfer price. Canadian, Italian, and Scandinavian managers have shown a preference for market prices, while U.S., French, British, and Japanese managers seem to prefer transfer prices based on cost. In general, transfer pricing systems of non-U.S. MNCs are less complex and more market based than those of U.S. MNCs.

The nationality of the parent company's management also influences the relative importance of various international transfer pricing objectives, some of which were discussed earlier in this chapter. U.S., Canadian, French, and Italian managers consider income taxes to be one of the most important variables affecting transfer pricing methods. U.S. and U.K. parent company managers consider it important that subsidiaries show a "reasonable" profit. Managers from most countries consider market conditions in the host country to be an important variable. The other major consideration of most managers is acceptability of the transfer price to both host- and parent-country governments.

The *Internal Revenue Code* and Transfer Pricing

All multinationals doing business in the United States must consider Section 482 of the *Internal Revenue Code* when pricing intercompany transactions (intracompany transactions from a headquarters' point of view). Section 482 gives the Internal Revenue Service (IRS) the authority to reallocate income and deductions among subsidiaries if it determines that this is necessary to prevent tax evasion, the illegal reduction of taxes, or to clearly reflect the income of the subsidiary. Intercompany sales of goods must appear to be priced at arm's-length market values. In addition, the IRS also scrutinizes the transfer of services, intangibles (such as trademarks, patents, and basic research), and R&D cost sharing arrangements among commonly controlled entities. Being required to use arm's-length transfer prices does not always allow an MNC to pursue the objective of worldwide profit maximization. According to the IRS, the arm's-length principle to be applied is whether unrelated parties with a reasonable level of experience, exercising sound business judgment, would have agreed to the same contractual terms. This principle does not always support the objective of MNC transfer pricing philosophy.

An MNC pursuing tax minimization must be careful to use transfer prices that appear to reflect arm's-length sales to avoid IRS scrutiny. The *Internal Revenue Code* and related regulations allow three pricing methods considered arm's length: (1) the *comparable uncontrolled price method*, better known as market price; (2) the *resale price method*, sales price received for the property by the reseller less an appropriate markup; and (3) the *cost-plus method*, better known as cost-based transfer price. Other methods are allowed if the MNC can show that they approximate arm's length.

The transfer price used by an MNC and the one required by the IRS may be the same, and then again they may not be. The IRS's objective is to determine the MNC's tax liability. The MNC's objective is after-tax profit maximization. The two are not always compatible. Thus, a U.S. multinational may use one transfer price for internal reporting purposes and another for computing its U.S. tax liability.

There has been concern in Washington, D.C., that foreign-controlled corporations operating in the United States are not paying their fair share of U.S. income taxes. They may be avoiding taxes here, by manipulating intercompany transfer prices. It is difficult for the IRS to use Section 482 as a defense against a foreign-controlled corporation because the corporation can simply refuse to present their records to the IRS. The IRS can fine the corporation, but that is about all.

INTERNATIONAL TAXATION—SELECTED TOPICS

International taxation has a pervasive effect on multinationals and, therefore, enters into most management decisions. Taxation affects where an MNC invests, how it markets its products, what form of business organization it selects, when and where to remit cash, how to finance—and of course—the choice of a transfer price.

Tax systems are used worldwide to effect economic policy, social issues, and the political scene; they are as varied as the nations developing them. International taxation is extremely complex and constantly changing. As tax treaties, agreements, laws, and regulations change, the multinational tax network must be reviewed and reworked to maintain relative worldwide advantages.

Philosophy of Taxation

A country may follow the territorial principle that income earned outside its domestic boundaries is not taxed. Other nations follow the worldwide principle that they have the right to tax income earned outside their boundaries when earned by an entity based in the country. The worldwide principle results in double taxation because the income is taxed where earned and then again to the parent company.

However, double taxation is mitigated by tax credits, tax treaties, tax havens, the "deferral principle," and tax exemption. A *tax credit* allows an entity to reduce the taxes paid to the domestic government by the amount of taxes paid to the foreign government. A credit is a direct reduction of the tax liability and reduces double taxation to a certain extent. A *tax treaty* between nations establishes what items of income will or will not be taxed by the authorities of the country where the income is earned. A *tax haven* is a country with an exceptionally low, or even no, income tax. It generally offers a company the right to earn or transfer income within its borders and pay little or no tax. Tax havens are normally used by MNCs to shift income from a country with a high tax rate to the tax haven. One way to accomplish this is by using transfer prices. The *deferral principle* works so that parent companies are not taxed on foreign source income until they actually receive a dividend. A *tax exemption* allows certain corporations to pay no tax on certain income.

Many MNCs were avoiding U.S. taxation by combining the tax deferral principle with the advantage of a tax haven and repatriating dividends to the tax haven instead of to the United States. As a result, the Controlled Foreign Corporation (CFC) rules were passed by Congress. These rules tax U.S. shareholders on CFC income when it is earned, regardless of when it is received, and thus eliminate the ability to avoid taxes in the manner described.

Congress also created the Foreign Sales Corporation (FSC) to encourage foreign sales by exporters. Part of the taxable income of the FSC is exempt from U.S. income tax. The requirements for qualifying as an FSC are extremely complex and beyond the scope of this book.

MNC Tax Avoidance

Tax avoidance is the legal reduction of one's tax liability and is accomplished by tax planning. We have already established that tax avoidance enters into most managerial decisions and, therefore, plays a role in the strategic planning process, the management control system, and performance evaluation. A *tax-planning information system* that attempts to accomplish worldwide tax minimization and tax avoidance should incorporate the following procedures: (1) stating the objectives of tax planning in MNC operations, (2) delegating responsibilities for tax planning to both headquarters and subsidiaries, (3) determining what operations are affected by tax considerations and how they are affected, (4) communicating necessary information to the tax planners and decision makers, and (5) evaluating the impact of tax considerations on an MNC strategic plan and management control system.

CONCLUSION

We have reviewed some of the objectives of MNC transfer pricing and international taxation. Accomplishing the objectives of transfer pricing is difficult without considering the applicable tax laws. These objectives are so important at times that they take precedence over the objectives of management control and performance evaluation. However, all are components of the strategic planning system and work toward the optimal achievement of a multinational corporation's comprehensive international plan.

KEY POINTS

1. The objectives of multinational transfer pricing include (*a*) minimizing income taxes and import duties worldwide, (*b*) avoiding financial restrictions, (*c*) managing foreign currency risk, and (*d*) winning host country government approval.

2. Transfer pricing methods will vary according to the characteristics of the multinational corporation. For example, smaller decentralized MNCs tend to use market-based methods, while larger centralized MNCs tend to use cost-based methods.

3. Tax regulations require arms-length market values for transfer pricing.

4. The objective of tax planning is minimizing taxes worldwide. It is part of the overall strategic planning process and must be supported by an effective information system.

CASES

The Monday Morning Korean Blues

You are the manager of a Korean subsidiary of a U.S.-based MNC. Your subsidiary has been operating quite profitably during the last year, and you have excess cash to invest. You expect to use this cash to strengthen your subsidiary's position in Korea and ultimately to make your performance look exceptionally good. Your subsidiary buys raw materials from other Pacific Rim subsidiaries of the U.S.-based parent to manufacture its product. You also have had permission to buy these parts from the competition if you can get a better price. Lately, you have been buying from the competition.

This morning, you had the following conversation with headquarters:

HQ:

We need cash transferred into France, and your Korean subsidiary has excess cash at the moment. We want you to facilitate the movement of these funds by Friday.

You:

You know that today is Monday?

HQ:

Yes, we know that it is Monday.

You:

How do you propose that I accomplish your request, considering the fact that my government has just stopped *all* movement of excess cash out of the country?

HQ:

That could be a problem. You know your country's system. Work around it. France needs the cash by Friday.

Questions

1. How could you facilitate the flow of cash from Korea to France, given the present restrictions in Korea?

2. If you are unsuccessful in transferring funds to France, how else could the parent facilitate this flow?

3. Why is your subsidiary allowed to operate so independently (i.e., investing its own excess cash where it chooses and buying raw materials from the least expensive source)?

4. What is meant by the phrase, "You know the system"?

Ah! the Tangled Webs We Weave

Seated around a table are Rhian Emmanuel, Welsh by nationality, and president of IBT-Europe; Patricia Rodary, French, and vice president of finance; and

Sarah Stevens, American, and vice president in charge of sales. IBT is a U.S.-based MNC that manufactures minicomputers. IBT-Europe is a very profitable, wholly owned subsidiary. As a result of its profitability, the president is given a great deal of autonomy from the parent company. Emmanuel manages eight geographically organized subsidiaries that are treated as profit centers when it comes to control and evaluation. Budgets are set in terms of pretax profit and local managers are largely evaluated on their ability to "beat the numbers." Transfer prices are determined at the annual budget meeting, where all subsidiary managers have input. If a complicated tax situation arises, headquarters steps in and determines prices. The following conversation takes place:

Stevens:

I received word from Ireland that the computers are en route to France at a price of $35,000. But France does not want to clear them through customs at this price, because machines from Belgium have been arriving at $25,000 and from the U.S.A. at $27,000. France wants a revised price from Ireland of $25,000.

Rodary:

Let's lower the price. It's only bookkeeping. We don't want the European Community investigating our transfer prices.

Emmanuel:

We can't lower the price. The whole point is to take advantage of the favorable tax deal we struck with Ireland. We have 12 years left on our exemption from income tax on all export sales. I thought this was all settled. We are in business to earn a profit.

Questions

1. What is going on here? Identify as many issues as you can.

2. Is this a centralization/decentralization problem?

3. Is minimizing payments to foreign governments an issue?

4. Can you suggest a solution?

Take It or Leave It

Henry Hothead has just been promoted to subsidiary manager of your German subsidiary that manufactures music boxes. He knows through experience that U.S. headquarters pays attention to bottom-line profit, after taxes, when evaluating managers and judging subsidiaries; therefore, he will too. The corporate income tax rate in Germany is 50 percent.

Hothead has inherited the outgoing manager's budget. He thinks that projected sales volume is low and also finds the sales prices to be low. Hothead figures that he will look good if he increases both volume and per unit price because his after-tax net income will go up. After all, it's not his fault that the German tax rate is so high.

The buyer from Japan, a subsidiary of the same U.S. parent, puts in an order at an expected purchase price of $25 per unit. The corporate tax rate in Japan is

37.5 percent. She quickly discovers that she is dealing with a new seller who wants a price of $35 per unit. If she pays this price, her cost of goods sold will be higher than budgeted and her gross profit will be lower. She too is evaluated on net income after taxes and, during the last several years, has looked like a shining star compared to other managers.

She puts in a call to headquarters.

Questions

1. What are the objectives of worldwide tax avoidance?
2. Do these objectives complement the objectives of the management control and performance evaluation systems?
3. You are the vice president of finance at headquarters. What will you suggest as a solution to this dilemma?

ADDITIONAL READINGS

Abdallah, W. M. "How to Motivate and Evaluate Managers with International Transfer Pricing Systems." *Management International Review* (First Quarter 1989), pp. 65–71.

Al-Eryani, M. F.; A. Pervaiz; and S. H. Akhter. "Transfer Pricing Determinants of U.S. Multinationals." *The Journal of International Business Studies* 21, no. 1 (1990), pp. 409–25.

Bodner, P. M. "International Taxation." *Handbook of International Accounting*. F. D. S. Choi. ed. New York: John Wiley, 1991. pp. 30/1–21.

Bradley, F. "International Transfer Pricing." *Handbook of International Accounting*. F. D. S. Choi. ed. New York: John Wiley, 1991. pp. 29/1–29.

Business International Corporation. *International Transfer Pricing*. New York: BI, 1991.

Khan, Z. U. "Transfer Pricing in Europe." *Journal of International Accounting, Auditing and Taxation* 1, no. 1 (1992), pp. 51–60.

O'Connor, W. F. "A Comparative Analysis of the Major Areas of Tax Controversy in Developed Countries." *Journal of International Accounting, Auditing and Taxation* 1, no. 1 (1992), pp. 61–79.

12

EMERGING ISSUES IN INTERNATIONAL ACCOUNTING

This chapter concludes a concise and nontechnical study tour of the subject matter of international accounting. The knowledge base created for the reader contains enough detail for general sensitivity to what the field is all about. Achievement of technical expertise in international accounting requires considerable further study and analysis. As a bridge toward potential further study, but also as a *synthesis* of the many open questions identified throughout the book, this final chapter offers an assessment of the key factors that seem to drive further emphasis on international accounting as well as a catalog of its emerging issues.

SELECTED FACTORS DRIVING INTERNATIONAL ACCOUNTING EMPHASIS

It is a truism that a computer keyboard manufacturer should consider itself part of the information technology industry rather than as a plastic materials converter. Similarly, it is critical to keep an eye on the factors pushing and reinforcing international accounting aside from the subject matter itself. For illustration purposes, a sketch of three such factors follows.

MNC Restructuring

In the preface of this book, we reported the growing shift away from self-sufficient multinational corporation (MNC) hierarchies to flexible, laterally organized *network structures*. The Japanese *Keiretsu* system (i.e., mutually supportive intercompany relationships) is finding more and more advocates among MNC managers. Strategic interdependent alliances are emerging where head-on competition formerly prevailed. The emphasis is on networks—from research and development (R&D), products and markets development, and employee training to systems design, sourcing of financial capital, and total quality management utilization. Information availability plays a key role in the new MNC organizational patterns. This clearly includes accounting information.

Another restructuring factor relates to *technology*. New technology of many different types is simply outpacing people and organizational capacities. As this new technology is becoming available at an increasingly rapid rate, MNC structures must be changed to capture and use it to the best possible advantage. Cross-cultural recognition is especially significant for MNCs. Global competitiveness suffers if applicable, available, and cost-effective technology is ignored.

A third element is the factor of *speed*. Things are happening so incredibly fast today that the slow are unable "to stay in the game." Just consider how many calculations a super computer can perform in one millionth of a second! Time, in the traditional sense, has lost all meaning. Therefore, MNCs must restructure themselves to cut reaction time to the shortest possible intervals. Management decisions have to be made almost concurrently with the first appearance of new opportunities and simultaneously with receipt of new critical information. To accomplish super-quick reaction patterns requires highly effective information processing and organizational structures oriented to information technology rather than to products, geographic areas, or the traditional business functions like manufacturing, sales, or finance. It goes without saying that the MNC push for speed impacts the full spectrum of international accounting.

More Regionalism

The news is mixed on economic regionalism. Late in 1992, the exchange rate mechanism of the *European Community* (EC) broke down. Early in 1993, a major international newspaper reported Asian perceptions of a decline of Europe's economic power. Influential Asian leaders were quoted to hold "views of the European Community as a declining global player" and that such views "are expressed with increasing frequency in East Asia."[1] The administration of President Clinton in the United States is less enthusiastic about the *North American Free Trade Agreement* (NAFTA) than was the predecessor Bush administration. Trade agreements in Eastern Europe have broken down, and there is little progress with economic integration in South America. Does this mean that regionalism has met its Waterloo?

Quite the contrary! It is a fact that some EC goals were overambitious and had to be slowed down. But the EC is not going to go away. While its economic fabric has unravelled somewhat, its political and regulatory grip has tightened. This is precisely the point. Bureaucracies of regionalism are gaining from Africa to the Pacific and from Scandinavia to Oceania. Regional agreements of cooperation are

---

[1]Michael Richardson, "East Asians See Europe's Power on the Decline," *International Herald Tribune* (Tokyo ed.), February 20–21, 1993, p. 1.

proliferating and with them accounting and financial reporting-related provisions. The accounting regulations of the EC are discussed in Chapter 3. The *U. S.-Canadian Free Trade Agreement* is spawning professional accounting licensing reciprocity between the two countries and has encouraged mutual recognition of each others' GAAP for financial reporting under the securities laws of the United States and the Province of Ontario. The *Association of South East Asian Nations* (ASEAN) operates an accounting standards committee, as do regional groups in East and West Africa. Political and regulatory regionalization is a major driving force behind the growing emphasis on international accounting.

Globalization of All Markets

Until the end of World War II, economic systems structured themselves around corporations, other large organizations, and national governments. Product availability drove consumption, large organizations were key sources of employment and pay-level setters, and governments regulated everything from foreign exchange rates to export/import policy. This system did not always provide goods and services really wanted by consumers and did not often offer the best possible prices. Thus, from 1950 to 1990, consumer demand drove the world economy to unprecedented expansion. There was a literal buying explosion culminating in the *great worldwide shopping spree* of the 1980s.

As the 1990s began, a new regime took over—globalization of all markets. In a perceptive op-ed piece, management guru Peter F. Drucker laid out where the more significant new global markets will be found.[2] These markets fall into the following four categories:

1. *A new market cluster around communication and information.* This involves telephone service in developing and former Soviet bloc countries. It also covers such items as school and office operations.

2. *The environmental market.* Here we have three separate components:
   a. The market for equipment to purify air and water.
   b. The agro-biology market for replacing chemical herbicides and pesticides with nonpolluting, mainly biological, products.
   c. The substitute energy market, which will seek to replace high-polluting energy sources with solar fuel cells and nonpolluting coalburning furnaces.

3. *The physical infrastructure market.* This market will be aimed at repairing and upgrading roads, railroads, bridges, harbors, and airports.

4. *The investment products markets.* People will need these to finance survival into old age.

---

[2]Peter F. Drucker, "Where the New Markets Are," *The Wall Street Journal* (April 9, 1992), p. A14.

It takes little imagination to translate the information needs of the new global markets into *drivers* for more emphasis on international accounting. Several of the emerging issues raised in the following section are directly related to the globalization of markets in general.

KEY EMERGING ISSUES

Throughout this book, many unresolved as well as critical emerging issues have been identified. Since the entire field of international accounting and financial reporting is still evolving, it is little wonder that quite a few issues are as yet unresolved or only partially resolved. The 12 topics selected for comment below are examples only. As indicated in the earlier chapters, there are many other critical issues. The emphasis here is on emerging issues.

1. Quality of National GAAP

Creating well-defined national *generally accepted accounting principles* (GAAP) and making sure that full enforcement occurs throughout the national economy are the first important steps toward reducing financial accounting practice diversity. But how do we know whether any set of national GAAP is of high quality (i.e., optimal) for the national environment being served? For the time being, the quality question is a judgment call. There is no theoretical/analytical model that tells when or if national GAAP are somehow "best." Setting financial accounting standards is basically a social policymaking process and therefore subject to political, social, and legal pressures just as much as to business and economic pressures. Is an accommodating response to all or most such pressures an indicator of quality achievement?

This issue is aggravated on two fronts. One is the *proliferation* of national financial accounting standard setting authorities. Chapter 2 pointed out that most industrialized countries, plus a few developing countries, now have their own accounting standard setting boards or committees. Each pursues its own individual agenda without knowing whether it is necessarily on "the right track." There are international conferences of national accounting standard setters, but they serve little more than information exchange purposes. The big question of what constitutes highest possible quality has not been addressed.

The second difficulty lies with the *process* involved. Chapter 2 illustrates some key national differences in the accounting standard setting processes utilized in selected countries. Is it good to have nonaccountants serve as members of national standard setting agencies? How much research and field testing should be undertaken before a new standard is put into force? Are fewer broad standards better than many detailed standards? All of these concerns bear on the quality of national GAAP issue, which is commanding some new urgency at present.

2. Further Regionalization

European regionalization dates back centuries. When the idea was seriously rekindled in the 1950s, most said it could not be done. Today, the EC thrust seems irreversible. Aside from its own successes (still too incomplete, to be sure), the EC has given impetus to several other regionalization proposals. On a more modest scale, there are already several regional setups like *ASEAN* (mentioned earlier). But a number of large-scale regional conglomerates appear in the making, which give the topic emerging issues status as far as accounting goes.

First, it seems useful to review those areas where real-term regional integration appears *unlikely* in the foreseeable future. This includes South America, the Middle East region, Eastern Europe, and the former Soviet Union, plus the Indochina subcontinent. Geopolitical and sociocultural forces and conditions militate against effective regionalization in the areas identified.

In contrast, the Asian Pacific area (from Oceania to Japan and from Malaysia to Guam), East Africa (Ethiopia to Malawi), West Africa (20-plus countries from Senegal to Gabon and including Nigeria and Zaire), plus a North Central American combination enjoy *good prospects* for some regional fusion. While, again, long-standing national, cultural, and language factors pose considerable obstacles, there are enough common interests within the regions identified to give full regionalization a chance. If further world separation into regions occurs, will (or should) there be corresponding regional accounting development? Will regional development take place concurrently with further national development (as demonstrated by current EC experience)? Are regional interests likely to gain dominance over international harmonization effects (Chapter 3)? It is unclear what further regionalization has in store for the next phase of accounting and financial reporting development worldwide.

3. Global Harmonization

The issue of global harmonization of accounting and financial reporting is posited in Chapter 3. Four possible policy directions exist:

1. Do nothing internationally and leave whatever harmonization efforts seem desirable to networking and adaptation among national accounting standard setting agencies.

2. Segment standard setting and reporting requirements between internationally active corporations and domestically focused companies. Through cooperative efforts between expert accounting professionals (the *International Accounting Standards Committee,* or IASC), securities markets regulators (the *International Organization of Securities Commissions*, or IOSCO), and regional political authorities (e.g., EC and ASEAN), define terms of reference for "internationally active" and negotiate a set of GAAP for all corporations falling within such a definition regardless of country of incorporation or other legal corporate domicile.

3. Establish international accounting standards as globally useful benchmarks that can either be used directly on their own terms, adapted into specified regional or national GAAP, or adopted as a whole or in part as local national GAAP. This alternative is the approach currently in effect.

4. Establish international accounting standards as a comprehensive set of GAAP and use market and political pressures to achieve universal acceptance.

While the present approach to global harmonization appears to be working and, in fact, gaining additional momentum, there are still many critics who would prefer something else. Another open point is *synergy* between IASC and EC activities. IASC would like its standards adopted by EC policymakers, while Brussels bureaucrats are reluctant to forgo their accounting harmonization autonomy over the 12 EC member countries. International harmonization is a sign of our time and firmly in place. Yet the process(es) of harmonization and the ultimate goals to be achieved are still open issues.

4. Mixed Economy Model Evolution

Privatization and movement toward market economics are the high-impact slogans circulating throughout the countries of the Mixed Economy accounting model. The geographic area covered by this model is substantial (see Chapter 1). What happens here in accounting and financial reporting is bound to be consequential.

Traditional forces in Eastern Europe and the former Soviet Union are most comfortable with national *uniform charts of accounts* and very prescriptive practice rules. In a sense, this would be a conceptual continuation of the system they had when their economies were still centrally controlled. A Western example of national uniform accounting is found in France and most Francophile African nations.

Committed reformers advocate adoption of the *British-American model*. They think that full parallels with practices prevailing in the English-speaking countries will help with better access to world financial and credit sources, quicker linkages to major markets for consumer products and all types of technology, and easier appeal for business investments and transfers of expert-level human resources. There is also the judgment that British-American types of education and training are more readily available at reasonable costs.

Finally, the idealists want international standards to start with. They want to create an accounting profession along the lines of the *International Federation of Accountants* (IFAC) and initiate a GAAP system on the basis of IASC standards. This comes through clearly in all the *United Nations*-sponsored workshops and study groups dealing with accounting in the mixed economy situations. It is also evident from the training demands addressed to Western institutions.

What will the winds of change ultimately bring? No clear directions have emerged so far, and questions of GAAP quality (see earlier section in this chapter) are clearly a big issue. Should the British-American model win the "competition," its world influence would be materially strengthened.

5. Special Disclosure Trends

As referenced throughout this book, measurement and disclosure are the "congenital twins" of accounting and financial reporting. Have the evolution and growth of these two components of the discipline been exhausted/completed? By no means. We have characterized accounting as a response mechanism to environmental factors and conditions. *As environments change, so must accounting*, in order to keep relevant. Disclosure advances are one way toward continued relevancy.

Chapter 5 puts the disclosure topic into full focus. Most interesting is the growing practice of voluntary disclosure—which means more disclosure than is required by laws and regulations. Concerned parties welcome this trend. But are more data always better? When do we start to worry about *information overload*? The whys and hows of voluntary (add-on) disclosure amount to an emerging issue in international accounting.

General disclosure questions aside, there are further considerations involving special disclosures. Chapter 5 makes the point of European attention to *social responsibility disclosures* addressing topics like employee safety, health and welfare records, consumer interests, environmental protection (i.e., "green" accounting), job security, employee training, research expenditures, equal opportunities in the workplace, or facilities for the disabled. Are any of these special disclosures more important than others? Should the IASC begin to address specific "social" disclosures? Is it time to export some special disclosure practices from Europe to the rest of the world?

Two special disclosure items deserve separate mention. These are *value-added* notes or statements, and earnings or *business activities forecasts* prepared by management. Both have received attention internationally, and both have been subjected to limited experimentation in several countries. There are, of course, pros and cons when it comes to such targeted disclosures. The consequences involved have not been sufficiently researched. But from the evidence available so far, net benefits appear to accrue from value-added and forecast disclosures. Hence, your authors support them.

6. Pace of Accounting Technology

A number of measurement issues have been addressed chapter by chapter. In the United States, new standards have been published on long future accruals. These involve employers' obligations for postretirement benefits other than pensions and postemployment benefits prior to retirement. Also in the United States, a mark-to-market requirement has been established for certain financial assets and liabilities of certain financial institutions. Most developing countries are struggling with formal recognition of the effects of changing price levels. The IASC's comparability project is redefining the measurement of research and development, and consolidation and lease accounting issues have high priority on the agenda of the *Business Accounting Deliberation Council* in Japan. Accounting technology is constantly changing—it is in a constant state of flux. The real question though is the rate of change. Is accounting measurement technology keeping pace with all of the demands placed upon it?

Each accounting measurement change is costly. When a change becomes official, all companies and other preparers of financial reports must change their manuals, retrain their employees, and reprogram their computers (or change or update applicable software). Auditors must change audit programs and retrain all professional staff. Financial analysts must learn to assess the effects of the changed measurements, as must loan officers at financial institutions. Reference books have to be updated and accounting textbooks rewritten. Even the *Uniform CPA Examination* has to incorporate the changes made. Cost is therefore a crucial factor.

The pace at which accounting measurement technology changes is a key issue. Should the change be incremental and more or less continual, or substantial and limited to specified time intervals? Is there any point in coordinating change between countries? How does one determine whether any set of accounting measurement standards are as up-to-date as they ought to be? Questions of this type are likely to be asked with increased frequency.

7. Information Content of Financial Statements

Financial reports derive their relevance and usefulness from the amount of information content they have. Since financial statements (i.e., balance sheet, income statement, cash flow statement, and all related explanatory notes) are the nucleus of a financial report, the information content of financial statements is critical. Ways to analyze this information content are explored in Chapter 7. Financial ratio analysis is the most widely used means of this type of information evaluation.

Why is this an emerging issue? Because an impressive amount of research has determined that the information content of conventionally prepared financial statements is less than statement users expect. This is obviously a dilemma of major proportions. The *American Institute of CPAs* has a blue ribbon committee working to assess objectives and structure of U.S. GAAP financial statements. In Europe, the *EC Commission* is continuously being challenged by the fact that *EC Directives* contain no requirements for cash flow or funds flow statements. The FASB has an ongoing priority project about desirable characteristics of consolidated financial statements. Form and content of financial statements have had attention on the working agendas of the IASC. These issues are all accentuated in international financial reporting when financial statements are translated in various ways, and even restated from one set of national GAAP to another. Clearly, change is in the air concerning information content of financial statements.

Going back to the earlier distinction between measurement and disclosure, one is tempted to attribute information content shortcomings to lack of disclosure. Chapter 5 pointed the way toward some innovative disclosure approaches likely to produce useful information for financial statement users. But that is not the full story. Maybe the entire financial accounting measurement model should be changed *from a historical cost to some current cost basis*. Maybe accruals of anticipated future events and transactions would be more relevant than present practice amortizations of past events and transactions. Maybe net income should be determined over periods shorter or longer than the presently customary 12 months. Thus, we can predict with some confidence that serious changes in the information content of financial statements are on their way in most GAAP jurisdictions. The open questions are what the nature of these changes will be and when they will arrive.

8. MNC Accounting Information Systems

The central issue faced by MNC accounting information systems developers was identified in Chapter 8. It was labeled *think globally and act locally*. This really means the simultaneous achievement of global synergy among many well-established, autonomously functioning multinational subsidiary companies and high levels of effectiveness at national levels. To quote from the Chapter 8 text:

> Today's international business environment is becoming increasingly complex and competitive. Transnational strategies, organizational structures, and attitudes that allow a company to think globally and act locally are necessary for survival. The *transnational* company of tomorrow must operate efficiently and economically through global-scale operations. It must be able to respond to both national and local differences, retaining local flexibility while achieving global integration.

Four component elements define the issue more specifically:

1. Transnational (as opposed to multinational or global—defined in Chapter 8) *organization structures* (networks) dictate transnational accounting information systems.

2. *Global synergy* does not automatically produce local efficiency and effectiveness.

3. With an increasingly complex and competitive business environment, accounting information systems must deliver decision-relevant information accurately and at *high transfer speeds*.

4. Today's *information technology* (IT) is costly and continuously changing. Using cost-effective IT and knowing when and how to change it have become key accounting systems design problems.

Aside from the operational systems design factors identified in the earlier chapter, there is the tactical issue of satisfying the foregoing four elements concurrently and as optimally as can be done. Here is where one meets the emerging issues challenge. Which of the four elements gets priority? Is higher transfer speed and low transfer accuracy better than the reverse? Is it a good policy to buy, and train employees for, the latest available technology even if that means frequent systems changes? Should global synergy get the nod over best possible local effectiveness? A new round of research, analysis, and field testing is needed before questions of this type can be answered with some confidence.

9. Integration of Strategic Planning and Control Systems

Strategic planning has been a buzz word among corporate executives worldwide for the last two decades. Billions of dollars have been spent setting up strategic planning departments and installing expensive computer systems and even more expensive data bases to feed the computers. Consulting firms have proliferated on lucrative strategic planning engagements. Yet despite all the strategic planning efforts, no one was able to forecast and plan for the abrupt demise of Marxism in Eastern Europe and the former Soviet Union! No one has ever been able to forecast, beyond broad general terms, future movements in interest rates or foreign exchange rates. Hence, strategic planning is at best subjective.

The real challenge, though, lies in translating whatever *strategic plans* are devised and accepted by senior management first into *tactical preparedness* and second into *actual ongoing operations*. Here is where management control systems come in. Control systems "provide useful information . . . so that the plan can be implemented, evaluated, and changed" (Chapter 9). What is not easily resolved is the constant and effective integration of strategic planning and management control systems. Again we quote from Chapter 9: "The management control system and the strategic planning process should be completely integrated."

How can one fully integrate when a strategic plan is broad and general in nature while tactical/operational processes have to address detail, often to the extent of minutia? Should one change tactical/operational detail (e.g., day-to-day operating budgets) every time a strategic planning assumption changes? The integration challenge is particularly severe in international operations. Business cycles typically have timing differences between major economies. For example, in 1993, the U.S. economy began recovery while the German and Japanese economies were further receding. Following closely a single overall strategic plan in all three major economies would have led to missed opportunities everywhere. Devising separate strategic plans for operations in each economy would defeat the overall strategy advantage. Thus, *integration must somehow capture essential local differences*, which is an issue yet to be resolved in transnational management practice.

10. Evaluating Managers or Their Organizational Units

Some emerging issues are "emerging" more quickly than others! Separating performance evaluations of managers from evaluations of the operating/organizational units they manage is a topic that has received attention in international business literature for at least two decades. But it is also a topic of disagreement. Researchers, analysts, and consultants generally favor separate evaluations. Senior managements of MNCs claim that this is difficult to do. Therefore, international operations managers are typically evaluated as one with the units they manage. This causes difficulties and thus keeps the topic on the key issues list.

What seems to be the difficulty? As explained in Chapter 10, *responsibility-based performance evaluation* is common in domestic business settings. Managers are evaluated in terms of the results they achieve through the operations they control. There is a clear link between resources made available to a manager, the manager's decisions about use of all available resources, and profit or loss results achieved. Here it makes sense to evaluate the manager and his or her organizational unit together.

Internationally, it is a different world. MNC coordination occurs across countries for many business functions including R&D, manufacturing, sourcing of financial capital, and marketing and distribution. The advantages gained from worldwide coordination are the very cornerstone of why MNCs exist. However, they are also important constraints with which transnational managers must work. Being in charge of a subsidiary company or a joint venture in another country necessarily requires conformance with a range of headquarters policies and directions. Moreover, local laws, business requirements, and environmental peculiarities must be observed, which also limit the managers' decision discretion. In other words, transnational managers *cannot act as independently* as their domestic operations colleagues. The results of operations of an offshore unit may well be largely the consequence of events and influences over which the local manager had little or no control. Thus, it would be unfair to evaluate managers specifically in terms of locally achieved results. The other side of this argument is presented in Chapter 10. *Shouldn't all managers be evaluated directly on the basis of the profit or loss results they achieve?* This issue continues to plague senior management of MNCs.

11. Currency Choice for Transnational Budgeting and Reporting

Another key issue springing from the discussion in Chapter 10 is the currency choice for MNC internal budgeting and reporting. First of all, there is no corresponding domestic issue. At home, companies always use the national currency unit to denominate all of their management accounting procedures.

However, there is a choice in transnational management accounting. In Chapter 10, we take a strong stand in favor of *local currency budgeting and internal reporting*:

> Managers should be evaluated on meeting primary *goals* in local currency, such as annual profits and sales forecasts, meeting projected production levels, managing the effects of inflation, and managing employees. . . .

Comparisons of the past, present, and future operations of a subsidiary are far more meaningful and valid if calculated in local currency. Comparing either the U.S.-dollar or local currency results of subsidiaries operating in different environments is useless. The environmental peculiarities of each operating environment need to be isolated and weighed in order to achieve a meaningful comparison.

So what happens in actual practice? There is no consensus. Europeans report mostly preferences for local currency procedures; developing country managements often dictate use of a "hard" currency like the U.S. dollar; and most *U.S. managers prefer their "own" U.S.-dollar measures* over local currency measures. By now, their argument is familiar to us—namely, we invested U.S. dollars to start with, we have U.S. investors who expect U.S.-dollar dividends, we finance our operations abroad from a U.S.-dollar risk management perspective, we prepare our annual report in U.S.-dollar denominated amounts, and we report to the SEC in terms of U.S. dollars. We want all of our transnational managers "to keep their eyes" on the U.S. dollar, think in dollar terms, and *manage toward dollar results*. In Chapter 10, we pointed out that for U.S.-based MNCs:

> Decision making by boards of directors and management headquarters is generally based on U.S.-dollar information. If one level of management bases decisions on U.S.-dollar information and another on local currency information, problems with goal congruency and optimization of resources may result.

This is the crux of the issue. Does it make sense to use both local currency and home currency budgeting and internal reporting in the same company at the same time and maybe even concurrently? Your authors have answered with a resounding yes. Practicing managements all over the world are not so sure. Multiple currency sensitivity is difficult, especially when dozens of different national currency units are involved in a company's transnational operations. So what is a bright MNC manager to do? The best he or she can do, given a company's management style and organization culture. But since the issue is unsettled, it is advisable to keep an open mind about it and expect changes.

12. Tax Aspects of MNC Transfer Pricing

Anyone with even cursory acquaintance with the 1992 U.S. presidential political campaign is aware of the controversy over the amount of income taxes paid by controlled foreign subsidiaries in host countries. Then-candidate Clinton claimed that tens of billions of federal corporate income tax dollars could be collected annually if the subsidiaries of non-U.S. corporations operating in the United States paid their "fair share." The issue, of course, is an acceptable definition of *fair share*.

Assume for the sake of illustration that Honda Motor Co., Ltd., of Japan fully owns a Canadian assembly plant company and a U.S. sales company. A given Honda automobile is market researched, designed, developed, and road tested in Japan. Fifty percent of the parts needed to produce this particular car are manufactured in Japan and shipped to Canada. In Canada, the rest of the needed parts are made and the car is fully assembled. It is then shipped to the United States, where it is sold to a local consumer. Assuming the eventual sale produced a profit, tax authorities in Japan, Canada, and the United States all want their *fair share* of taxes on the transaction. Since the tax laws differ substantially between the three countries involved, what might be "fair" in one country is most likely unfair in the next. Therefore, we have a highly emotional issue begging for a solution.

Transfer pricing is obviously the key. If the transfer price of the car involved is set so high in Canada that the U.S. sale just covers this price plus selling expenses, there is no taxable income in the United States and therefore zero tax collection. Thus, any taxes paid are paid in Canada and Japan. Is that fair? It clearly depends on whose perspective is taken as the point of departure.

To grapple with the inevitable confrontations this important issue involves, the U.S. Internal Revenue Service (IRS) has launched its *Advance Pricing Agreement* (APA) program vis-à-vis non-U.S. corporations with operating subsidiaries in the United States. After comprehensive review of corporate procedures and data (some of them highly confidential), the IRS and the non-U.S. corporation agree *in advance* on a transfer pricing mechanism that both parties will honor. Matsushita Company in Japan is party to such an APA. Maybe this approach represents the beginnings of a solution toward the onerous taxation aspects of MNC transfer pricing.

KEY POINTS

1. The forces of internationalization are irreversible. The key factors driving an emphasis on international accounting are the increasingly multinational structure of business organizations, the political and regulatory development of regionalism, and the globalization of all markets.

2. The direction that the global harmonization of accounting and financial reporting will take is an open issue. It is also uncertain how existing national and regional standard setting processes will affect global harmonization and which one(s) will dominate. The direction of accounting in the Mixed Economy model is also unclear.

3. Disclosure trends, especially those of a voluntary nature, bear watching. There is also the question of whether accounting measurement technology can keep pace with the increasingly complex transactions that MNCs engage in. Many such issues need attention, because the information content of conventionally prepared financial statements is less than users expect.

4. The challenge in designing an MNC accounting information system is resolving the inherent conflicts in "thinking globally and acting locally." Integrating strategic planning and control systems is also problematic. Finally, designing a

system that allows the performance of managers to be evaluated separately from that of their operating units is a long-standing, but still unresolved issue.

5. Two issues unique to multinational (versus domestic only) operations are the choice of currency for transnational budgeting and reporting, and the international tax aspects of MNC transfer pricing. The first issue affects internal operations, while the second one has political overtones.

ADDITIONAL READINGS

Brown, V. H. "Accounting Standards: Their Economic and Social Consequences." *Accounting Horizons* (September 1990), pp. 89–97.

Choi, F. D. S. "Economic Effects of Multinational Accounting Diversity." *Journal of International Financial Management and Accounting* (Summer 1989), pp. 105–29.

Gyllenhammar, P. "The Global Economy: Who Will Lead Next?" *Journal of Accountancy* (January 1993), pp. 61–67.

Krugman, P. R. "A Global Economy Is Not the Wave of the Future." *Financial Executive* (March/April 1992), pp. 10–13.

Meek, G. K., and S. M. Saudagaran. "A Survey of Research on Financial Reporting in a Transnational Context." *Journal of Accounting Literature* 9 (1990), pp. 145–82.

Ndubizu, G. A. "Accounting Disclosure Methods and Economic Development: A Criterion for Globalizing Capital Markets." *The International Journal of Accounting* 27, no. 2 (1992), pp. 151–63

Wallace, R. S. O. and H. Gernon. "Frameworks for International Comparative Financial Accounting." *Journal of Accounting Literature* 10 (1991), pp. 209–63.

Q–R

S

T

U

Thank you for choosing Business One Irwin for your business information needs. If you are part of a corporation, professional association, or government agency, consider our newest option: Business One Irwin Custom Publishing. This allows you to create customized books, manuals, and other materials from your organization's resources, select chapters of our books, or both.

Business One Irwin books are also excellent resources for training/educational programs, premiums, and incentives. For information on volume discounts or Custom Publishing, call 1-800-448-3343, ext. 2715.

Other books of interest to you from Business One Irwin . . .

THE ACCOUNTANT'S GUIDE TO LEGAL LIABILITY AND ETHICS

Marc J. Epstein, Ph.D., and Albert D. Spalding, Jr., J.D., C.P.A.

A major liability loss can severely damage or cause the complete failure of large and small accounting firms alike. This practical guide tells how public accountants can steer clear of liability danger. (300 pages)

ISBN: 1-55623-993-9

EVENT-DRIVEN BUSINESS SOLUTIONS
Today's Revolution in Business and Information Technology

Eric L. Denna, David P. Andros, J. Owen Cherrington, and Anita Sawyer Hollander

Here is a unique blueprint for implementing the solution-oriented structure of the future within your organization today, by focusing less on processes and more on defining the impact of every business event—and using that information to develop new and better ways to do battle in today's economic world. (400 pages)

ISBN: 1-55623-942-4

A MANAGER'S GUIDE TO GLOBALIZATION
Six Keys to Success in a Changing World

Steven H. Rhinesmith

Co-published with the American Society for Training and Development

Discover the six key skills needed to effectively compete in an increasingly internationally challenging environment. Rhinesmith shows how to cope with the complexities and uncertainties arising from globalization, as well as how to manage and lead multicultural teams to success. (150 pages)

ISBN: 1-55623-904-1